CULTURE AND
CITIZENSHIP

Politics and Culture
A Theory, Culture & Society series

Politics and Culture analyses the complex relationships between civil society, identities and contemporary states. Individual books will draw on the major theoretical paradigms in politics, international relations, history and philosophy within which citizenship, rights and social justice can be understood. The series will focus attention on the implications of globalization, the information revolution and postmodernism for the study of politics and society. It will relate these advanced theoretical issues to conventional approaches to welfare, participation and democracy.

SERIES EDITOR: Bryan S. Turner, *University of Cambridge*

EDITORIAL BOARD
Jack Barbalet, *University of Leicester*
Mike Featherstone, *Nottingham Trent University*
Engin Isin, *York University*
Stephen Kalberg, *Boston University*
Andrew Linklater, *University of Wales, Aberystwyth*
Carole Pateman, *University of California, Los Angeles*
Tony Woodiwiss, *City University, London*

Also in this series

CULTURE AND CITIZENSHIP

Edited by
Nick Stevenson

SAGE Publications
London • Thousand Oaks • New Delhi

Editorial arrangement and Chapter 1 © Nick Stevenson 2001
Chapter 2 © Bryan S. Turner 2001
Chapter 3 © Nick Crossley 2001
Chapter 4 © Anthony Elliott 2001
Chapter 5 © Stephen Frosh 2001
Chapter 6 © Maurice Roche 2001
Chapter 7 © Jude Bloomfield and Franco Bianchini 2001
Chapter 8 © Jim McGuigan 2001
Chapter 9 © Anna Yeatman 2001
Chapter 10 © Diane Richardson 2001
Chapter 11 © Deborah Marks 2001
Chapter 12 © Shane Blackman and Alan France 2001
Chapter 13 © John Solomos 2001

First published 2001

SAGE Publications Ltd
6 Bonhill Street
London EC2A 4PU

SAGE Publications Inc
2455 Teller Road
Thousand Oaks, California 91320

SAGE Publications India Pvt Ltd
32, M-Block Market
Greater Kailash - I
New Delhi 110 048

British Library Cataloguing in Publication data

A catalogue record for this book is available from
the British Library.

ISBN 0 7619 5559 3
ISBN 0 7619 5560 7 (pbk)

Library of Congress catalog record available

Typeset by SIVA Math Setters, Chennai, India
Printed in Great Britain by Biddles Ltd, Guildford, Surrey

CONTENTS

CONTRIBUTORS

Franco Bianchini is Reader in Cultural Planning and Policy, and Programme Leader for the MA in European Cultural Planning at De Montefort University, Leicester. His publications include *Cultural Policy and Urban Regeneration: The Western European Experience* (with M. Parkinson) (Manchester University Press, 1993) and *The Creative City* (with C. Landry) (1995).

Shane Blackman is Reader in Applied Social Sciences, Canterbury Christ Church University College. He is the author of *Youth: Positions and Oppositions* (Avebury Press, 1995) and has published papers on ethnography, feminism, youth culture, youth training, youth 'underclass' and homelessness.

Jude Bloomfield is currently Senior Visiting Research Fellow in the Department of Sociology at the University of East London and a freelance writer and researcher on urban cultures and European citizenship. She was formerly Political Science Lecturer in Modern European Studies at UCL.

Nick Crossley is Lecturer in Sociology, University of Manchester. He has published two books: *The Politics of Subjectivity: Between Foucault and Merleau-Ponty* (Avebury, 1994) and *Intersubjectivity: The Fabric of Social Becoming* (Sage, 1996).

Anthony Elliott is Professor of Social and Political Theory at the University of the West of England, Bristol. He is the author of *Social Theory and Psychoanalysis in Transition* (Free Association Books, 1999, 2nd edn) and *The Mourning of John Lennon* (1999).

Alan France is Lecturer in Applied Sociology in the Department of Sociological Studies at the University of Sheffield. His main areas of interest and writing are: the sociology of youth and children and the life course; youth and citizenship; and youth, social policy and inclusion and evaluation methodologies for youth intervention programmes.

Stephen Frosh is Professor of Psychology at Birkbeck College, University of London, and Consultant Clinical Psychologist and Vice Dean in the Child and Family Department at the Tavistock Clinic, London. His recent publications include *For and Against Psychoanalysis* (Routledge, 1997) and the second edition of *The Politics of Psychoanalysis* (Macmillan, 1999).

Jim McGuigan is Reader in Cultural Analysis and Programme Director for Sociology in the Department of Social Sciences at Loughborough University,

UK. His books include *Cultural Populism* (Routledge, 1992), *Culture and the Public Sphere* (Routledge, 1996), *Cultural Methodologies* (Sage, 1997) and *Modernity and Postmodern Culture* (Open University Press, 1999).

Deborah Marks is Course Co-ordinator of the MA Disability Studies, Centre for Psychotherapeutic Studies, Sheffield University and is training to be a child psychotherapist. She is the author of *Disability: Controversial Debates and Psychosocial Perspectives* (Routledge) and co-author of *Challenging Women: Psychologies Exclusions and Feminist Possibilities* (OUP).

Diane Richardson is Professor of Sociology in the Department of Sociology and Social Policy at the University of Newcastle. Her previous books include *Theorising Heterosexuality* (Open University Press, 1996), *Introducing Women's Studies: Feminist Theory and Practice* (Macmillan, 1997), co-edited with Victoria Robinson, and most recently, *Rethinking Sexuality* (Sage, 2000).

Maurice Roche is Reader in Sociology at Sheffield University and has held posts at the LSE and McMaster University. In the field of cultural policy and citizen-ship he is the author of *Mega-Events and Modernity: Olympics and Expos in the Growth of Global Culture* (Routledge, 2000) and *Rethinking Citizenship: Welfare, Ideology and Change in Modern Society* (Polity Press, 1992).

John Solomos is Professor of Sociology at South Bank University. Among his publications are *Race, Politics and Social Change* (with Les Back) (Routledge, 1995) and *Racism and Society* (with Les Back) (Macmillan, 1996).

Nick Stevenson is Lecturer in Sociological Studies at the University of Sheffield. He is author of *Understanding Media Culture* (1995) and *The Transformation of the Media* (Longman, 1999).

Bryan S. Turner is Professor of Sociology at the University of Cambridge. His recent books include *Classical Sociology* (1999) and *The Blackwell Companion to Social Theory* (2000).

Anna Yeatman is currently Professor of Sociology at Macquarie University in Sydney. She is the author of *Postmodern Revisionings of the Political* (1994) and of a forthcoming book with Routledge, *The Politics of Individuality*.

ACKNOWLEDGEMENTS

The production of this edited volume has taken a long time given that it was interrupted by my own ill health and a multitude of other delays. In this respect I would particularly like to thank Bryan S. Turner, Robert Rojek and Chris Rojek for their patience. In the final stages the encouragement of Lucy James, Anthony Elliott, Mike Kenny, David Moore and Maurice Roche has been particularly helpful.

The book is dedicated to Jagdish Patel and Gaye Flounders, two of the best 'cultural' citizens I know.

Nick Stevenson

1

CULTURE AND CITIZENSHIP: AN INTRODUCTION

Nick Stevenson

Recent debates within cultural studies and citizenship studies might suggest that these areas have little in common. The term 'culture' is usually associated with a mix of public and private institutions including museums, libraries, schools, cinemas and the media, while more specifically being connected with the dialogic production of meaning and aesthetics through a variety of practices. Citizenship, on the other hand, is more often thought to be about membership, belonging, rights and obligations. In institutional terms the terrain of citizenship is usually marked out by abstract legal definitions as to who is to be included and excluded from the political community.

Indeed, under certain circumstances, claims to an identity and rights of residence should indeed be kept separate. A liberal view might propose that the rights of citizenship and substantive cultural commitments need to be clearly distinguished from one another. It has been the remit of cultural racism to argue that access to citizenship criteria depends upon particular cultural persuasions. Such a view then would warn against linking 'culture' and 'citizenship'. However rather than suggesting that citizens' entitlements are conditional on certain cultural criteria we might think of ways of bringing these ideas together to promote a more inclusive society. For example, as both Bryan Turner (1993) and Maurice Roche (1992) have argued, in addition to civil, political and social rights we might now start to talk of cultural rights. These dimensions expand legal frameworks and questions of governance into the cultural sphere. Yet how these rights (and possibly obligations) are to be elaborated remains an open question. Conversely, in cultural studies, many writers such as Douglas Kellner (1995) and Jim McGuigan (1996) have become closely associated with the need to respect the diversity of modern popular cultures, while linking them to more political and economic questions. Generally speaking the ground does seem fertile for exploring the interconnections between these different domains. To talk of cultural citizenship, as we shall see, invites a dialogue across disciplinary boundaries and maps out some of the key developments currently taking place within the modern world.

In particular, the notion that culture is now a key site of contestation forcefully brings questions of citizenship to the fore. As Beck (1992), Castells (1996) and Melucci (1996) have all argued the 'cultural' dimension can no longer be conceived as an add on after the 'real' dimensions of politics and economics have been satisfactorily explained. Whether we are talking about the risk society, network capitalism or the concerns of social movements, ideas of symbolic challenge and exclusion remain central. The power to name, construct meaning and exert control over the flow of information within contemporary societies being one of the central structural divisions today. Power then, as we shall see throughout this collection, is not solely based upon material dimensions, but also involves the capacity to throw into question established codes and rework frameworks of common under-standing. This means that the locus of cultural citizenship will have to occupy positions both inside and outside of the formal structures of administrative power. To talk of a cultural citizenship means that we take questions of rights and responsi-bilities far beyond the technocratic agendas of mainstream politics/media. That is, we should seek to form an appreciation of the ways in which 'ordinary' under-standings become constructed, of issues of interpretative conflict and semiotic plurality more generally. However, this can not be achieved without also appreci-ating how dominant systems and institutions seek to establish the power of master codes, meaninglessness and dominant viewpoints. Such a position then requires us to consider the ways in which more formal definitions of citizenship have been maintained within modernity. Such notions arguably join together sociology's attempt to map the 'big' transformations of modernity with cultural studies' attempt to capture more subtle shifts within meaning and aesthetics.

Theories of Cultural Citizenship

How then might we talk of questions of culture and citizenship? The academic literature, leading up to the publication of this volume, has begun to explicitly debate many of the ways that these interconnections might be articulated. Renato Rosaldo (1994) writes of 'the right to be different' while enjoying full member-ship of a democratic and participatory community. From this view the solidified national community views cultural citizenship as a threat. A cultural citizen is a polyglot who is able to move comfortably within multiple and diverse communi-ties while resisting the temptation to search for a purer and less complex identity. Conversely, John Urry (1995) suggests that we become cultural citizens through the growth of a 'surface' cosmopolitanism that has helped produce a certain 'openness' to the rich patterns of geographical and historical cultures the globe has to offer. On this reading, 'cultural' citizenship is more the product of the free mobility of goods and peoples than legally formulated rights and obligations.

The arguments of Rosaldo and Urry are an interesting starting point. Whereas Rosaldo connects up questions of citizenship to the public sphere and issues related to rights, Urry is more concerned to link the global traffic of goods and symbols to questions of consumption. This I think makes an important point in that to talk of culture and citizenship or 'cultural' citizenship is to be mutually concerned with both political as well as economic practices. That is, notions of cultural citizenship offer an opportunity to link the way changes in the economic and political sphere have had impacts upon the ways in which citizenship is commonly experienced. However, we could also argue that both Rosaldo and Urry connect culture and citizenship in ways which begin to think about difference and diversity within a shared community.

This point has been picked by Bryan Turner (1994) arguing that the postmodernization of culture and the globalization of politics have rendered much of the literature in respect of citizenship inadequate. First, the attack on traditional divisions between high and low culture poses serious questions in terms of the common or national cultures that might be transmitted by public institutions. The diversification and fragmentation of public tastes and life styles have undermined a previously assumed 'cultural' consensus. Secondly, the development of transnational spheres of governance, instantaneous news and global networks amongst new social movements has questioned the assumed connection between citizenship and the nation-state. These dual processes undermining, or at least calling into question, the correspondence that citizenship has traditionally drawn between belonging and the nation-state.

More recently, Jan Pakulski (1997) has argued that 'cultural' citizenship should be viewed in terms of satisfying demands for full inclusion into the social community. Such claims should be seen in the context of the waning of the welfare state and class identities, and the formation of new social and cultural movements focusing on the question of the rights of groups from children to the disabled. Cultural rights, in this sense, herald 'a new breed of claims for unhindered representation, recognition without marginalization, acceptance and integration without "normalizing" distortion' (Pakulski, 1997: 80). These rights go beyond rights for welfare protection, political representation or civil justice and focus on the right to propagate a cultural identity or life style. These claims, however, are likely to be as problematic as the implementation of social rights. Pakulski suggests that there is already a perceived backlash against 'politically correct' programmes and unease about bureaucratic attempts to regulate the cultural sphere.

Elsewhere, I have similarly argued that the demands for cultural citizenship both focus on the spheres of media and education and have been influenced by the dual processes of postmodernization and globalization. The partial break up of previously assumed homogeneous national cultures has opened questions of cultural inclusion and exclusion. To be excluded from cultural citizenship is to be excluded from full membership of society. This converts cultural citizenship into a more normative set of criteria:

> Cultural citizenship can be said to have been fulfilled to the extent to which society makes commonly available the semiotic and material cultures necessary in order to make social life meaningful, critique practices of domination, and allow for the recognition of difference under conditions of tolerance and mutual respect. (Stevenson, 1997a: 42)

Such a view would argue that 'cultural' citizenship needs to include dimensions other than the recognition of difference. That is while the recognition, if you like, of our right to be different remains key, cultural citizenship also requires a set of public institutions that are both democratic and protected from the excesses of the free market. Arguably this points to the continued links between social and cultural forms of citizenship. In the section below, I seek to trace out what I consider to be the key questions at stake in this arena.

The Dimensions of Cultural Citizenship

During the past decade, questions of citizenship have come increasingly to the fore. This has been widely recognized as being connected to the growing crisis of the welfare state in Western democratic nations, the demise of actually existed socialism, the critical questioning of liberalism and social democracy and the development of informational capitalism. All of these social developments and others have helped put citizenship studies on the map. There is renewed interest across a range of academic specialisms in the study of citizenship. The question of membership and belonging in terms of our common rights and duties has arguably been heightened in an age where the liquidity of capital and the demise of communism have brought into question older Left/Right binarisms. This has led to the rediscovery of the politics of citizenship, which is neither tied to free market liberalism nor state socialism. Notions of citizenship then more sharply focus our attention on questions of rights, democratic participation and notions of duty as we move into the more uncertain terrain of the post-Cold War era. These debates open out key questions in respect of our political cultures, as the main ideologies that dominated the twentieth century come under increasing critical scrutiny from both inside and outside of the academy.

Yet to conceive of citizenship in these terms is both at once important and overly narrow. While it matters greatly whether we need to rethink our ideas in respect of social democracy and liberalism we also need to address the emerging 'cultural dimension' of citizenship. The emergence of new social movements and critical questions that can be related to 'identity' politics have been crucial in this respect. Social movements in respect of race and ethnicity, gender and sexuality, disability and others have all sought to interrupt the construction of dominant cultures. These movements have sought to challenge widely held stereotypes that once permeated the symbolic cultures of civil society. The deconstruction of ideas that have been associated with the 'normal' citizen has sought to widen the 'inclusive' fabric of the community while creating space for difference and otherness. Questions of 'cultural' citizenship therefore seek to rework images, assumptions and representations that are seen to be exclusive as well as marginalizing. At heart then these dimensions ask what does it means to belong to society, and how might modern society be made more 'inclusive'? This not only adds more voices to the debate in terms of the maintenance of our collective identities, but also opens traditional views and practices up for critical scrutiny. Public issues as widely diverse as date rape, gay cinema, children's rights, the black communities monitoring of the police, lad culture and wheelchair ramps all have issues connected to 'cultural' citizenship at their heart. Notably these issues have all been brought onto the agenda by political and cultural formations that have their organizational basis outside of mainstream political parties. This is not to argue that more mainstream agendas can not become hegemonically reformulated, but that the social forces that have pressed these issues, for the most part, have come from outside of establishment circles. Adding a cultural dimension to citizenship therefore points towards the deepening and broadening of questions related to the politicization of everyday life.

The discursive construction of these ongoing conversations has a further 'cultural' dimension. That is, the arena in which they are mostly likely to be fought out is within the media of mass communication. The progressive enframing of key political debates within print and radio, and the dominant medium television has been one of the major 'cultural' transformations of the twentieth century. The development of a sophisticated array of visual codes and repertoires that interrupt the agendas of more hegemonic institutions and cultures is an essential armament within the semiotic society. To have access to cultural citizenship therefore is to be able to make an intervention into the public sphere at the local, national or global level. The debate concerning young people's 'cultural' literacy in respect of drugs could feature a range of debates including the national press, a school magazine and CNN news all at once. This issue may link reports of trans-national drug cartels, a debate of the risks involved in taking particular life style drugs, pronouncements by leading politicians and the views of young people themselves. This example then not only underlines the increasingly political nature of cultural questions, but the diversity of arenas that debate and represent these questions.

The other key social development that has ignited questions of cultural citizenship has been globalization. The 'cultural' aspects of globalization are by now well known and include a number of processes encompassing the growing intensification of the movement of people and symbols across national boarders. This has fostered a number of complex and often contradictory developments. The first and most obvious has been the growing penetration of the cultural sphere by economics and instrumental reason. Huge conglomerates specializing in the production of a range of cultural goods now dominate world markets. However new levels of cultural intermixing partially breaking down older more homogeneous cultures have also coupled this development. This has helped foster claims for cultural rights from a variety of sites including opera houses and organizations that aim to protect minority languages. An increasingly commercial as well as a more multi-cultural public sphere has produced claims for special protection from the domains of high culture and minority cultures alike. Processes of globalization then can be read ambivalently in that they have provided new zones of cultural intermixing while progressively commodifying the cultural realm. These claims for rights will primarily be addressed towards the nation-state, despite recent reports of its demise, as well as more trans-national and local levels of governance. The claim that we protect languages, cultures and aesthetic pursuits from the logics of both capital and the state are likely to be heard ever loudly as we progress into the next century.

The provision of a pluralistic and electrically charged public sphere would seemingly have resonance in this regard. The availability of public places where ideas, perspectives and feelings can be shared in modern societies is crucial for the development of the self, the creation of social movements and the fostering of a critically informed public more generally. Again the spaces and places where this sort of interaction can take place may combine different kinds of communication from face to face interaction to that of a more mediated variety. Open-ended and reflexive forms of dialogue can be as much a part of the Internet as it can the local town hall. However there are many other pressures within modern society that would seek ideological closure and ensure topics for debate that do not receive the chronic forms of scrutiny they evidently deserve. The provision of public spaces, in terms of a genuinely 'cultural' citizenship, that have achieved at least relative forms of autonomy, needs to be added to and preserved against more colonizing impulses.

The questions raised above have an obvious connection to issues of cultural policy. This area has been one of growing concern both within and outside of the academy. States and societies face choices in terms of the museums they fund, the mix of public and private forms of television they allow and the languages they teach in the classroom. These policy areas then arguably broaden the remit of public governance into the domain of culture. Cultural policy is centrally concerned with the kinds of 'culture' that are deserving of public protection and the kinds of policies that are best fit to achieve these objectives. These questions, as I have commented elsewhere, are likely to require fresh forms of thinking to accommodate the mixing of popular and elite culture (Kenny and Stevenson, 1998; Stevenson, 1997b). Since the advent of postmodernism it is no longer automatically clear the sorts of culture that should be offered public forms of protection. This poses the question as to what set of public criteria would indeed be applicable to the domain of cultural policy? While this inevitably raises questions of quality, diversity and democracy the unfreezing of the 'cultural' domain does not automatically tell us which of these principles have a priority over others, and the order of their importance. Now that cultural policy can no longer be simply the preserve of an elite culture or left to the market to define the tastes of the vast majority of the population these questions come increasingly to the fore.

Finally to raise issues of culture and citizenship is to be intimately concerned with the potential creativity or otherwise of the self. To be concerned with the 'cultural' dimensions of citizenship then is to try and foster the social conditions that make such creativity possible. The twin threats of bureaucratization and fundamentalism even within advanced industrial economies should not be underestimated. That is, it is not enough to point to processes of cultural democratization, as important as these might be, but one should also be concerned with questions related to meaningfulness, quality and aesthetics. These dimensions could come into play in the funding of adult evening classes, centres for inter-cultural understanding and meaning, and the development of places and spaces within audio and visual culture that can be opened up to more experimental purposes. The arrival of more niche-marketed cultures has not yet displaced some of the predictable and conformist features of mass culture (Stevenson, 1999). This again necessitates a set of normative criteria that would point to the evident danger of allowing our common cultures to be determined by more instrumental agendas.

While the specific way of linking these issues remains my own they do provide a context for *most* of the concerns available within this volume. My thoughts here are perhaps an initial example of *one* of the available ways we might have in tying them together.

Social Theory and Citizenship

A useful starting point for thinking the links between culture and citizenship lies with social theory. The chapters by Turner, Crossley, Elliott and Frosh consider many of the *theoretical* issues at stake in the 'cultural' turn in citizenship studies. In particular, Turner seeks to map a wider conception of what a genuinely 'cultural' citizenship might mean. Turner argues that we have come to a theoretical turning point in our consideration of the cultural dimension of citizenship. Due to globalization and the fragmentation of homogeneous national cultures it has become increasingly difficult to describe cultural citizenship as our capacity to be able to participate in the reproduction of a national culture. These processes have meant that the state has become challenged from both above and below. Instead we might reconceive cultural citizenship as those processes that allow us to participate as democratic citizens. Here Turner discusses the provision of mass education and the possible development of an electronic democracy via the Internet. The prospects for cultural citizenship, on this reading, being caught between evidence of cultural democratization and the continuation of cultural hierarchies and cultural deprivation.

Crossley, Elliott and Frosh also pick up the question as to the cultural preconditions of citizenship. For Crossley to be a citizen means that one is capable of acting both autonomously and responsibly. That is the 'rights' of citizenship are conditional upon 'common attributes' like taking 'the attitude of the other'. There is then, in Crossley's terms, no point attributing the status of citizenship on those, like animals, which can not claim rights and uphold obligations. This means then that in order to nourish the conditions ripe for citizenship we need to think beyond more formal legal criteria. That is citizenship is dependent upon meaningful criteria that give the concept its vitality in the horizons of ordinary people. Elliott similarly calls attention to the intersubjective basis for citizenship. However he skilfully asks us to attend to a number of opportunities and dangers in respect of new dimensions which are opening out within modernity. Here Elliott argues that 'individuation' processes have paradoxically led to claims that institutions need to be restructured to enhance space for emotional literacy and more ambivalent feelings. Yet cultural privatization and the operation of global economics has made it increasingly difficult to press the case for notions of the common good upon which citizenship ultimately depends. These considerations lead into a rethinking of the domains of citizenship deconstructing older oppositions between public and private, while linking questions of personhood and more global forms of governance.

Frosh, like Elliott, thinks that we need to attend more closely to some of the unconscious aspects of citizenship. In this respect, psychoanalysis offers important resources in helping us unpack how citizens live their relationship to the wider community through rights and duties, but also, through feelings and fantasies. Here Frosh argues that a 'cultural' understanding of citizenship would help us understand the emotional investments people make in wider collective identities where no rational interests are perceivable. These issues are particularly pertinent given the centrality of identity to new domains of constructed subjectivity. These directions help us to more fully understand the lure of different kinds of fundamentalism in terms of their emotional rather than their purely intellectual appeals.

The chapters in this part of the volume all draw attention to the preconditions and preunderstandings that make citizenship possible. This is done by pointing to a diversity of cultural resources from the creative potential of the self to cultural goods like the media and education system provided by the community. Further, these chapters, also point to the changed 'cultural' conditions within which citizenship now operates as we move into an increasingly global and postmodern age.

Culture, Policy and Citizenship

The contributions by Roche, Bloomfield and Bianchini and McGuigan all seek to relate the practice of cultural citizenship to the key domain of cultural policy. In this context, Roche also picks up on the theme of globalization, but more explicitly relates this question to Europeanization. Against those who would overstate the significance of the nation-state he points to an emergent European dimension in respect of popular culture and the public sphere. In this respect, the key cultural site has proved to be sport. Television's role in restructuring sport has helped transmit a genuinely popular European culture that may eventually be seen as complementary and in competition with the culture of the nation-state. Alternatively Bloomfield and Bianchini argue that the city in the European context remains an important location for the expression of cultural citizenship. Contemporary postmodern and multi-cultural times mean that cultural citizenship needs to be thought less in terms of access to a literary sensibility and more around issues of inter-cultural understanding. Further, the city in terms of cultural policy, has gone through three definite stages in terms of the cultural provisions it has made for its citizens. These different periods have ended with cultural policy becoming a tool utilized to attract economic capital into urban areas. In order to promote more inter-cultural forms of literacy, policies are needed to attend to local cultural production, the provision of genuinely multi-cultural public spaces and civic participation more generally. Finally, in this section, if Roche's focus is trans-national, Bloomfield's and Bianchini's local, McGuigan's is national. It is not that any of the chapters ignore the links between these different domains, more that specific levels are emphasized. McGuigan unfashionably argues that the nation-state, despite globalization, remains the main domain we should seek to address when it comes to questions of cultural policy. In this important chapter, McGuigan identifies three discourses of cultural policy that can be located in terms of state engineering, the free market emphasis upon a language of market opportunities and managerialism, and civil discourses that seek to open cultural policy and cultural practices up for democratic discussion. This is key, as despite the three chapters' different spatial emphases, it is inevitably to more democratic forms of cultural engagement that we are asked to look in the policy arena.

Difference, Culture and Citizenship

Finally the chapters by Yeatman, Richardson, Marks, Blackman and France, and Solomos inevitably bring us back to questions related to difference and diversity. All of the perspectives covered here are concerned that 'mainstream' views of citizenship have traditionally had at their core a white, heterosexual, adult, able-bodied male that has helped define the 'normal' dimensions of citizenship. However the chapters under review offer markedly different responses to this perceived problem. For example, Yeatman argues that the feminist movement initially sought to extend citizenship to include women by suggesting that they were just as capable of autonomous forms of self-government as men. The problem with this view being that the capacity for independence and self-determination is a tough test for citizenship. Indeed it is one that many human beings would fail, and is ideologically modelled on the male head of the household. Instead what Yeatman calls a post-patrimonial conception of citizenship should be based upon securing respect for individualized personhood. The need to break with masculine and heterosexual definitions of citizenship is also emphasized by Richardson. She connects these arguments into questions of sexual rights. Here the public circulation of symbolic material in respect of the production, representation and consumption of sexuality has brought these questions into the public sphere. The increased visibility of gay and lesbian narratives and life styles in popular culture has helped open a complex set of questions. These social transformations have all put issues concerned with the commodification of sexuality and the deconstruction of hetrosexism onto wider social agendas.

A similar concern to deconstruct 'normality' is also evident in the contribution made by Marks on the themes of disability and citizenship. This important chapter argues that the disabled rights movement has done much to challenge widely held assumptions in terms of who is fit to be called a citizen. Like Yeatman, Marks emphasizes the importance in breaking with the bodily fit and autonomous citizen in favour of a more ambivalent social imaginary. However, whereas Richardson identified primarily social barriers to this process, Marks argues that these may be supplemented by unconscious dimensions. The able bodied in this respect need to maintain certain psychic fantasies of bodily perfection to keep less secure constructions of the self and others at bay. These identifications provide the social terrain upon which the disabled movement attempts to revalue stigmatized identities and argue for the right to be different. However as Blackman and France observe, these rights still have to be won on a terrain that is largely determined by the imperatives of late capitalism. These crucially include, for young people in particular, the operation of social exclusion in the labour market and the commercialization of popular culture. These features perhaps warn us from offering overly postmodernized accounts that are exclusively concerned with the semiotic dimensions of culture and identity.

The question of difference is also central to any consideration of multi-culturalism. There are, according to Solomos, perhaps two key questions a genuinely multi-cultural politics has to address in the face of mono-cultural hegemony. These are policies that effectively protect minorities against social exclusion, discrimination and racism. In particular these policies would need to tackle the social and economic issues and questions of immigration that invariably face minority groups. Secondly, we need to question the degree of cultural relativism that is actually compatible with the maintenance of a democratic state. This issue, as Solomos well understands, has important consequences, both theoretically as well as practically. Avoiding cultural homogenization, respecting a diversity of genuinely multi-cultural associations, while making them compatible with the wider values of liberty, democracy and justice is likely to be a difficult task to achieve.

As will by now be apparent, the book offers a number of different readings and interpretations of the theme of cultural citizenship. This collection then marks the beginning of a wider debate that will increasingly see the linking of culture and citizenship. While there is much disagreement in the approaches taken here there are also some common features present. The first is that the normative features of citizenship remain central to debates across a whole range of academic disciplines. That is that the term is both useful and dangerous as it groups together questions of belonging, rights, obligations and crucially democracy. Secondly, that the cultural dimension in an era of postmodern culture, globalization and fragmentation amongst other features opens important questions that citizenship studies can ill afford to ignore.

References

Beck, U. (1992) *Risk Society*. London: Sage.

Castells, M. (1996) *The Rise of the Network Society*. Oxford: Blackwell.

Kellner, D. (1995) *Media Culture: Cultural Studies, Identity and Politics between the Modern and the Postmodern*. London: Routledge.

Kenny, M. and Stevenson, N. (1998) 'Cultural Studies or Cultural Political Economy? Cues from the Long Revolution', *Cultural Policy*, 4 (2): 249–269.

McGuigan, J. (1996) *Culture and the Public Sphere*. London: Routledge.

Melucci, A. (1996) *Challenging Codes: Collective Action in the Information Age*. Cambridge: Cambridge University Press.

Pakulski, J. (1997) 'Cultural Citizenship', *Citizenship Studies*, 1 (1): 73–86.

Roche, M. (1992) *Rethinking Citizenship: Welfare, Ideology and Change in Modern Society*. Cambridge: Polity Press.

Rosaldo, R. (1994) 'Cultural Citizenship and Educational Democracy', *Cultural Anthropology*, 9 (3): 402–411.

Stevenson, N. (1997a) 'Globalization, National Cultures and Cultural Citizenship', *Sociological Quarterly*, 38 (1): 41–66.

Stevenson, N. (1997b) 'Global Media and Technological Change: Social Justice, Recognition and the Meaningfulness of Everyday Life', *Citizenship Studies*, 1 (3): 365–388.

Stevenson, N. (1999) *The Transformation of the Media: Globalisation, Morality and Ethics*. London: Longman.

Turner, B.S. (1993) 'Contemporary Problems in the Theory of Citizenship', in B.S. Turner (ed.), *Citizenship and Social Theory*. London: Sage.

Turner, B.S. (1994) 'Postmodern Culture/Modern Citizens', in V.B. Steenbergen (ed.), *The Condition of Citizenship*. London: Sage.

Urry, J. (1995) *Consuming Places*. London: Routledge.

2

OUTLINE OF A GENERAL THEORY OF CULTURAL CITIZENSHIP

Bryan S. Turner

Citizenship may be conceptualized as a bundle of rights and obligations that formally define the legal status of a person within a state. This formal status is important because it is from this legal basis that individual citizens claim entitlements to national resources through such institutional arrangements as retirement, unemployment provisions, social security and welfare. There is an important reciprocal relationship between the possession of citizenship status and community membership. Because the modern state has been typically a national state, citizenship is derived ultimately from membership by birth within an ethnic community, where the entitlement to citizenship is typically inherited from parents. Israel may be the extreme example of acquiring citizenship within a nation-state by virtue of having a Jewish mother, but the issue of citizenship as a right of birth is fairly common. Gender, nationhood and citizenship are closely related (Yuval-Davis, 1997). Having citizenship involves having a family name, which is enscribed upon one's passport as a legitimate status within a kinship system and the state. It is for this reason that citizenship is normally a patriarchal legacy of households, where names are handed down from father to children. This right to citizenship through community membership defines one's identity as a public person. Although citizenship is a formal legal status, it is, as a consequence of nationalism and patriotic sentiment, intimately bound up with the sentiments and emotions of membership. Finally, this ensemble of relations (legal status, resources, communal membership and identity) describes a field of moral behaviour, social practices and cultural beliefs that are collectively known as civic virtue, because they define what constitutes the virtues of the 'good citizen'. The earliest notions of contract involve ideas about proper conduct. Thus, Samuel Pufendorf in his *On the Duty of Man and Citizen according to Natural Law* (Tully, 1991) warned the citizen not to contemplate revolution, but to live with dignity and scrupulousness. The notion of 'civic virtue' is closely associated with civic republicanism, but there is no form of citizenship which does not also imply moral conduct. Citizenship is a status position which interpellates specific characters and identities. Generally speaking, obligation, not right, is the corner-stone of civic culture (Selbourne, 1994).

A cultural component informs each of these dimensions. One's formal legal status is closely associated with the particular cultural forms of law in a given society (with its peculiar and unique notions of person, property or privilege).

Similarly, social resources definitely include cultural resources or broadly what Pierre Bourdieu (1977) has called 'cultural capital'. Community membership and personal identity are obviously cultural attributes of modern citizenship, and civic culture can be defined as the cultural arena of citizenship practices which ultimately interpellate citizens and categorize individual behaviour within a code of public values and virtues. Despite this intimate relationship between culture and citizenship, cultural citizenship and the cultural underpinnings of modern citizenship remain neglected aspects of contemporary studies of citizenship (Pakulski, 1997). Of course, there has been a traditional concern about the education of the citizen as a foundation for the development of the cultural life of civil society, which goes back to the liberal critique of industrial civilization by J.S. Mill. It lies behind the educational theories of J.-J. Rousseau and in contemporary political theory the failure of the state to provide for the education of the citizen is seen to be one cause of political apathy and an explanation for the general failure of mass democracy (Bobbio, 1987: 35). The absence of a robust tradition of political theory on culture and citizenship is problematic, because cultural citizenship is undoubtedly one of the key components of the politics of identity and globalization. It is also fundamental to debate about the role of the Internet in participation and communication in the advanced societies, namely cultural membership is a significant feature of the analysis of electronic democracy. The question and the possibility of cultural citizenship have become major issues of contemporary society as a consequence of globalization, decolonization and multi-culturalism. Globalization raises new questions about individual identity and therefore brings into prominence questions of multi-cultural membership and cultural empowerment through the possession of citizenship status.

Initially cultural citizenship can be described as cultural empowerment, namely the capacity to participate effectively, creatively and successfully within a national culture. Superficially such a form of citizenship would involve access to educational institutions, the possession of an appropriate 'living' language, the effective ownership of cultural identity through national citizenship membership and the capacity to hand on and transfer to future generations the richness of a national cultural heritage. The role and function of museums and the formulation of heritage strategies, for example, would be critical to such a pattern of civilizational inheritance. In these terms, one can immediately perceive the problem of modern cultural citizenship, namely the question mark which hangs over the idea of a unified, homogeneous and integrated national culture. Can one have cultural membership in a context of multi-cultural and multi-national diversity (Aron, 1974)? In contemporary societies, cultures proliferate, fragment and diversify through political and social experimentation. While aboriginal and nativistic cultures may die, new commercial, diversified, postmodern expressions of culture extend, simulate and multiply modern identities. This multiplication of cultures raises the problems of diverse and different forms of cultural membership. While social positions in traditional societies were stratified by a number of finite and specific structures (tribe, class and status), identity in modern societies is complicated by cultural simulation; it appears to be fluid, transferable and reversible (Baudrillard, 1987).

Historically, citizenship is associated with the growth of the city as a corporation and later with the emergence of the nation-state as a unified political system. Cultural homogeneity was accepted as a principle of communal solidarity with the nation-state, and ethnic homogeneity was imposed by the state through political methods ranging from language policies and compulsory membership in the national church to ethnic cleansing; it was political membership within the national community which, often by default, defined cultural membership, primarily as the possession of a dominant language. The politics of language evolved in tandem with the politics of nation-state citizenship. If language, religion and the state formed the building blocks of the 'grand narratives' of political modernization, then the emergence of mass cultures, globalization and multi-culturalism has produced a postmodern cultural environment which questions and probes the idea of a unitary cultural system of which one might have, as it were, 'naive' membership. The traditional presumption that cultural membership is or can be spontaneous, natural and naive is incompatible with the simulation of cultures by the modern culture industry through advertising, marketing and public relations.

The problem of aboriginal rights within a nation-state paradigm of citizenship emerges clearly and distinctively at this historical conjuncture. The notion on the part of colonizing powers, that the lands which they sought to occupy were in fact empty, was a convenient political mythology which permitted the automatic identification of legitimate settlement with colonization and the unopposed rights of the dominant language, the dominant culture and the dominant class. Diversity and difference were ruled out by the subjection and exclusion of aboriginal communities from within the national community. Alexis de Tocqueville's exclusion of the aboriginal inhabitants of North America on the grounds that they had not produced property or civilization is a classic illustration of the role of the universal doctrine of the rights of man in the exclusion of subordinates (Connolly, 1995). For de Tocqueville, Christian monotheism became the necessary social glue which pulled together the territorial basis of the nation-state as a unified but exclusionary community. The solidarity of this political community created scarcities and exclusions through the maintenance of cultural borderlines and boundaries. Against this dominant and homogeneous culture, slaves, women and minority groups have laboured to find a pattern of inclusion (a voice) into the world dominated by white Christian males. Although similar patterns of state building through a national culture can be found in the cases of Australia, Canada, Israel and New Zealand, there are also important variations in terms of the strength and character of native opposition to white settlement.

Obligations of Culture

The notion of cultural citizenship raises two interesting problems. The first is a sociological issue about the unified character of the cultural foundations of the nation-state, namely the problems of multi-culturalism and postmodernism. The second problem is a philosophical one. If one can in fact articulate a notion of cultural rights, is there a cultural obligation which corresponds to or matches this assertion of rights to cultural resources? While the sociological problem has been addressed by writers on multi-culturalism, the philosophical issues have been rather neglected with the exception of an influential argument by Onora O'Neill in her essay on 'Practices of Toleration' (O'Neill, 1990). Generally speaking, philosophers have argued that rights necessarily entail obligations, and vice versa. In the case of cultural rights (for example, freedom of expression and freedom of information), it is often difficult to think of a clear and direct cultural obligation. O'Neill approaches this issue with the question of how are we entitled to express ourselves? She shows that cultural rights are typically couched within a rights discourse, but she intends to derive them more effectively from an ethical theory that takes obligations rather than rights as its foundation. Indeed much of the debate about cultural rights has been dominated by a tradition of individual liberalism which excludes the notion of obligation in favour of an individualistic theory, thereby concentrating on freedoms. In this approach, O'Neill argues that legal institutions which only address these individualistic freedoms without a corresponding notion of obligation produce a collection of rights which are merely shams.

This focus on obligations is particularly important, she claims, in the area of the media because the assertion of the rights of tolerance and freedom of expression do not protect us from negative and damaging consequences such as pornography and the trivialization of culture, which are promoted by the commercialization of the media. A definition of cultural rights from the perspective of obligation would raise questions about how we ought to communicate and what type of practices of representation ought to be promoted.

O'Neill's approach is useful from a sociological point of view, because it indicates the possibility of cultural risk and the growth of a communications environment which is hazardous and culturally contaminating. Recent sociological approaches to risk (Beck, 1992) have adopted an ecological approach which in fact fails to address the central question of social risk in the cultural as opposed to the natural environment. Beck's theory of risk works best when he provides an analysis of environmental hazard, not when he is trying to understand social risk. Unlike Mary Douglas (1966), he has no adequate understanding of cultural pollution. As a consequence, Beck's risk theory fails to consider and cannot analyse social risks, which involve or produce the contamination of cultural heritage, the simulation of authentic traditions and the erosion of cultural authority. While one can in principle measure environmental hazards with some degree of neutrality and precision, the measurement of cultural risk inevitably involves an element of moral judgement.

Our obligations towards the natural environment in terms of industrial policies to control pollution can be translated back into a set of obligations about the social environment in terms of the concept of cultural risk. For O'Neill, communicative obligations in a democracy are associated with maintaining the conditions for public communication as such. She notes that 'languages can be debased and killed: cultural traditions, dispersed and vulgarized; technologies can be introduced and others displaced in ways that destroy possibilities of communications without coercing or deceiving individuals' (O'Neill, 1990: 167).

Communicative obligations directly raise questions about the ownership of the media, the shaping of public space, the silencing of minority opinion, and the manipulation of information by powerful sectors of the communications industry. If cultural rights are to be fostered alongside, for example welfare rights, we need to think more seriously about both rights and obligations. Such an analysis of the rights and obligations of communication would help to develop the notion of corporate citizenship, namely the idea of a corporate responsibility for genuine and critical public debate rather than a cynical policy of communication management.

The Sociology of Cultural Democratization

In this analysis of cultural citizenship, I pursue a constructive critique of the legacy of T.H. Marshall's model of citizenship. While Marshall (1950) identified civil, political and social dimensions of citizenship which correspond to the jury system, parliament and the welfare state, he did not articulate a view of the cultural dimensions of citizenship as a further extension of the evolution of citizenship rights. Sociologists have generally not addressed the issue of cultural rights and in so far as there is a literature on the possibility of cultural democratization, it has been negative and critical. For example, the influence of critical theorists like Max Horkheimer and Theodor Adorno indicates that modernization in industrial capitalism involves the inauthentication of culture. Commercialization and the growth of a mass culture undermine authentic, distinctive and appropriate aesthetic appreciation. In more recent years, globalization theory has taken an equally negative view of the possibility of and prospects for authentic global cultures. The globalization of culture is associated with the growing interconnectedness of the world economy alongside which there has been an associated development of a world market of cultural goods (Robertson, 1992). The communication requirements of world trade and modern warfare have had the consequence of creating the basis for a global system of symbolic interaction and cultural exchange. We inhabit a world of nearly constant and instant news. Indeed we have moved into a politics of the sceptical as the most significant form of political debate in this semiotic system (Wexler, 1990). Globalization challenges the sovereignty of the state over the control of national cultures. With globalization, more and more social groups become rootless and homeless with the expansion of a world labour market, tourism and geographical mobility. At the same time that the state is eroded in terms of its political sovereignty and cultural hegemony, localism as a response to such changes squeezes the state from below. The state is caught between these global pressures which challenge its cultural monopoly from above, and local, regional and ethic challenges to its authority, as it were, from below. The traditional discourse of nation-state citizenship is confronted by an alternative discourse of human rights and humanity as the normatively superior framework of political loyalty.

The principal exceptions to this theoretical lacunae are probably in the sociology of Talcott Parsons and the analysis of ideology by Karl Mannheim. For Parsons (1966, 1971) the growth of a mass, comprehensive and national system of education in the United States was an important stage in the modernization process. This 'educational revolution' was as significant historically and sociologically as the industrial and French revolutions in an earlier period. A comprehensive education system was the necessary prerequisite for the education of citizens as active participants in democracy, just as information and freedom of exchange are viewed in economic theory as necessary conditions for economic participation for consumers. There is therefore a direct parallel between the freedom of the consumer in an economic market and the freedom of the citizen within the education system.

In a similar fashion, Mannheim (1956) adopted a positive view of democratization in the twentieth century in his sociological explorations of the idea of rational planning. For Mannheim, the democratization of culture was an inevitable stage in the growth of modern societies. This educational revolution in cultural democracy would be based upon notions of the ontological equality of human beings, pedagogic optimism, the idea of individual autonomy and the principle of open recruitment to elite positions. Cultural democratization would be based upon pedagogical optimism, namely the belief that all children have the capacity to achieve the highest levels of excellence and a similar scepticism towards expert knowledge and a monopolistic authority over knowledge production. Such a cultural democratization would lead to the erosion of the caste-like distinction between high and low cultures which in turn undermines the authority of universities and intellectuals over high culture. The modernization of cultural citizenship requires the replacement of an aristocratic ethos by a democratic one characterized essentially by pedagogical optimism.

There are several arguments against the possibility of cultural democratization. There is, for example, the criticism that cultural divisions between social classes are inevitable and irreducible. The high/low distinction in culture is simply an expression of the existence of social stratification and if social stratification cannot be significantly and systematically reduced, then cultural distinctiveness is inevitable. For example, Thorstein Veblen's notion of a leisure class suggests that the high culture/low culture division is likely to persist in an industrial society where subordinate groups derive their livelihood from manual labour and are therefore characteristically referred to as the 'working' or 'labouring' class. Similar negative cultural assumptions lie behind the expressions 'white-collar employee' or 'blackcoated worker'. Because the mental/manual dichotomy has been a fundamental feature of social stratification, a dominant status group is likely to assume a leisure life style as a mark of distinctiveness against subordinate labouring groups, and the existence of elite cultural capital ultimately precludes a radical democratization of cultural empowerment and participation.

Another criticism of cultural citizenship comes from the mainstream sociology of education which has shown that competitive education systems which were created in the post-war period, far from achieving a major democratization and equalization of social outcomes, tend merely to reproduce the existing class structure through educational stratification. Formal equality of opportunity in the educational system was an important feature of the post-war extension of citizenship rights to the whole population, but the continuity of cultural deprivation and class differences meant that actual social mobility through education attainment was well below the level which was anticipated by post-war educational reformers.

The result has been that the educational system has merely reproduced the cultural stratification of society as a whole (Bourdieu and Passeron, 1990). Furthermore, Pierre Bourdieu's development of a theory of distinction (Bourdieu, 1984) provides an analysis of the social distribution of symbolic goods which largely match the distribution of economic capital. The scarcity of cultural goods produces a hierarchy which is controlled and regulated by cultural intermediaries who regulate the distribution of symbolic value through the social structure.

Bourdieu's argument about cultural capital is clearly powerful and raises serious questions about the value of Mannheim's optimism with respect to the democratization of culture and the spread of pedagogic optimism. There are, however, a number of objections to Bourdieu's sociology of culture which to some extent protect Mannheim's position as a starting point for a theory of cultural rights. First, Bourdieu's sociology is over-deterministic and structuralist because the relationship which he draws between the appreciation of cultural objects (such as a preference for Van Gogh's 'Corn Flowers') and social class fractions is too tight, precise and mechanistic. In modern societies, there is generally a greater fluidity between particular cultural goods and specific locations in the social system of stratification. Secondly, Bourdieu's theory may be valid in the case of the French cultural system, but it is less relevant in other societies where, for example, the cultural elite is not so clearly identified with the capital city or with a national educational system. In many modern societies, the cultural influence of the elite may well be dispersed through a variety of large cities, particularly where a federal political system is in operation. For example, in Australia there is clearly cultural competition between Sydney, Canberra and Melbourne where the elite structures have rather different patterns, cultures and constitutions. The same competition exists in Canada between Ottawa, Montreal and Toronto. Thirdly, Bourdieu's theory of symbolic goods depends upon the view that intellectuals still perform a crucial service as cultural intermediaries of the national culture. Zygmunt Bauman's study of intellectuals and culture (Bauman, 1987) suggests that a fissure has opened up between the state and the national culture with the consequence that intellectuals no longer have an effective monopoly and authority over cultural capital. They have lost a considerable degree of political power as a result of this separation of politics and culture, and the conversion of intellectuals from cultural legislators into interpreters is associated with the postmodernization of cultures, that is their fragmentation and pluralization. In general therefore, the cultural field is more fluid and fragmented than Bourdieu suggests and as a result it is more difficult for cultural elites to impose their taste over the entire field of cultural capital.

Bourdieu's somewhat mechanistic view of the relationship between culture and structure suggests that cultural consumers are passive recipients of cultural taste. There are of course alternative views of popular culture as an oppositional force in modern societies. The notion that mass culture is associated with passive reception has been successfully challenged by sociological research which shows that social actors adapt and manipulate cultural objects to their own specific social circumstances (Featherstone, 1991). In popular culture, punk and heavy metal subcultures can be sites of cultural resistance to incorporation into commercial mass culture. The high-street consumer boom of the 1980s was constructed around a variety of specific target groups, especially young, single men, and developed a strategy towards youth which was seen to be opposed to traditional, middle-class cultures (Mort, 1996). Postmodern culture is fragmented and contested rather than hierarchical and dominant.

Measuring Cultural Citizenship

Although cultural identity and cultural citizenship as political issues are an important consequence of the development of mass education systems, multiculturalism, globalism and decolonization, there appears to be a dearth of sociological literature on the themes of cultural citizenship and cultural rights. There is as yet no clear or explicit body of knowledge which problematizes cultural citizenship in terms of its positive freedoms or in terms of its educational underpinnings. However, aspects of a debate about cultural citizenship have emerged in the area of mass consumption in the sociology of culture and it plays a part in the sociology of art with respect to the debate about art and its publics. In other spheres of sociological inquiry such as international relations and legal discourse, the cultural dimensions of democracy are frequently treated in terms of the rights of ethnic minorities and their rights to cultural autonomy through a process of decolonization and thus numerous United Nations declarations on the legitimacy of diverse cultural traditions and the national right to preserve cultural heritage have been debated in the literature (Kartashkin, 1982). When cultural rights are examined within these domains, they are often discussed within a legal framework in terms of the problem of maintaining individual privacy within an information society (Lury, 1993). Cultural rights within this discourse are seen in terms of the right to access information freely within an information society. In the mainstream political science literature, there is no explicit treatment of cultural rights and cultural citizenship under the broad heading of cultural politics and cultural identity. In Chandran Kukathas' (1992) discussion of community rights (under the question, are there cultural rights?), he is primarily concerned with the issue of ethnic diversity in political theory and thus in general the cultural rights debate is located in the evolution of liberal political theory towards an evaluation of collective rights in multi-cultural societies. Kymlicka's (1995) *Multicultural Citizenship* is the classical illustration of this cultural debate in political theory.

While many important collections on the rights of citizenship neglect the cultural dimension (Beddar and Hill, 1992; Blackman, 1993), sociological notions about cultural rights can be inferred from debates about electronic participatory democracies (Abramson et al., 1988; Barber, 1984; Rodota, 1993), the cultural politics of contemporary pedagogy (Giroux, 1991, 1992) and the debate about political literacy in institutions of learning (Senate Standing Committee, 1989, 1991; United Nations, 1993). Apart from these sources, two general problems emerge in this type of research. First there is the rather amorphous use of the word 'culture' which is employed variously and indiscriminately. The relationship between citizenship and culture cannot be properly delineated without some definite idea as to what the term 'culture' refers. Both Prott (1988) and Blau (1989) admit to the difficulty in defining culture precisely when making reference to cultural rights, cultural production and participation. For instance, Blau concentrates on the institutional and organization structures of modern art consumption and production (Geiryn, 1990). The second problem is that citizenship and democracy are concepts which are neither examined nor evoked outside of their more conventional contexts and thus there is a hiatus in the literature between traditional analyses of democratic participation and the sociological analysis of the cultural industry and its associated patterns of consumption. Hence a considerable part of Blau's work on sociology of art dwells neither on the issue of modern citizenship nor on the more extensive question of cultural democratization. *The Shape of Culture* (Blau, 1989) is primarily concerned with patterns of cultural consumption and the relative diffusion of various high and low art forms. To the extent that this sociology of art and art institutions deals with inequalities of cultural consumption (for instance unequal access to and attendance in diverse cultural institutions and activities), it can be inferred that social class, race, gender and educational attainment in contemporary America still severely restrict access to patterns of cultural consumption and to a lesser extent participation in cultural production. The sociology of cultural consumption more generally is concerned with the role of social inequality in the dissemination of artistic forms, performance and appreciation.

Similar themes emerge in the cultural sociology of Pierre Bourdieu. *The Love of Art* (Bourdieu and Darbel, 1990) shows very effectively the impact of class and educational achievement on the definition and determination of cultural 'need' and aesthetic appreciation with respect to museums in European societies. Similarly Bourdieu's *Homo Academicus* (1988) shows the importance of hierarchies in the reception of intellectual products in the higher educational field and how hierarchy, generations and cliques are crucial in the legitimation of academic authority. Against the legacy of Kant's analysis of the neutrality and independence of aesthetic judgement, Bourdieu (1984) adopts in his study of distinction a social constructionist perspective on taste and what he calls cultural need. 'Objects are not rare', but the propensity to consume them is, and 'cultural need' in contrast to 'primary needs' is the result of education (Bourdieu and Darbel, 1990: 37). 'Cultural inequalities or unequal appetites for cultural works are only one aspect of inequalities at school, which create the cultural need at the same time as it provides the means of satisfying it' (Bourdieu and Darbel, 1990: 37). Hence against rational choice theory, liberal notions of free choice and postmodern suppositions about cultural diffusion, Bourdieu maintains that if 'it is indisputable that our society offers to all the pure possibility of taking advantage of the works of display at museums, it remains the case that only some have the real possibility of doing so' (Bourdieu and Darbel, 1990: 37). Both *Distinction* (Bourdieu, 1984) and *The Love of Art* (Bourdieu and Darbel, 1990) offer powerful criticism of the cultural diffusion or democratization thesis. Bourdieu has not directly addressed the problem of cultural citizenship or cultural democracy, because these notions are largely antithetical to Bourdieu's sociological orientation and his intellectual position. Bourdieu is specifically concerned to understand how the field of art is structured by endless struggles, particularly between generations, to control scarce resources, namely the effect of symbolic violence over the pattern of social interaction (Bourdieu, 1993). Although both Blau and Bourdieu's work, and the sociology of art generally, largely focus on consumption patterns (namely on the quantity of the various dimensions of cultural practices), it could be argued that a more qualitative distinction can be drawn from these forms of social closure that define contemporary patterns of cultural consumption. In other words, citizenship benchmarks can include measures which either preclude or restrict citizens, not only from cultural participation, but also from culture exposure to or enjoyment of the arts, higher learning, political literacy and so forth.

In these debates on the sociology of art and in the associated analysis of postmodernity, there is much contention about the relative openness or exclusivity of contemporary cultural institutions and practices. We can conceptualize cultural citizenship in terms of the ownership and control of the means of cultural production: how is citizenship participation expressed with respect to the ownership, production, distribution and consumption of cultural goods? So far we have noted that the sociology of culture, which has been inspired by Bourdieu, is implicitly pessimistic about the possibilities of a democratization of consumption. Many studies maintain that there still exists a noticeable gap between the producers and consumers of culture, whether it be high or low. Paul Gillen (1984), Judith Blau (1986, 1989) and Paul Dimaggio and Michael Useem (1983) posit the existence of such a cultural gap which has been traditionally expressed in terms of a city/country distinction. Dimaggio and Useem in particular reject what they call the cultural democratization thesis, suggesting that there are in fact no indications that the democratization of arts funding is bringing about a democratization of arts consumption, because there are real economic and social barriers to the mobilization of cultural participation. They argue that a proper pedagogy would be an essential aspect of such a cultural mobilization, involving a democratic acquisition of symbolic goods. Moreover, where Dimaggio and Useem dispute the efficacy of state sponsorship of art activities, Blau (1989) believes that it has had some beneficial effects. Although Blau questions Bourdieu's thesis concerning the success of elite resistance to cultural diffusion, she nevertheless concludes that 'cities with relatively little inequality and a substantial middle class have more culture of all kinds' (Blau, 1989: 177). Her study also debunks some of the common place myths about the ubiquity of so-called popular culture indicating how spatial and place theory make important corrections to mass society theory and implicitly about the postmodernization of culture (Goodall, 1995). Against Bourdieu, Blau (1988: 280) had earlier argued that cultural development is not fostered by small elites but by a substantial middle class with relatively little experience of socio-economic inequality, that is while individuals may accrue social and cultural prestige by exhibiting a certain degree of cultural sophistication, the growth of culture on a grand scale may well depend upon the widespread distribution of social and educational resources, not on their concentration. Extensive organization, standardization and declining differences in education have significantly and effectively connected the masses with the elite at least in America. These arguments may re-state the conventional view in the social sciences from de Tocqueville onwards that the deep social class divisions of industrial Europe were not reproduced in the United States where, apart from caste-like divisions between black and white, status and community differences formed a continuous scale of social stratification.

The pedagogical critical theorist Henri Giroux (1991, 1992) also vacillates between the postmodern emphasis on rupture, proliferation and plurality, and the hegemonic thesis of traditional Marxism. While Giroux provides us with a way of linking citizenship with the cultural politics of education in which education is considered to be critical in understanding modern patterns of cultural consumption, he nevertheless remains uncertain to what exactly a radical conception of citizenship and pedagogy would involve. Although Giroux intends to move towards the postmodern pedagogy which is delineated fundamentally by a discourse of radical democracy, he at the same time wants to extend and deepen these democratic values and ideals which are already embedded within a modernist project of liberal freedoms. In the politics of identity movements, Giroux (1992) finds a democratic thrust that will help to rupture the conventionally conservative discourses on education and educational policy, thereby permitting various forms of transgression of borderlines between citizenship and pedagogy. While barriers do exist in the form of eurocentrism, sexism and racism, Giroux sees popular culture as a radical challenge to existing ideologies of pedagogy. His notion of a critical pedagogy thus approximates the idea of cultural citizenship. He argues that 'critical pedagogy as a cultural politics points to the necessity of inserting struggle over the production and creation of knowledge as part of the broader attempt to create a public sphere of citizens who are able to exercise power over their lives and the social and political performance through which their society is governed' (Giroux, 1991: 50).

United Nations declarations of cultural rights also emphasized the importance of the universality of education, especially as it relates to the right to participate fully in the cultural life of the community and therefore also to maintain those traditions and heritages which constitute any cultural community. Both Prott (1988) and Kartashkin (1982) raised the significance of cultural identity through a discussion of universal cultural rights, being mindful nevertheless of the paucity of empirical research on this subject. Prott in fact identifies eleven cultural rights in existing declarations between nations, which are binding in international law. Five of these rights are rights of individuals and there are another six which he classifies as the collective rights of the people. Apart from the rights to respect cultural identity and the right of people to their own artistic, historical and cultural wealth, they include the respect of the cultural rights of minorities, the right to avoid or to resist cultural imperialism, and the equal enjoyment of the common heritage of humanity. Interestingly enough, only Prott acknowledges that contradictions may indeed arise as a result of these two sets of cultural rights, between minority and universal rights. Cultural citizenship may well help to stem or to control cultural imperialism, but it may also implicitly articulate conflicts between local or particular rights and the right to enjoy the universalistic legacy of humanity. The right to maintain one's historical culture may well contradict other universalistic claims about economic and social rights. The controversy about the existence and importance of cliterectomy in certain Muslim communities is an important, if extreme, version of this tension between the particular and the universal. However, these specific examples fall under the general problem of whether the law should focus on sameness or difference (Olsen, 1996), the problem which constitutes the core of the analysis of cultural rights in contemporary societies.

Kartashkin (1982) recognizes the interdependence of social rights, namely the right to an education with cultural rights and his rather truncated discussion of the latter draws on J.S. Mill's treatment of the need to have secure civil liberties that will allow full artistic, literary and scientific expression, as well as the production of and access to information and communication networks and media that will enable citizens to participate fully in the cultural life of their society. Although Kartashkin notes the general importance of cultural rights in various universal declarations of rights, he does not sufficiently problematize either the idea of cultural identity or cultural rights as such. While both Kartashkin and Prott raise the difficult question of heritage in terms of ownership and cultural decolonization, they do not connect cultural rights to those aspects of cultural policy relating to media formats and communication systems.

Electronic Democracy

This traditional debate over cultural imperialism and cultural rights, which we might see as an extension of the nineteenth-century liberal debate over conscience and individual freedoms in a mass society, has been in recent years transformed by the revolution of communication media and information production and distribution systems. Aspects of this debate can of course be traced back to Daniel Bell who in his concept of the industrial society and postindustrialism developed a sophisticated theory of the information revolution and the centrality of the university and tertiary education systems to knowledge production and knowledge control (Bell, 1974). Postindustrial society was defined in terms of the axial principle of the centrality and codification of theoretical knowledge which became the basis of economic growth and social stratification. These changes in the social structure meant that the primary institutions of society were the university, the academy and the corporate research institutes. The principal planning issues of such a society were organized around science and education policies, and its major social issues concerned questions of access to education. Its major political problems were the effects of the cohesiveness or otherwise of the 'new class' (Bell, 1974: 114–119). Bell's contribution to this debate has been neglected in favour of more recent approaches to the electronics revolution, but his treatment of the postindustrial revolution established many of the principal theoretical issues of both postmodern social theory (Lyotard, 1984) and the theory of the virtual community.

The same argument would apply to the writings of Marshall McLuhan. McLuhan's imaginative analysis of the media revolution was somewhat spurned by Bell, despite their obvious similarities. Bell's claim that McLuhan's own form of analysis was itself a product of cultural trivialization which it sought to analyse, only served to obscure the breakthrough which McLuhan had achieved. McLuhan's contribution was in fact complex and diverse but in essence he argued that the medium is the message, that is the form of the media actually is constitutive of the content of the message itself. Furthermore, there are radically different forms of media, such as 'hot' and 'cold', and we need to understand the radically different implications of these distinctive forms of communication. The electronic revolution has brought with it a profound change in both life style and consciousness, and the problem is that much conceptual thinking is stuck in print medium. Finally, he developed an early and influential argument that the electronic media have resulted in the globalization of culture, leading to the global village (McLuhan, 1964). McLuhan's work paved the way towards contemporary media theory which indicates that we can no longer think, for example, about the problems of democracy and literacy as if we still inhabited a print-based culture.

The important issue here is whether there has been a revolution in the means of communication which is such that all previous modes of thinking about communication and information are rendered obsolete and irrelevant. If McLuhan's argument is correct, then we need to re-think not only the specific idea of cultural citizenship but the basic premises of democratic theory as such. McLuhan's theory of communication indicates that we need to reconceptualize democratic theory in order to understand the impact of globalized electronic media on identity, participation and culture. In general, much conceptualization of democratic citizenship, as illustrated by the differences between, for example, Bobbio and Wexler, still assumes the dominance of print-based culture. This recognition underlines the importance of the discussion of electronic democracy.

Social theorists of the global media believe not only that we have arrived at a new cultural threshold, but that we have arrived at a unique opportunity to side-step the legacy of the administrative state and to revive participatory democracy through an extension of the impact of electronic communication systems to the wider community. Rejecting anti-technological criticisms and interpretations of culture in the community, Ben Barber (1984), Richard Lanham (1993), Mark Poster (1994) and Ted Becker (1993) have recognized the enormous scope of the digital-satellite-electronic media of communication and their interaction for a revitalization of democratic participation. Each of these writers welcomes rather than laments the arrival or intervention of technology in modern civil society, suggesting that an electronic commonwealth can be realized through the use of numerous cable and satellite services, and television- and consumer-based formats of interaction. Such a commonwealth would bring together individuals otherwise largely disenfranchised from political life by powerful institution elites and media systems, that way reinstating the political subject into modern life.

They believe that the new media of the communication revolution can overcome a fundamental problem of modern democracy, namely space. The classical democracies of Greece and Rome could be participatory because, in principle, face-to-face dialogue was possible. In the ancient polis, space did not prohibit dialogue, which was the medium of character development for the citizen

(Dahl, 1989: 14). However, with the exception of Walter Wriston (1992) most observers failed to address the spatial or geographical impact which electronic democracy might have on existing definitions of citizenship. Whether or not the electronic commonwealth will indeed constitute a de-territorialized and de-nationalized entity is neither posed adequately nor successfully analysed. Poster (1994) largely concentrates on how the subject as a political being is constituted within this second media age, as he calls it, an age marked simultaneously by a multiplicity of identities and social interactivity which will displace the priority of organic communities and effective solidarities within various modern projects. Poster's enthusiastic endorsement of second-age technologies of interactivity is tempered by a number of caveats. First 'neither of these technologies has been fully constituted as cultural practices; they are emerging communication systems whose features are yet to be specified with some permanence or finality' and secondly 'it is conceivable that the information super-highway will be restricted in the way the broadcast system is restricted. In that case, the term second media age' is unjustified (Poster, 1994: 80). This restriction will most likely be culturally consonant with wealthy, white male values and ideas. Finally its restrictiveness owes to the fact that 'new technologies, even after two decades of the new social movements, are likely to have been conceived, designed and produced by white males' (Poster, 1994: 89).

Richard Varn (1993), although anxious to see an increase in citizenship participation, expresses a realistic caution about the merits and possibilities of electronic democracy in the information revolution. Varn, formally majority political whip in the Iowa Senate, is worried that citizens may drown in a sea of irrelevant data and information churned out by inordinate distribution points in large bureaucracies and government agencies. Secondly, he is concerned that opinions will override political action if electronic roads to democracy are taken. More enthusiastically, D. Elgin (1993) and Ted Becker embrace the concept of the Electronic Town Meeting(s), the rejuvenation of local identities by reactivating political awareness of participation, and the revitalization of modern politics in and through electronic dialogues. Becker was one of the earliest advocates of electronic democracy and localistic experiments in electronic dialogues and teledemocracy, namely 'democratically aided, rapid, two-way political communication' and he envisages that 'advances in interactive electronic communication technologies would empower the American citizenry and lead to a much stronger democracy at the national, regional, state and local levels' (Becker, 1993: 14). Becker asserts that with the origin of the mass television system, political life is now in every citizen's lounge at their finger-tips. He finds evidence in the electronic dialogues of electronic town meetings (ETMs) which took place in Hawaii, Georgia, Oregon, New Mexico and Nova Scotia for a recreation of local, regional and national politics. Combinations of public broadcast programmes, cable television channels and public educational telecommunication networks connect meeting sites potentially providing every citizen with the means to enter a dialogue. His advocacy of electronic democracy preceded the contemporary fascination with the Internet and sparked off numerous debates and analyses of the possibilities for democracy of these developments.

Although Ben Barber (1984) shows more reserve than Becker with regard to electronic democracy, he recognized its important contribution to the debate on ETMs and the argument that contemporary politics is significantly in need of redevelopment and resuscitation by such new media of dialogue, communication and interaction. Indeed the very foundation of the American republic was always about the problems of communication in a nation of strangers. Barber's work is a useful contribution to how citizenship can be empowered by these technological modes of dialogue, exchange and policy construction. Within his 'strong argument' for democratic citizenship lies an appropriation of the techno-culture thesis which advocates, such as Becker, have developed in the United States for the last decade. The creation of the medium to facilitate civic participation in an active democratic programme would require significant linkage among neighbourhood assemblies that permitted equal discussion of shared concerns as well as national and indeed international discussions among individuals on national and local initiatives. Barber argues that there already exists a body of evidence which supports the view of the civic utility of ETMs and answers the fears of its critics about the abuses of power made possible by these interactive systems. 'The technology exists to develop even more sophisticated uses' (Barber, 1984: 275) and thus he believes that a civic communications co-operative should be established in America. Barber's views laid the foundation for contributions by Wriston (1992) and Feather (1994) on the transformative capacity of the information revolution for democracies. Feather (1994) in particular, provides an interesting and vigorously written analysis of techno-culture in the postindustrial environment.

Other writers have seen the impact of the electronic revolution in terms of the instability and uncertainty of the authority of the intellectual over establishment values. The contribution of the electronic revolution is to popularize truth(s). For example, Richard Lanham's *The Electronic Word: Democracy, Technology and the Arts* (1993), taking a more literary approach to the examination of the visual and literary arts and the humanities, wants to collapse what he sees as several invidious dichotomies in the humanist traditional treatment of the arts and literature and its more hegemonic control over the 'secrets of truth' found within the Western literary canon. He seeks to deconstruct unnecessary oppositional dichotomies in the approach to the arts and the teaching of humanities by public intellectual gatekeepers. Herein lies the usefulness of 'the electronic word', the latter to be used metaphorically to cover an electronic rendering of paintings. It is effective in breaking down the traditional distance between professional authority within the academy and the everyday world of mundane communication. For example, the 'criticism/creation dichotomy automatically becomes, in a digital world, a dynamic oscillation: you simply cannot be a critic without being in turn a creator' (Lanham, 1993: 107). Digitization renders the world of music making it 'infinitely more accessible than it was, accessible to people who before had not the talent or the resources to make music and how it sounds' (Lanham, 1993: 107). He therefore argues, and surprisingly, that the digitization of the arts radically democratizes the artistic field. This argument clearly places Lanham in the cultural dissemination/democratization camp which raises doubts about the relevance and scope of Bourdieu's approach and other structuralist interpretations within cultural sociology. Lanham's intention is not to flatten out the Western canon of literature but rather to deconstruct the dualistic or oppositional set of contrasts which has regulated debate within the arts, artistic pedagogy and liberal humanism generally. He argues that 'Western Lit is in no danger from Westerns. They are both going interactive' (Lanham, 1993: 106). Here therefore we see once more that the issue of pedagogy is central to any realization of the democratic impulse and that interactivity provides a very effective way of reducing the formal and informal barriers to cultural literacy, the production of cultural works and political dialogue.

Perhaps the most extensive treatment of the connection between democratic practice and electronic worlds of communication has been undertaken by Abramson, Arterton and Orren in *The Electronic Commonwealth* (1988). As the title indicates, the authors are interested in a re-examination of the communitarian ideal but they approach this tradition from the perspective of a pluralized communitarian politics. This electronic commonwealth is not a hi-tech politics manifesto but rather it 'harks back to the old democratic ideal of congregating the people together' and looks to the new technologies of communication not to change or to update that ideal but instead to establish the practice of a 'lost democratic arts' (Abramson et al., 1988: 31). This approach successfully problematizes what is new about the 'new' media of electronic communication and concludes that we are indeed at another major turning point in global history, one which is analogous to the impact which the Guttenberg press had.

Two distinctive aspects are identified. First there is a marked shift in time travelled across tracks of transmission and convergence, and secondly there is the decentralization and devolution of the means of communication, that is the means of political discourse. Like Lanham and other 'cultural democrats', the authors argue that individual identification need no longer be wholly circumscribed by traditional dimensions such as class, status, gender, ethnicity or bureaucratic jurisdictions. In addition they are not circumscribed by the messages of the traditional forms of mass media. This anti-utopian commonwealth celebrates the empowerment of a previously apathetic citizenry who now possess the means to enter directly into political dialogue and opinion formation via various multimedia sites such as videotext, videoconferencing, capital VCR time delayed monitoring, cable services, e-mail and the Internet. In general terms, the authors hold that uniformity and monopolistic measures of control have failed and will not win out in the final analysis. Dissemination, diversity, literacy, political consciousness and anarchic use of infocommunication media predominate in this analytical and normative paradigm.

There is however an important caveat in relation to 'information classes' where the issue of hardware availability raises certain difficulties in the rate of participation in ETMs and thus in 'electronic political dialogue'. For example, the Alaska Reading Project raises important issues in this field. At the time they anticipated that hardware availability would rise, while the cost of information services and networks were expected to decline gradually. Part of this evidence came from the previous history of the domestic telephone, television, wireless, radio and, of course more recently, PCs and VCRs where there had been significant reductions in unit costs. Concentrating on the American data, they of course identified restrictions which arguably apply to other societies. While the authors are interested in reviving these lost democratic arts, the Electronic Common-wealth abdures any notion that these new technologies can be used simply to enhance opinion poll taking, elite governance (both in the corporate and government fields) or self-interested rational action. Neither the organic community nor the self-interested utilitarian actor can prevail in their idea of an electronic utopia. Thus, 'empowering citizens to participate in local government and bringing them the sometimes distant information to participate intelligently. …is the goal of the Electronic Commonwealth' (Abramson et al., 1988: 277). It envisages various levels of interactivity and various commonly shared channels of popular culture and symbolic acculturation. In short, it argues 'the microphone enlarged partici-pation in meetings but did not explode the constraints of numbers and distance' something which the electronic age does with 'all the threats and promises for democracy implicit in mass participation' (Abramson et al., 1988: 278).

The theme of these theoretical and empirical analyses is to point to the effect which class, gender, ethnicity, educational attainment and geography have on the consumption and, to a lesser extent, production of cultural works and practices. Although academic opinion is divided over the extent to which these typical soci-ological categories of analysis (especially social class) shape patterns of cultural literacy and cultural need, there is some convergence in opinion on the salience of education for the acquisition of cultural competence and cultural capital. Restrictions to these forms of acquisition are quantifiable, making it possible to arrive at quantitative and qualitative distinctions or judgements on the basis of who is excluded or included in divergent modes of cultural consumption and pro-duction. Since social actors need audiences and vice versa, cultural participation could encompass both forms of cultural competency, that is the citizen is both subject and agent of cultural life. On this basis, it should be possible to create indices which could be constructed to measure to what extent location, education, social class, gender, race and linguistic knowledge stand in the way of full access to and participation in either the high or low cultural spheres of any particular state or society.

From this debate, at least three criteria of measurement emerge. First there is the question of the relative exclusivity in the consumption and production of cul-tural objects. Simple illustrations such as the extent of literacy are relevant to the measurement of such exclusivity or inclusivity. Secondly, there is the question of the diversity of cultural forms, objects of symbolic significance, and high and low cultures. It was generally held that mass culture, however democratic, resulted in a reduction of diversity or alternatively an increase in standardization. The theo-rists of the electronic commonwealth suggest that this issue is no longer relevant. Thirdly, there is the absolute level of cultural production as opposed to consump-tion and the issue of the ownership of the means of production. Once more, the new wave of electronics is seen to bypass the traditional issue of unequal owner-ship. Finally, there is the issue of the relative spatial concentration of cultural lit-eracy and production, for example, in capital cities. Electronic communication is thought to minimize the conventional problem of space in classical approaches to democracy. Although these debates take us somewhere towards the measurement of the idea of cultural citizenship, much of the literature is unfortunately specific in that it often fails to take into account the globalization of culture and the impact of such globalization on national cultural politics. Whether localistic strategies can survive globalization is somewhat neglected in favour of more optimistic interpretations of democratic opportunities within the local community and the local state. An alternative negative scenario would have to take into account, for example, the role of global communication systems for military surveillance. Finally, much of this literature is devoted to the advanced, industrial societies of the northern hemisphere. In Latin America, the construction of unified nation-states on the basis of considerable internal diversity (between rural and urban, pre-colonial and colonial, dominant and subordinant, Christian and pagan) means that the centralized media function to impose political domination in the name of cultural citizenship. Museums become strategies for confining 'folklore' and 'popular cultural antiquities', with their alternative visions of nationhood, to the safe and distant past as part of the collective memory (Rowe and Schelling, 1991). Enthusiasm for electronic democracy has to be qualified by a comparative awareness of the dangers of cultural McDonaldization and electronic imperialism.

Conclusion: Towards a Theory of Cultural Citizenship

In this discussion of cultural citizenship, I have concentrated on two issues: the importance of culture in understanding identity in relation to the formal or legal status of the citizen, and secondly I have examined problems about the rights and obligations of participation in the political community in the age of the digital revolution. Where there has been any analysis of democracy and cultural rights, debates about cultural citizenship have been traditionally housed within debates about education and progressive pedagogies. Communitarian theories have been used to extend some of the individualistic assumptions of J.S. Mill and others. However, in recent years the question of cultural citizenship has been raised primarily around the notion of identity. Political identities have become problematic as a consequence of multi-culturalism, decolonization and globalism. Attempts to provide a theory of cultural identity have typically turned to postmodernism and feminism for some analytical guidelines. These developments in the theory of citizenship provide an important extension and criticism of the simplistic notion of identity in Marshall's influential account of the development of citizenship.

The traditional issue of community participation in the large democracies of modern society has been revolutionized by the advent of global electronic communication systems. Whereas the prohibition of space was a conventional limitation of democratic dialogue, the new electronics can in principle overcome such constraints of space. We could argue that space is no longer a scarcity in modern political theory, but time is in short supply as the wave of electronic communication overwhelms existing social systems.

Theorists of the electronic democracy are of course divided between those who believe that the limitations of access to the hardware will reproduce existing hierarchies and inequalities, and those who are optimistic about access, given assumptions about inevitable cost reductions. It is certainly the case that these new means of communication have transformed traditional assumptions about political and economic limitations to dialogue. In summary, there are three broad areas of criticism of the electronic 'virtual community' (Rheingold, 1993). First, there is the commodification of information, resulting in the erosion of a public sphere. Secondly, there is the argument that high-bandwidth interactive networks increase the level and sophistication of political surveillance, resulting in a loss or decline of personal liberties. Finally, there is the view that we have already moved into a hyper-reality, where the politics of spectacle and entertainment construct the citizen as a passive, hypnotized subject, resulting in a simulation of political reality.

The nature of 'community' in the modern electronic world becomes a crucial issue in political theory and public debate. Who are 'the strangers' with whom we can have communion in the electronic commonwealth? It is suggested that the notion of 'thick' and 'thin' communities might be a useful distinction to further analysis (Turner, 1998). The traditional (thick) *gemeinschaft* was an organic community based on hot communication in which members were bound together by propinquity, common cultural inheritance and shared memories. The electronic (thin) community and cool communication can be an association of strangers, who never physically connect with each other, share only a computer language, and 'visit' each other's sites merely out of idle curiosity. The modern web site, in this respect, could be regarded as the modern equivalent of the 'market' which dominated nineteenth-century discussions of association versus community. The contemporary Internet could be regarded as a global market of strangers exchanging information and as a consequence creating a thin community. As local cultural identities thicken in response to decolonization, political networks extend through thin channels of exchange.

One issue with optimistic theories of the electronic democracy is that, by emphasizing the innovative and unique features of the technology of communication, they have forgotten or ignored many of the valid conclusions of traditional communications theory. These questions can be divided around (i) the everyday world as a mediator of (public) communications and (ii) the security of everyday identities. These questions take us back to McLuhan and Mannheim. Given recent transformations of the university system by new management practices and global marketing strategies, there can be little hope that a free-floating intelligentsia can provide moral leadership over the Internet. The state through the university system has been divorced from high culture, leaving intellectuals in the cultural market place to sell their intellectual services to global corporations. Mannheim's optimism about an effective democratization of culture was based on assumptions about national sovereignty, an independent intelligentsia, the authenticity of high culture in Europe and the benevolent effects of rational planning for democracy. There is a globalization of culture and communication which creates both risks and opportunities for democratic participation, but these participatory opportunities are filtered through social stratification (class, gender and age) and through the life-chances and the exigencies of everyday life. Educational attainment appears to be crucial to participation in the emerging electronic democracy, and thus active citizenship in the virtual community presupposes the existence of a mass education system. Employment opportunities in the global labour markets of the symbolic analysts will be constrained by the high level of 'down-sizing' and 're-structuring' which are characteristic strategies of the large corporations in the 1990s (Reich, 1991). In this respect, the opportunities for radical change in the pattern of cultural participation will prove to be more limited than optimistic Mannheimian theories of democracy currently predict.

Note

I would like to thank Dr John Mandelios, Griffith University, Queensland for assistance in writing this chapter, especially for his exploration of the literature on electronic democracy.

References

Abramson, J.B., Arterton, F.C. and Orren, G.R. (1988) *The Electronic Commonwealth: The Impact of New Media Technologies on Democratic Politics*. New York: Basic Books.

Aron, R. (1974) 'Is Multinational Citizenship Possible?', *Social Research*, 41 (4): 638–656.

Barber, B. (1984) *Strong Democracy*. Berkeley: University of California Press.

Baudrillard, J. (1987) *The Evil Demon of Images*. Sydney: The Power Institute.

Bauman, Z. (1987) *Legislators and Interpreters. On Modernity, Post-modernity and Intellectuals*. Cambridge: Polity Press.

Beck, U. (1992) *Risk Society. Towards a New Modernity*. London: Sage.

Becker, T. (1993) 'Gathering Momentum in State and Local Goverance', *Spectrum*, 66 (2): 14–19.

Beddar, R. and Hill, D.M. (1992) *Economic, Social and Cultural Rights: Progress and Achievement*. London: Macmillan.

Bell, D. (1974) *The Coming of Post-Industrial Society. A Venture in Social Forecasting*. New York: Basic Books.

Blackman, R. (ed.) (1993) *Rights of Citizenship*. London/New York: Mansell.

Blau, J. (1986) 'High Culture as Mass Culture', *Society*, 23 (4): 65–69.

Blau, J. (1988) 'Study of the Arts: A Reappraisal', *Annual Review of Sociology*, 14: 269–292.

Blau, J. (1989) *The Shape of Culture: A Study of Contemporary Cultural Patterns in the United States*. Cambridge/New York: Cambridge University Press.

Bobbio, N. (1987) *The Future of Democracy*. Minneapolis: University of Minnesota Press.

Bourdieu, P. (1977) *Outline of a Theory of Practice*. Cambridge: University of Cambridge Press.

Bourdieu, P. (1984) *Distinction. A Social Critique of the Judgement of Taste*. London: Routledge & Kegan Paul.

Bourdieu, P. (1988) *Homo Academicus*. Stanford: Stanford University Press.

Bourdieu, P. (1993) *The Field of Cultural Production*. Cambridge: Polity Press.

Bourdieu, P. and Darbel, A. (1990) *The Love of Art: European Art Museums and their Public*. Stanford: Stanford University Press.

Bourdieu, P. and Passeron, J.-C. (1990) *Reproduction in Education Society and Culture*. London: Sage.

Connolly, W.E. (1995) *The Ethos of Pluralization*. Minneapolis: University of Minnesota Press.

Dahl, R.A. (1989) *Democracy and its Critics*. New Haven and London: Yale University Press.

Dimaggio, P. and Useem, M. (1983) 'Cultural Democracy in a Period of Cultural Expansion: The Social Composition of Arts Audiences in the United States', in J. Kamerman and R. Martorella (eds), *Performers and Performances: The Social Organization of Artistic Work*. New York: Praeger.

Douglas, M. (1966) *Purity and Danger. An Analysis of Concepts of Pollution and Taboo.* London: Routledge & Kegan Paul.

Elgin, D. (1993) 'Revitalizing Democracy Through Electronic Town Meetings', *Spectrum,* 66 (2): 6–13.

Feather, J. (1994) *The Information Society.* London: Library Association.

Featherstone, M. (1991) *Consumer Culture and Postmodernism.* London: Sage.

Geiryn, T. (1990) 'What Happens when Culture is Separated from Society?', *Contemporary Sociology,* 19: 505–506.

Gillen, P. (1984) 'Reading, Writing and Cultural Democracy', *Meanjin,* 43 (4): 525–530.

Giroux, H. (ed.) (1991) *Postmodernism, Feminism, and Cultural Politics: Redrawing Educational Boundaries.* Albany: State University of New York Press.

Giroux, H. (1992) *Border Crossings: Cultural Workers and the Politics of Education.* New York and London: Routledge.

Goodall, P. (1995) *High Culture, Popular Culture: The Long Debate.* St Leonards: Allen & Unwin.

Kartashkin, V. (1982) 'Economic, Social and Cultural Rights', in Philip Alston (ed.), *The International Dimensions of Human Rights, Vol. 1.* Connecticut and Paris: Greenwood Press and UNESCO.

Kukathas, C. (1992) 'Community, Rights and Society: Are There any Cultural Rights?', *Political Theory,* 20 (1): 105–139.

Kymlicka, W. (1995) *Multicultural Citizenship.* Oxford: Clarendon Press.

Lanham, R.A. (1993) *The Electronic Word: Democracy, Technology and the Arts.* Chicago: University of Chicago Press.

Lury, C. (1993) *Cultural Rights: Technology, Legality and Personality.* London: Routledge.

Lyotard, J.-F. (1984) *The Postmodern Condition.* Manchester: University of Manchester Press.

Mannheim, K. (1956) *Essays on the Sociology of Culture.* London: Routledge & Kegan Paul.

Marshall, T. (1950) *Citizenship and Social Class.* Cambridge: Cambridge University Press.

McLuhan, M. (1964) *Understanding Media: The Extensions of Man.* London: Routledge & Kegan Paul.

Mort, F. (1996) *Cultures of Consumption. Masculinities and Social Space in Late Twentieth-century Britain.* London and New York: Routledge.

Olsen, F. (1996) 'Do (only) Women have Bodies?', in P. Cheah, D. Fraser and J. Grbich (eds), *Thinking Through the Body of the Law.* St Leonards: Allen & Unwin, pp. 209–226.

O'Neill, O. (1990) 'Practices of Toleration', in J. Lichtenberg (ed.), *Democracy and the Mass Media.* Cambridge: Cambridge University Press, pp. 155–184.

Pakulski, J. (1997) 'Cultural Citizenship', *Citizenship Studies,* 1 (1): 73–86.

Parsons, T. (1966) *Societies. Evolutionary and Comparative Perspectives.* Englewood Cliffs, NJ: Prentice Hall.

Parsons, T. (1971) *The System of Modern Societies.* Englewood Cliffs, NJ: Prentice Hall.

Poster, M. (1994) 'A Second Media Age?', *Arena,* 1 (3): 49–91.

Prott, L. (1988) 'Cultural Rights as Peoples' Rights in International Law', in James Crawford (ed.), *The Rights of Peoples.* Oxford: Clarendon Press.

Reich, R.B. (1991) *The Work of Nations. Preparing Ourselves for 21st Century Capitalism.* New York: Alfred A. Knopf.

Rheingold, H. (1993) *The Virtual Community. Homesteading on the Electronic Frontier.* Reading, MA: Addison-Wesley.

Roberston, R. (1992) *Globalization. Social Theory and Global Culture.* London: Sage.

Rodota, S. (1993) 'Sovereignty in the Age of Techno-Politics'. Interparliamentary Conference on Citizens, Representative Democracy and European Construction. Paris: Senate Palais de Luxembourg.

Rowe, W. and Schelling, V. (1991) *Memory and Modernity. Popular Culture in Latin America.* London: Verso.

Selbourne, D. (1994) *The Principle of Duty. An Essay on the Foundations of Civic Order.* London: Sinclair-Stevenson.

Senate Standing Committee on Employment, Education and Training (1989) *Education for Active Citizenship in Australian Schools and Youth Organizations.* Canberra: Commonwealth of Australia.

Senate Standing Committee on Employment, Education and Training (1991) *Active Citizenship Revisited*. Canberra: Commonwealth of Australia.

Tully, J. (ed.) (1991) *Pufendorf: 'On the Duty of Man and Citizen According to Natural Law'*. Cambridge: Cambridge University Press.

Turner, B.S. (1998) 'The Airport Departure Lounge Metaphor; Towards an Ironic Theory of Communication', *Australian Journal of Communication*, 25 (1): 1–18.

United Nations (1993) The Vienna Declaration and Programme of Action. Adopted 25 June by the World Conference on Human Rights. Geneva: United Nations Department of Public Information.

Varn, R.J. (1993) 'Jeffersonian Boom or Teraflop?', *Spectrum*, 66 (2): 21–25.

Wexler, P. (1990) 'Citizenship in the semiotic society?', in B.S. Turner (ed.), *Theories of Modernity and Postmodernity*. London: Sage, pp. 164–175.

Wriston, W. (1992) *Twilight of Sovereignty: How Much the Information Revolution is Transforming our World*. New York: Scribner.

Yuval-Davis, N. (1997) *Gender and Nation*. London: Sage.

3

CITIZENSHIP, INTERSUBJECTIVITY AND THE LIFEWORLD

Nick Crossley

This chapter contributes to our understanding of cultural citizenship by examining the intersubjective-lifeworld aspects of citizenship qua status, role and identity. The main part of the chapter focuses on the work of G.H. Mead (1967). Notwithstanding some problems, which I examine, Mead's work makes an important contribution to the sociology of citizenship which has not received the attention it deserves; it allows us to see that citizenship is necessarily rooted in the intersubjective nexus of the lifeworld. Following Habermas (1987), however, I contend that a lifeworld perspective is not sufficient, on its own, for critical social theory. A systems perspective is also required. I therefore begin the chapter with an outline of the 'systemic' aspect of citizenship and I end with an account of the relationship between system and lifeworld.

Citizenship and the Social System

Citizenship fits with a systems perspective in a number of respects. First, it belongs to a specifically differentiated sub-system of society (the administrative–political sub-system), which, in turn, is the product of social evolution and differentiation (Habermas, 1987; Marshall, 1992; Parsons, 1966, 1971). Citizenship, as we know it, only exists in societies with a differentiated and rationalized political system. Secondly, the role of citizens, as tax payers, electorate and welfare recipients, is central to the process of system integration, as defined by Habermas (1987, 1988). To be a citizen is to engage in the basic exchanges of money and power which facilitate co-ordination between the economic, political and cultural sub-systems. The citizen qua citizen finances the state through their taxes and exercises power in relation to it (constituting *its* power) through their voting behaviour and mass loyalty. They are also subject to its power, however, through its imposition of political decisions and the consequences of its organizational accomplishments. These interactions constitute systemic aspects of society because they are performed, quasi-automatically, through strategic actions in reified action contexts.[1] They are not, routinely, open to communicative negotiation.[2] As rights and duties of citizenship they are legally defined and fixed, and bureaucratically provided for by the courts, Parliament and welfare institutions.

The systems perspective is important because many contemporary citizenship issues derive from shifts within economic and political systems. The globalization of capital and labour markets and the corresponding growth of international political (and military) organizations, for example, have been identified as processes which undermine current, national forms of citizenship and necessitate the development of international or global forms (Held, 1991; Roche, 1992); or, to give another example, some writers have identified a structural tension within the citizenship system (qua system) between welfare and democracy (Offe, 1996).

Citizenship and Intersubjectivity

The systems perspective only captures one aspect of citizenship, however, and it is not self-sufficient. Many of the concepts used in the systems account rest upon an intersubjective base. In the first instance, the rights and duties of citizenship are a legal formalization of intersubjective relations of mutual recognition (Fukuyama, 1992; Honneth, 1995; Kojeve, 1969). As Marshall (1992: 6–7) argues, the 'status of citizenship' entails 'full membership of a community' and 'basic human equality of membership', and it therefore depends upon one being recognized by one's community as an equal member of it. Like any other status, citizenship is a marker of one's standing in the community and the respect one commands. More specifically, the status of citizenship entails that one is recognized as an autonomous, self-conscious being, whose projects and beliefs are owed a duty of respect. A citizen is an equal. The status of citizenship is not granted automatically, of course. In many circumstances it must be fought for, as is exemplified by the many emancipatory (citizenship) movements of the nineteenth and twentieth centuries, e.g. working class movements, the suffragettes and feminist movements, the black civil rights movement and other civil liberties groups. These struggles too embody an intersubjective element, however. They are precisely 'struggles for recognition' (Fukuyama, 1992; Honneth, 1995).

Intersubjectivity is equally integral to the other side of the citizen relation – duty. The recognition that it involves is two-way, 'mutual recognition'. To be a citizen is to recognize the other as an autonomous, self-conscious being. This entails that citizens assume responsibility within their community and bestow the same respect towards their fellow citizens that they expect in return. To quote Marshall again:

> If citizenship is invoked in the defence of rights, the corresponding duties of citizenship cannot be ignored. These do not require a man to sacrifice his individual liberty or to submit without question to every demand made by government. But they do require that his acts should be inspired by a lively sense of responsibility towards the welfare of the community. (Marshall, 1992: 41)

There is an almost mathematical logic behind this point – as well as a resonance of the universalization principle expressed in Kant's (1991) 'categorical imperative'. Citizens can only take from the community, in the form of rights, what they put into it in the form of duties, since the rights of any one citizen are constituted through the duties of every other. The right to free speech, for example, rests upon the duty to tolerate and respect the expression of views that one does not share.

The Citizen as Intersubject

Deeper reflection upon the concepts of duty and membership takes us further in the direction of an intersubjective conception of citizenship and towards an appreciation of its lifeworld basis. The work of G.H. Mead (1967), in particular his theory of self-hood, provides a useful starting point for such reflection. The acquisition of language and consequent entrance of the child into the symbolic world of a particular speech community are essential to the development of self-conscious self-hood for Mead. By means of language the child is able to think and simultaneously gain access to their own thoughts, i.e. they 'hear' their own thoughts as they utter them. This process constitutes the reflexivity which is central to self-hood as Mead defines it. Self-hood, he argues, is a temporal, reflexive process, in which the individual ('I') turns back upon and reflectively objectifies their self as 'Me'. In addition to language acquisition, however, Mead stresses the importance of learning to 'take the role' or 'the attitude' of 'the other' for the development of self-hood. If, as children, we are to achieve full self-hood, he maintains, then we must come to recognize that our experience of the world is one amongst many and we must learn to see ourselves from the point of view of the other. This is both because a sense of self necessarily presupposes a sense of what is not self (i.e. what is other) and because the process of becoming conscious of oneself requires that one gain critical distance from oneself. One cannot turn back upon oneself, thus becoming self-conscious, other than by assuming an outside perspective, and this is achieved, according to Mead, by imaginatively assuming the perspective of the other. Furthermore, he argues that we learn to see ourselves both from the point of view of specific others and from the point of view of what he calls 'the generalized other' – that is, from the point of view of the community as a whole, its laws, moral codes etc. This process, which I have discussed and evaluated in detail elsewhere (Crossley, 1996), involves two stages according to Mead. First, in play, the child learns to take different roles and to assume the attitude or role of specific others (e.g. playing 'Daddy' allows the child to see itself from 'Daddy's' point of view). These others are likely to be those close and important to the child and those who exert some power or control over its life. Secondly, building on the achievement of the play stage, the child learns through games, particularly team games, to assume the attitude of the 'generalized other'.

Having said that we become self-conscious by becoming other to ourselves and assuming the views of our community, it is important to add that the perspective of the other does not necessarily prevail in the self-process, dominating decisions about action and suppressing spontaneity or individual agency. Obediance to some basic rules, such as those governing communication, and a basic awareness of the other are necessary to the basic constitution of the self but many of the 'attitudes' of the other are presented to the individual as possibilities (which could be rejected). Although the anticipated response of the other may be keenly felt by the individual they are not forced to submit to it. The internalized view of the other is, in effect, only one participant in a two-way dialogical action, always initiated from the point of view of the individual. What is important for Mead is that we are able to consider the view of the other and recognize that there is another view, not that we necessarily submit to it. Indeed, his discussion of 'I' and 'Me' emphasizes agency. The self-dialogical process is, in his view, constitutive of reflective thought and decision making. To think is to dialogue with oneself and to do this one must have learned to assume the role of the other in relation to oneself. The decentring of the individual perspective in relation to that of the other is thus a condition for the individuation and autonomy of the self.[3]

This particular description of the pathway to self-hood is important in relation to the concept of citizenship because, in contrast to other possible pathways, such as the Lacanian 'mirror stage' (Lacan, 1989), it explains how self-hood can both integrate an individual into a community, affording them a sense of belonging, and also give rise to responsible, reflective and argumentative agency. Like Lacan, Mead views the emergence of self as a form of alienation in which the lived 'I' only has access to itself as a reflective object ('Me') but for him this is the price of both a new form of integration and belongingness (to a social community) and the constitution of a reflective-reflexive agent. It is the process by which one becomes an autonomous and self-conscious member of a social–political community. Moreover, in contrast to Lacan, Mead argues that critical reflection and dialogue between communicative agents can give rise to some genuine self-understanding. In this respect, given the appropriate political structures,[4] the development of one's self is coterminous with becoming a citizen: 'It is this that gives to the man what we term his character as a member of the community; his citizenship...' (1967: 270). Indeed, Mead argues that citizenship is conditional upon recognition of and respect for the communal view: '...the individual maintains himself as a citizen only to the degree that he recognizes the rights of everybody else to belong to the same community' (1967: 270). Or again:

> We cannot be ourselves unless we are also members in whom there is a community of attitudes which control the attitudes of all. *We cannot have rights unless we have common attitudes*. That which we have acquired as self-conscious persons makes us such members of society and gives us selves. (1967: 164, my emphasis)

This statement (above) can be read as an analytic argument, similar to that made earlier – namely, that a system of rights is impossible to sustain, socially, without certain shared attitudes, because rights depend, for their existence, upon being recognized and respected by everyone in the community. It has normative implications too, however. Mead is arguing that citizen rights *should be* conditional upon internalization of certain 'common attitudes', which manifest as laws and duties (i.e. 'the generalized other'). This normative aspect is brought into sharp focus elsewhere in Mead's account, where he argues that animals, because they do not have (intersubjectively mediated) self-consciousness and cannot therefore take on responsibilities and duties, cannot have citizenship rights. Indeed, he suggests that they have no rights at all: 'We are at liberty to cut off their lives; there is no wrong committed when an animal's life is taken away' (1967: 183).

Few today share this stance regarding animals without some qualification. It is commonly believed that animals should be afforded some rights. Notwithstanding this, however, Mead is right to argue that the specific status of citizenship is and should be founded on this conditional intersubjective principle. There is no point in affording the status of citizenship to a being who is incapable of assuming the 'basic structures' of the community because they would be incapable of assuming the role that accompanies that status. Moreover, they could not honour their duties as citizens and their enjoying such a status would therefore, at the very least, constitute a social injustice at the heart of citizenship, and at the most, collapse it from within. They would be a group who had rights without duties, but in not fulfilling their duties they would effectively undermine the rights of everybody else. Nobody would have proper rights because there would be a class of beings at large in the polity who lacked the capacity to respect those rights. This is why citizenship is and must be a conditional status – that is, conditional upon the capacity to fulfil the obligations associated with it and upon the fact of actually doing so.

It may be objected that a consequence of adopting this position is that citizenship is constituted as an exclusive rather than an inclusive status – some critics have already made this point to me. I accept that this is a consequence but have three lines of response to the criticism. First, citizenship is necessarily exclusive – if the term is to have any meaning and is to function as a status then it must demarcate. If everyone and everything were a citizen then being so would amount to nothing. Secondly, being a citizen is not the only way of enjoying rights. As I have already suggested, animals may be afforded rights without being citizens. Thirdly, it is an open matter where, precisely, one would draw the lines of demarcation for those deserving citizenship status and how much flexibility could and should be built in to them (e.g. to accommodate groups of individuals who might periodically or temporarily be incapable of assuming the role) but my contention is that these lines should only exclude those who either cannot take up the role of citizen or who violate the rights of other citizens to the extent that they render citizenship meaningless – in the first case nothing is lost for the excluded individual since they could have no use for citizenship anyway and in the second case the excluded individual does not deserve citizenship. This is an exclusive conception of citizenship then, but its exclusivity is not a problem.

My argument then, following Mead, is that citizenship is bound, both analytically and normatively, to the intersubjective nature of human beings. We are and can be citizens because we can 'take the attitude of the other', transcending our individual particularity and assuming a communal view. This is one of the most central reasons why citizenship must be viewed from the point of view of the lifeworld and intersubjectivity. The citizen is, of necessity, an intersubject. There are problems with Mead's position as it stands, however. One problem is that he tends to emphasize the intersubjective-lifeworld aspects of citizenship and social integration without giving full attention to systemic mechanisms. I am attempting to overcome this problem in the present chapter by considering both system and lifeworld but the omission is too considerable to deal with fully and explicitly here. I will, however, consider two further problems with Mead's approach – the lack of elaboration in his image of the citizen and the problems associated with his notion of 'the generalized other'.

Citizens of the Lifeworld

From Mead we get a basic sense of the social-intersubjective basis of citizenship. To be a citizen, he argues, one must recognize the perspective of specific and generalized others and this recognition, in turn, is dependent upon a specific process of socialization. Citizenship is dependent for its survival upon the basic processes of symbolic reproduction within the lifeworld and cannot be understood independently of this context. Mead's perspective is very general and vague however. He says very little, for example, about the manner in which 'the generalized other' is represented within the lifeworld. Representations are clearly required to afford citizens an image to identify with, appeal to and manipulate in arguments and political contests. But how is such an abstract entity represented? At a concrete level we could answer this question by reference to flags, anthems and to concepts like 'nation' and 'citizen' itself. Each of these can be invoked in communication to represent the generalized other. Indeed the concept of citizenship is fundamental to its social realization. To be a citizen one must know what a citizen is and does. 'Citizenship' must be a meaningful category in one's discursive repertoire, a category which one uses to make sense of one's place in the world and to orient to it. And it must be kept alive as a concept, invoked in discourse and transmitted through socialization, if the institution of citizenship is to remain intact. At a more theoretical level, however, these concepts and icons need to be understood as 'symbols', in the specific sense given that term by Alfred Schutz (1973). A symbol, for Schutz, signifies a transcendent entity – that is, something which is not immediately given to our experience. In particular it signifies those entities that we cannot experience *in toto* because we belong to them (e.g. a 'we' relationship or a community). Symbols don't just represent for Schutz, however. They function within 'we' relations to constitute or bind those relations. The symbol 'family', for example, may precisely be invoked by family members as a means of promoting intra-familial solidarity and binding the group. The icons and concepts of citizenship are symbols in precisely this sense – they signify a transcendent phenomenon ('the generalized other' or, to use a different name for the same thing, the political community) and, at the same time, function to constitute and bind that phenomenon, realizing it.

It is not just symbols which are missing in Mead's account however. The citizen role involves a range of forms of tacit knowledge, competence and taken-for-granted assumptions, all of which are overlooked in his account. Citizens must know how to engage in citizenship activities. They require basic working knowledge of the political system and skills in accessing and processing information, interpreting political talk and debating public issues. All of this must be contained in the taken-for-granted knowledge which comprises their (shared) lifeworld. Citizenship is not just about taking things for granted, of course. It is about identifying and contesting assumptions. And this may extend to contesting the meaning of 'citizenship' itself. Indeed, it is perhaps a central feature of the concept of citizenship, at the level of the lifeworld, that it is always open to contestation. Such questioning activity involves taking up a role and engaging with and from within a specific cultural tradition of citizenship, however, and my point is that Mead fails to elaborate upon this culture of citizenship.

A further point, which stems from this, is that citizenship is a rather more precarious phenomenon than Mead accounts for. It is not achieved, once and for all, but must be sustained and nurtured within the lifeworld. Marshall (1992) recognizes this, in a roundabout way, when he considers 'duty' and the problems it poses. Some duties are easily guaranteed for the polity, he claims, because they are effected more or less automatically, are unambiguous and require little in the way of motivation or sentiment on the behalf of the citizen (e.g. paying taxes and national insurance contributions). Other duties are more problematic, however, since they are either vague or require habits which can be difficult to instil and maintain. These duties and more specifically the question of how citizens are to be persuaded to fulfil them is something of a problem: 'A successful appeal to the duties of citizenship can be made in times of emergency, but the Dunkirk spirit cannot be a permanent feature of any civilization' (Marshall, 1992: 46). Amongst the duties that are difficult to sustain, Marshall singles out the obligation to work in particular, but it is clear that he has a wider conception of these duties which involves having a sense of loyalty to one's community, a loyalty which, he argues, stems from a sense of belonging.

It is because of the precarious nature of the cultural basis of citizenship that writers such as Habermas (1987) express concern about the 'colonization of the lifeworld' by expanding economic and administrative sub-systems.[5] The corrosive effects of this process could undermine the culture of citizenship and, with it, citizenship itself. And it is perhaps for this same reason that citizenship remains a concern for many social movements and political parties. The Communitarian movement in the USA, at least as represented by Etzioni (1995) in *The Spirit of Community*, for example, is highly critical of the decline of a citizen culture and calls for its renewal. Likewise in Britain, a number of campaigns have developed in recent years, criticizing the lack of a sense of duty and loyalty within certain sectors of society. Following the highly publicized murder of her husband (headmaster Philip Lawrence) by a gang of youths with knives, for example, Frances Lawrence launched a (well publicized) campaign to open up public debate on morality and promote citizenship values in British society, particularly in the education and socialization of the young. These are not isolated efforts. Throughout the century one can see evidence of fears regarding the decline of a culture of citizenship and attempts to reinvigorate it (e.g. Rose, 1985, 1989).

Having said that these points go beyond Mead's position, it is important to add that his dynamic and dialogical conception of self-hood is integral to what is being said here. Although it is central to citizenship that individuals are able to and actually do internalize the views of the community, *including their culture of citizenship*, it is equally important that they are not subordinated to those views, that they can step back from them and oppose them or rather engage with them in dialogical fashion. This, to reiterate, is integral to what citizenship is about. Indeed, this is precisely what Etzioni, Frances Lawrence and others are doing.

The Culture of Citizenship: Lifeworld and System

The culture of citizenship within a society is clearly very important. Citizenship in every era depends upon it. Every era must confront a distinct range of problems in this respect however. In our own era the process of globalization demands additional knowledge and familiarity of political systems, by citizens, whilst the constant revolutions in information and communication technologies require ever new forms and degrees of I-Tech literacy if citizens are to be well informed (see Schutz (1964) for a discussion of the 'well informed citizen'). The citizen in the information age requires a quite different range of skills and taken-for-granted knowledge to his/her predecessor and those required skills and assumptions are constantly shifting. Without these skills individuals cannot properly perform their citizen role. They lack the knowledge which would allow them to choose and argue on public–political issues and are therefore excluded from full citizenship.

These issues are posed here as problems for the citizen, in the sense that they are problems experienced by citizens. As such they may form a potential axis for social critique. These issues can also be posed from the systems perspective which was discussed at the beginning of the chapter however. From a systems perspective, the (lifeworld-based) culture of citizenship secures the action orientations, motivations and legitimation necessary for both social and system integration – any 'damage' to the lifeworld thus automatically threatens the system. Furthermore, new forms of global citizenship, which are necessitated, as I have already briefly noted, by the globalization of economic and political systems (see also Held, 1991; Roche, 1992), will only be fully possible (and meaningful) to the extent that the symbols and taken-for-granted assumptions that secure the citizens' role and identity develop a global orientation. We can briefly illustrate this latter point by considering the case of British integration with Europe. British citizens are slowly becoming European citizens at the level of institutions and the European social system. They have the right to vote in European elections, for example, and the right to appeal on legal and human rights issues to the European Courts. Many of the structural components of basic European citizenship are either in place or are developing. There is a common perception, however, that European citizenship has largely failed to 'catch on' in Britain, as is evidenced by low electoral turnouts at European elections, disputes over questions of sovereignty and the widely perceived distrust and lack of enthusiasm for integration amongst the British general public and some politicians. 'Europe' has not entered the tacit horizon of meanings and taken-for-granted assumptions within which the British public conduct themselves politically. It is an explicit concern, about which very little is either taken for granted or agreed upon, but unlike other such debates on citizenship it is conducted from an external viewpoint. The British question as to whether 'we' should be in Europe and if so how far, makes clear that 'we' is Britain rather than Europe and that Europe is still other. There is of course a sense in which this national 'we' is itself amplified by the perceived threat of the other (Europe), but it is interesting in this respect that Europe does not seem to benefit in the same way when the focus is shifted to a global level. If international alliances are sought in the global context 'we' British are as happy forming a 'we' with the USA or the Commonwealth as with 'them' Europeans. The symbol or concept of Europe is not paired with the concept of citizenship in the shared structures of relevance of the British life-world. I am not claiming that British reluctance to stay in Europe can be reduced to our socialization, history or sentiment. These are important factors in relation to 'gut instincts' but there are serious issues to be debated about the likely politi-cal and economic consequences of closer integration, whose validity claims rest upon less particularistic and sentimental criteria. The point is, however, that whether or not it is right to be in Europe, shifts will be required in the lifeworld if European citizenship is to be meaningful and politically effective in Britain; that is, if people are to appropriate and act out European citizenship, making it real. Institutional provision and shifts at the system level alone will not suffice.

Formalism and the Generalized Other

Returning to Mead, the second problem area with his work concerns the notion that citizens must, to qualify as citizens, have internalized the attitudes of the gen-eralized other. It could be objected that this position is overly formal, in the sense that it says nothing substantive about the ethics, rights and duties of citizenship; that is, it says nothing about what the view of the generalized other *should* be. I will not dwell upon this issue because it is not, in my view, a problem. Developing Habermas' (1992) view, I contend that the cultural pluralism of con-temporary societies necessitates a formalistic approach. There is, in effect, a diverse range of substantive views of citizenship at large within modern Western societies, particularly if we include international societies, and the job of acade-mic theories of citizenship should be to engage with this diversity and consider procedures through which it might be reconciled. Formalism and proceduralism are precisely what is required for a normative approach to citizenship in the con-temporary era.

Cultural plurality does pose problems for Mead, however, in so far as it seems to undermine the idea of a 'generalized other'. There is, we might argue, very little that is generalizable about 'the other' in contemporary societies. Self and others live and have been socialized within a wide variety of different cultures and communities. Putting this another way – there is a variety of generalized others, each belonging to the different communities within modern Western soci-eties. Religions are an obvious and significant source of communal differentiation in this respect, since they usually involve clearly articulated systems of substan-tive ethics, rooted in specific worldviews. They are not the only sources of dif-ferentiation, however. Political groupings (including those usually termed 'New Social Movements') are another important source. Posed in one way, this is an analytic problem in Mead's work, which can be formulated as a question: how are we to identify a generalized other in such a pluralistic context? But the ques-tion has normative implications too. Mead can be read as calling for cultural homogenization of groups who do not wish to be homogenized or as suppressing difference in the name of a specific cultural tradition. His citizens orient to *the* generalized other.

To tackle this problem we must begin by stating clearly what Mead means by taking the attitude of the 'generalized other'. On my reading, the bottom line is that there should be a common law and administrative process to which we all defer. Mead is not suggesting that we need common attitudes in the lay sense. His is basically a liberal position which values the fact that individuals and groups within society have different beliefs and perspectives on a range of issues, but which recognizes the need for each group to recognize the others and to work together in creating a common system of law, justice etc. This is not a value free judgement. Liberalism does not stand above the fray. It is itself one amongst the variety of perspectives that it recognizes as existing within society and it has different values (e.g. freedom of belief) to some other perspectives. But in Mead's case it is a perspective which appeals to certain sociological facts, as well as values. One's community and communal belongingness is not, in the first instance, a matter of choice but rather of mutual interference: 'The question whether we belong to a larger community is answered in terms of whether our own action calls out a response in this wider community, and whether its response is reflected back in our own conduct' (Mead, 1967: 271). Whether we like it or not our behaviours (informed by our value systems, etc.) interfere with those of others. This is one reason why Sartre claims that 'Hell is other people!' – that is, because, as the title of his play suggests, there is *No Exit* from social relations and the mutual interference they entail. Furthermore, Mead contends that some sort of solution to this interference *will* be arrived at. Some stable mechanism for co-ordinating interference will emerge. His reading of both history and Hegel make him aware that the solution is often a 'fight to the death', resulting in either annihilation or domination of one party by the other. He also presents a more optimistic possibility however. Contact of any one culture or community with another initiates new forms of social relationships, he notes, and these forms of social relationship are the basis upon which a common system of communication, a cultural bridge, can be established, so giving rise to a bigger, inclusive community. Human beings cannot help but communicate in Mead's view. Communication is part of human nature, an evolutionary adaptation. Moreover, systems of communication rest upon 'forms of life' (to borrow a term from Wittgenstein (1953)) and are constantly changing as forms of life change and new circumstances and interlocuters are encountered. Wittgenstein coveys this aspect of language well: 'Our language can be seen as an ancient city: a maze of little streets and squares, of old and new houses, and of houses with additions from various periods' (Wittgenstein, 1953: 18). This conception allows for the possibility of negotiation and dialogue between cultures and communities because it identifies them as fluid and open, with no definite boundary around them. Indeed, Mead's view of the communicative nature of human beings leads him to believe that cultural merger and mutation is an inevitable consequence of contact between communities.

The mutual interference of communities, often motivated by economic expansion, is a constant theme of world history for Mead. Families, clans, communities, regions, societies have all expanded, mutually encroached and been forced to resolve their difficulties. This has often resulted in war and domination, he argues, but it can result in real communication and negotiation too and in both cases it results in the formation of new, bigger communities. At his time of writing, prior to the Second World War, the League of Nations was in the process of forming and he saw this as the beginning of a world communicative community. The experience of wars, combined with the growth of international trading (i.e. mutual interference) he argued, was giving rise to an international community.

The critic may reply to this that communication can equally function as a system for securing relations of domination between cultures and often takes the form of cultural imperialism. Mead would have no reason to disagree with this. Indeed, his Hegelianism would perhaps lead him to predict that cultures must 'struggle' before mutual recognition can be achieved between them, and even perhaps to argue that recognition that is not struggled for is not true recognition. What his perspective does offer, however, is a radical antidote to the reified conceptions of language and culture which make issues of difference appear unsolvable. Languages and cultures are constantly undergoing change, for Mead, because they are rooted in the life of communication communities, communities whose boundaries are porous and whose ways of life and contexts of interaction are diverse and changeable. Co-operation is always possible from this perspective and, given the facts of mutual interference, the choice between conflict and co-operation must be made.

If we return to my earlier example of British integration into Europe it is clear to see that cultures are quite sticky, as well as porous. Changes aren't necessarily welcomed or speedy. The importance of Mead's position, however, is that it reminds us to put the nationalistic opposition to European integration into wider perspective. There is nothing natural about any particular national boundary. National sentiments and loyalties are relatively recent historical achievements which, at the time of their inception, were strongly resisted (and sometimes still are) by regional groups. A (relatively) homogenized British language, culture and political system was arrived by way of mutual interference and conflict between local groups and there is no reason to believe that it will stay as it is. Indeed, it simply could not because qua cultural phenomenon it must consist in dynamic interaction – and therefore change. Moreover, Mead's position equally reminds us that we cannot avoid forming social–political relations with those societies and communities whose actions interfere with our own, that our only choice is how we do so.

The Generalized Other and the Public Sphere

We can advance this position on the issue of domination and cultural imperialism by asking how the attitude of the 'generalized other' is and should be generated. *Can a common view (a truly generalized other) be arrived at, between diverse groups, in an equitable way?* If it can't then citizenship can never be anything but an ideological function – sectional beliefs masquarading as general views. Or rather, it cannot be citizenship at all in terms of the intersubjective definition that was offered earlier in this chapter – citizenship as mutual recognition. It is integral to the notion of mutual recognition that everybody has an equal say in determining the communal view. That is precisely what equal membership implies. In the context of large complex social systems this is very likely to involve some sort of representative system of course. But the principle must apply at some level if citizenship is to be said to be realized; there must be equality of opportunity for participation in the process of determining the communal view.

My own response to this question is to advocate a critical position. Following Mead and Habermas I contend that it is possible, in principle, for conflicts to be resolved in a just fashion, by means of dialogue. There is, in my view, nothing *essential* to communication or culture which would prevent this. Furthermore, I would contend that the democratic systems of the modern Western world go some of the way towards achieving this state of affairs. Nevertheless, it is clear that this realization is partial and that we should remain committed to the identification and removal (where possible) of the obstacles that stand in its way. Central to this position is a normative commitment to the notion of the 'public sphere' – to an arena or arenas constituted through the communicative efforts and initiatives of citizens, using various forms of media, wherein issues of public concern can be defined and debated, and through which influence can be brought to bear upon government and legislative bodies. A public sphere is one potentially democratic way in which the view of the community, 'the generalized other', could be formed and determined. This is not to say, to repeat, that there is a fully effective public sphere in any of the Western democracies. We must draw a distinction between the normative advocation of the (perfect) public sphere and the belief in its actual existence or rather, in the effectiveness of the public sphere as it stands in modern societies. There *ought* to be an effective public sphere if citizenship is to be fully realized, but that doesn't mean that there *is*. There certainly are groups of 'active citizens' whose activities, which involve the lobbying of the media, Parliament and the courts, constitute a public sphere of sorts, but there are many obstacles which stand in their way and many of the mechanisms which these groups require to realize a fully functioning public sphere are simply absent.[6] Moreover, though the public sphere is perhaps not quite so one-dimensional as Habermas (1989) describes in his classic study, *The Structural Transformation of the Public Sphere*, there is reason to believe that the political need to secure votes and legitimation often overrides the demand for reasoned debate over serious political issues. This gap between is and ought is more than just an interesting dichotomy, of course: it needs to be filled by social research, critique and reform.

The Public Sphere as a Medium Between System and Lifeworld

The concept of the public sphere is important if we are to capture the agency that is essential to citizenship. Whilst citizenship rests in a lifeworld bedrock, a 'culture of citizenship', it equally rests upon the active engagement of citizens, who take an interest in public issues, constitute them as 'citizenship' issues and argue over them in public (sphere) contexts. The public sphere exists only in and by means of such debate and only for so long as it continues. It is a publicly created phenomenon or nothing at all. In addition, however, it is or rather should be the vehicle which mediates between the lifeworld and the social system. The public sphere 'short circuits' the process of automatic and bureaucratically regulated legitimation, noted at the start of this chapter, and ties the process back into lifeworld argumentation and discourse. The process of collective will formation that it can or at least should entail, can and should also be generative of a pressure which works upon government; the lifeworld currency of ideas and opinions should be transformed into the systemic currency of effective political power.

Conclusion

I have suggested that there is something necessary about citizenship in this chapter, at least at the normative level; the sociological fact of our 'mutual interference' forces upon us the necessity to form social relations with other inidividuals, communities and societies. Isolation and separatism are not options for social animals, particularly when they live in complex divisions of labour. There is a choice to be made, however, between relations of domination and relations of citizenship (qua mutual recognition). We may choose the former and there are many examples where we have but there is nothing inevitable about this. If we choose citizenship, however, then we must confront the implications of its contingency; that is, the fact that one is made, not born, a citizen, and the fact that the culture of citizenship needs to be constantly nourished within the lifeworld and the public sphere. Without the reproduction of identities, role expectations, information and the necessary know-how and taken-for-granted assumptions one cannot be or remain a citizen. Moreover, full citizenship demands an effective public sphere. If we are to follow up and expand upon the notion of cultural citizenship in a critical and constructive fashion then it is these matters that we need to address. We need to consider how effective our public sphere is and how effectively the constituents of citizenship are nourished within the lifeworld. Furthermore, we need to be aware of the scale of our mutual interference. Effective communities are not bounded by the limits of our imagination and identifications but by the reach of the consequences of our actions.

Notes

1 Following Habermas (1987) I see the system aspect of society as being constituted through instrumental actions in reified action contexts.

2 They may, as I note later, be contested in the public sphere of society, but at the point of delivery they are routinized and enforced by non-negotiable laws.

3 Lest this version of self and agency sound overly reflective, it should be emphasized that, for Mead, we can and do act without reflection in our ordinary mundane contexts of actions and we need to do so given the unpredictable gap between the world as we account for it in our plans and the world as we find it when we come to act. This is how we are able to surprise ourselves or find ourselves wondering how we got to be where we are. Furthermore, reflection and planning are always situated for Mead; though they may precede and anticipate some of our actions, they always emerge out of contexts as a function of those contexts and they necessarily utilize shared lifeworld resources.

4 I do not mean to suggest by this that full self-hood necessarily coincides with full citizenship; this is only the case in societies which, first, have an institution of citizenship which, secondly, recognizes the group to which any particular individual belongs as being worthy of citizenship. One can enjoy reflexive self-hood without being a citizen.

5 Briefly stated, the colonization of the lifeworld involves the replacement of forms of linguistically achieved and negotiable mechanism of social integration by forms which rely upon money and power.

6 My own empirical work in this area has been on psychiatric groups and movements.

References

Crossley, N. (1996) *Intersubjectivity: The Fabric of Social Becoming*. London: Sage.

Etzioni, A. (1995) *The Spirit of Community*. London: Fontana.

Fukuyama, F. (1992) *The End of History and the Last Man*. Harmondsworth: Penguin.

Habermas, J. (1987) *The Theory of Communicative Action Vol II: Lifeworld and System*. Cambridge: Polity Press.

Habermas, J. (1988) *Legitimation Crisis*. Cambridge: Polity Press.

Habermas, J. (1989) *The Structural Transformation of the Public Sphere*. Cambridge: Polity Press.

Habermas, J. (1992) *Moral Consciousness and Communicative Action*. Cambridge: Polity Press.

Held, D. (1991) 'Democracy, the Nation State and the Global System', *Economy and Society*, 20 (2): 138–172.

Honneth, A. (1995) *The Struggle for Recognition*. Cambridge: Polity Press.

Kant, I. (1991) *The Moral Law: Groundwork of the Metaphysic of Morals*. London: Routledge.

Kojeve, A. (1969) *Introduction to the Reading of Hegel*. New York: Basic Books.

Lacan, J. (1989) *Ecrits*. London: Routledge.

Marshall, T.H. (1992) *Citizenship and Social Class*. London: Pluto.

Mead, G.H. (1967) *Mind, Self and Society*. Chicago: University of Chicago Press.

Offe, C. (1996) *Modernity and the State: East, West*. Cambridge: Polity Press.

Parsons, T. (1966) *Societies: Evolutionary and Comparative Perspective*. New Jersey: Prentice Hall.

Parsons, T. (1971) *The System of Modern Societies*. New Jersey: Prentice Hall.

Roche, M. (1992) *Rethinking Citizenship*. Cambridge: Polity Press.

Rose, N. (1985) *The Psychological Complex*. London: Routledge & Kegan Paul.

Rose, N. (1989) *Governing the Soul*. London: Routledge.

Schutz, A. (1964) 'The Well Informed Citizen: An Essay on the Distribution of Knowledge', in M. Natanson (ed.), *Collected Papers II: Studies in Social Theory*. The Hague: Martinus Nijhoff.

Schutz, A. (1973) 'Symbol, Reality and Society', in M. Natanson (ed.), *Collected Papers Vol I: The Problem of Social Reality*. The Hague: Martinus Nijhoff, pp. 287–356.

Wittgenstein, L. (1953) *Philosophical Investigations*. Oxford: Blackwell.

4

THE REINVENTION OF CITIZENSHIP

Anthony Elliott

'In the twentieth century', wrote T.H. Marshall (1973: 84), 'citizenship and the class system have been at war.' The advancement of the democratic potential of modernity, according to Marshall's classic analysis, has occurred as a complex, negotiated trade-off between the evolution of capitalism (and the oppressive effects of class inequalities) on the one hand, and the integrative effects of an extension of citizenship to social rights and social equality on the other. 'The expansion of social rights', Marshall says, 'is no longer merely an attempt to abate the obvious nuisance of destitution in the lowest ranks of society…It is no longer content to raise the floor-level in the basement of the social edifice, leaving the superstructure as it was. It has begun to remodel the whole building' (1973: 96–97). On this view, the development of citizenship as a cluster of social and political rights has provided sources of social solidarity for processes of democratization. Civil society, underpinned by an appreciation of civil or legal rights, is based upon the widening and deepening of rationality and solidarity.

Marshall's work on citizenship provided a powerful alternative interpretation of modernization and modernity to that offered by radicals on the left. As Anthony Giddens develops this point:

> Marshall's views were strongly shaped by a critical reaction to Marx and Marxism. Marshall wanted to defend the claims of reformist socialism as contrasted to its bolder and violent cousin, revolutionary communism. He wanted to show also that class conflict was neither the main motor of social transformation nor a vehicle for political betterment. With Max Weber, Marshall accepted class inequality as an inherent element of a capitalistic industrial society. Class division, however, in Marshall's view is only one dimension of such a society. The other, integrative, dimension is that of universal involvement in the national community, given concrete form in the welfare state. (1996: 208)

Marshall's account of the formation of citizenship rights, as Giddens emphasizes, is intricately interwoven with the nation-state and welfare institutions. In Marshall's conception, citizenship rights, and the political and cultural struggles associated with them, have a certain parallel with the principles of the national community as understood in the liberal tradition.

The foundations of citizenship, then, belong to the nourishing sphere of the nation-state and its welfare systems. Yet identifying the institutional locus of Marshall's analysis allows us to see that such an approach can no longer grasp the core prospects and risks for civil society at the turn of the twenty-first century. For ours is the era of globalization, reflexive meta-modernism and postmodernization. The nation-state today has to react to the twin forces of globalism and localism, and its associated transformation of the world economy. One comprehensive result of these trans-national events or structures is that the nation-state is no longer the main regulator of socio-systemic order, and thus no longer politically accountable for finding solutions to major and traumatic crises. 'The Welfare State is dead', or so argue the neo-liberals. Such critics have attacked welfare systems for promoting dependency and apathy – and, by implication, socio-economic stagnation. While many question and critique the glaring inadequacies of the neo-liberal interpretation of the world of the late twentieth century, one would surely have to conclude that a model of citizenship contextualized in the frame of the national state no longer holds good, if it ever did.

Some social theorists argue that the deep impact of globalization and new media technologies on mass culture signifies that citizenship is best approached as an ideology, a kind of hangover from the Enlightenment's privileging of rationality and individuality. Hence, reports are spreading about the 'death of the citizen' (see Turner, 1993: 10–12). However, the post-structuralist or semiotic critique of the end of citizenship is based on mistaken, and somewhat simplistic, assumptions about the eclipse of modernity and modernism in the light of postmodernist theory. In this chapter, I propose to analyse some very general trends affecting the cultural conditions of citizenship in the context of a mixed model of modernity and postmodernization. As Bauman (1991, 1992, 1997) has argued, postmodernization does not spell the end of the project of modernity – postmodernity is rather 'modernity without illusions' – as social practice is increasingly geared to reflect back upon itself, to examine its guiding assumptions and aspirations. Accordingly, I want to examine the concept of citizenship in the frame of both modern and postmodern life strategies, set within the broader institutional possibilities and risks inaugurated in an age of globalization. My suggestion is that citizenship need not be theorized pessimistically (despite the hazards and dangers confronting cultural communities and the global social order), but can instead be located as a new departure point for the chronic tension and struggle of civil (or intersubjective) interchange.

Strategies of Identity, Modern and Postmodern

Much talk these days is about identity: identity and its problems, the transformation of identity, and, perhaps most fashionably, the end or death of the subject. Nowadays notions of identity seem inevitably to capsize into either modern or postmodern forms of theorizing. In modern theorizing, the catchword for identity is that of 'project'; in postmodern theorizing, it's that of 'fragmentation'.

The 'project' of modern identity is that of identity building. By identity building I mean the building up of conceptions of oneself, of one's personal and social location, of one's position in an order of things. It is such restless self-activity that replaces the ascriptions of tradition and custom. Freed from the rigidities of inherited identity, human beings are set afloat in the troubled waters of modernity – in its unpredictability and flux, its global transformations, cultural migrations and communication flows. Modernity, we might say, is much preoccupied with identity as an end in itself: people are free to choose the kind of life they wish to live, but the imperative is to 'get on' with the task and achieve. To put it in another way, the order-building, state-constructing, nation-enframing ambitions of modernity require human subjects capable of picking themselves up by their own bootstraps and making something of life, with no rationale beyond the market driven imperatives of constructing, shaping, defining, transforming. Perhaps the most comprehensive analysis to date that we have of this modern conception of identity building has been provided by the British sociologist Anthony Giddens (1991, 1992), who lists 'life-planning', 'internal referentiality' and 'colonization of the future' as defining features. But the paradox of self-construction, if we read Giddens against himself, is that modern craving of identity-maintenance or identity-preservation results in a drastic limiting of life stories, the denigration of meaning in the present and its projection into the future. What Giddens calls the future colonized is a spurious form of self-mastery, if only because the predictable, the routine, and the determined always involve destructive forms of unconscious repetition.

Indeed, the psychic costs of life lived as project are grave. For the founder of psychoanalysis, Sigmund Freud, the crux of the problem is that of delayed gratification. In *Beyond the Pleasure Principle* (1921), Freud argues that psychic violence erupts in that gap between demand for pleasure and pleasure actually attained. 'What we call happiness', writes Freud, 'comes from the (preferably sudden) satisfaction of needs which have been damned up to a high degree, and it is from its nature only possible as an episodic phenomenon.' The more culture presents itself as future-colonizing and project-orientated, the more life becomes repressive: the very contingencies of human experience are imagined insured against by the promise of future certainty, a certainty always tantalizingly out of reach. Elsewhere, in his magisterial cultural analysis *Civilization and its Discontents* (1930), Freud speaks of the modern adventure as a drive for order, a drive which he links to the compulsion to repeat. The trimming of pleasure into that of order, says Freud, spares us the painful ambivalence of indecision and hesitation. So too, the French psychoanalyst Jacques Lacan sees the human subject as marked by the impossibility of fulfilment, an empty subject constituted through a primordial lack or gap of the Other. Indeed, such a decentring of the subject is at the heart of 'Lacan's Freud'. Lacan (1977: 171) states: 'If we ignore the self's radical ex-centricity to itself with which man is confronted, in other words, the truth discovered by Freud, we shall falsify both the order and methods of psychoanalytic mediation; we shall make of it nothing more than the compromise operation that it has, in effect, become, namely, just what the letter as well as the spirit of Freud's work most repudiates.'

In broader social terms, Lacanian theory has often been unproblematically inserted into the whole discourse of postmodernism, as if the critique of the withering of imaginative cultural production could be generated up from unconscious desire itself. But it might be just as plausible to see Lacanian psychoanalysis as symptomatic of the modern adventure in identity building. For the Lacanian Mafia, without knowing it, offer up a superb portrait of the limits and dead-ends of *life lived as project*. A subject marked by lack and gap is, one might say, an accurate portrayal of that brand of modern identity which is always on the move, hungering for new (and better) destinations, but never actually arriving. From the National Socialism of Hitler's Germany to the present-day resurgence of nationalism in Europe, identity building is framed upon an exclusivist, violent negation of the Other. Life lived as an identity project, then, is defined by *pleasure in discontent*. This is a discontent which leads modern women and men to the view that 'things can always be better', to the denigration of the here-and-now, and to the desire for smooth-functioning, regulated identities (always in the future, or around the next corner).

By contrast, in what are increasingly called 'postmodern' times, the status of identity projects diminishes. Postmodern sentiments recognize that the socio-political consequences of modernity clash strongly with its programmatic promises (see Bauman, 1991, 1995, 1997). Instead of the search for the ideal identity (complete, finished, self-identical), we find a celebration of cultural heterogeneity and difference. Ours is the age of what Jean-François Lyotard (1988: 31–36) describes as 'open space-time', by which he means that identities are liquidated into episodes, a flow of drifting moments, eternal presents, transitory encounters. The postmodern condition – with its globalization of the market, its proliferation of media simulations, its cult of technologism, its self-reflexive pluralism – unleashes a multiplicity of local identities without any 'central' or 'authoritative' co-ordination.

The American cultural critic Christopher Lasch (1984) some years ago made a crab-like move towards the idea of a postmodern life strategy, which he summarized as a 'minimal self'. This new self is one drained of ego-strength and autonomy, a narcissistic self focused only on the experience of living 'one day at a time', the comprehension of reality as a 'succession of minor emergencies'. Daily life, in the postmodern, becomes a matter of shifting anxieties and drifting concerns, always changing, always episodic. It is as if we live in a constant state of information overload. Crisis, in short, has become the norm. Living in a world of constant crisis means, necessarily, adjusting one's emotional response level. There is no citizen that can adequately monitor all that is going on; and any attempt to do so can only lead to psychic burn-out. So, players in the postmodern game of life develop an air of indifference and aloofness, sure only in the knowledge that all new improvements, social and technological, will create further problems down the track.

Postmodern life is episodic, a fractured and fracturing world, with little in the way for continuity or the making of meaningful connections. And yet one can also view the personal consequences of the postmodern in a somewhat more positive light. Imagination, it appears, has been given a considerable boost as a result of new technologies and electronic advances. Computers, word processors, faxes, the Internet, DAT – we now have technology which ushers in the possibility of different kinds of pleasures, different thoughts and feelings, different imaginings. In psychical terms, one may say that the trademark of postmodernity is a radical 'decentring' of the human subject – the limiting of omnipotence, not in Lacan's sense of a separation of subject and Other, but rather in terms of a *reflexive scanning of imagination* (see Elliott, 1996). By reflexive scanning, I mean to draw attention to the complexity of fantasy itself, as a medium of self-construction and other-directedness. This fantasized dimension of our traffic with meaning is underscored powerfully by contemporary theorists such as Julia Kristeva (1995), who speaks of 'open psychic systems', Cornelius Castoriadis (1997), who speaks of 'radical imagination', Christopher Bollas (1995), who speaks of 'personal idiom', and Jessica Benjamin (1995), who speaks of 'the shadow of the other subject'. Viewed from this perspective, the postmodern can promote a heightened self-understanding of imagination and desire in the fabrication of meaning in daily life. Against this backdrop there are risks and opportunities. The risks are that there is no guarantee that the reflexive scanning of imagination will prove solid enough to sustain interpersonal relationships; but the gains are the capacity to proceed in personal and cultural life without absolute guidelines – in short, an increased toleration of ambivalence and contingency.

But perhaps the most important feature to note concerns the durability of human imagination. New technologies and postmodern aesthetics can extend the richness of the sense-making process, furthering the questioning of pre-existing categories by which we make sense of personal and social life. In people's changing attitudes to technology and globalization, identity has become problematic all over again. From the most intimate, personal relationships through to global processes of political governance (such as the UN), social life has become more and more structured around ambivalence and contingency. The dynamics of mind and world are increasingly treated as puzzling, and simple descriptions and explanations of social processes are discarded.

These identities of which I've spoken, the modern and postmodern, represent different ways of responding to the globalization, bureaucratization and commodification of contemporary culture – of which I'll say more about in a moment. But let me stress now that we should not see these identity strategies as simple alternatives – the postmodern as something that eclipses the modern. Modern and postmodern identities are better seen, as Zygmunt Bauman (1991, 1997) has powerfully analysed, as simultaneous strategies deployed by contemporary societies. Constructing a self today is about managing some blending of these different modalities of identity: a kind of constant interweaving, and dislocation, of modern and postmodern states of mind. If, for example, the signifier 'America' can today be used to fashion identities framed upon a sense of global interconnectedness, democratic cosmopolitanism and a post-national way of belonging, it can also easily be deployed in a more defensive manner, the production of identities held in thrall to the foetus and the flag.

Individualization: or, Structurally Necessitated Identity Creation

What are the broader social transformations underpinning such modern/postmodern identity strategies? What are the institutional reference points marking out the dimensions within which identities are fabricated today? And how might these modernist and postmodernist identity strategies affect citizenship?

There has recently emerged a massive level of interest in the notions of globalization, globalism and global culture. Indeed theory in the space between globalization and culture has been on the boil for some time now, having reached a level of pressure which is at once a deepening and a displacement. On the one hand, the discourse on globalization opens up new political, social and economic flows that classical notions of nation, state and society seem ill-equipped to comprehend. On the other hand, the attention theory has lavished on globalism has often been at the cost of denying the significance of the regional, local and contextual, the long-running post-structuralist emphasis on difference and otherness notwithstanding.

What has fueled such interest has been the emergence of a range of socially produced, institutional transformations. These include trans-national communication systems, new information technologies, global warming, holes in the ozone layer, acid rain, the industrialization of war, the collapse of Soviet-style socialism and universal consumerism. The globalization of financial markets, the increasing importance of international trade, and the advent of new technologies, in particular, define the contours of an advanced capitalist order, in which general deregulation and the marketization of culture reigns supreme. The political ambivalence of globalism is nowhere more obvious than in the split it introduces between macro and micro levels of social life. In terms of macro considerations, it can be said that, if globalism has bulked so large in contemporary theory, it is because the deregulation of society and economy is fundamental to late capitalism. But deregulation is only one aspect. The other side of a labour market that demands complete flexibility and mobility is that of an increasingly regularized and standardized micro world. In this respect, social integration is portrayed as a blending of normalization (as described by Foucault) and the seductions of the market, the thrills of simulated pleasure-seeking (as described by Baudrillard).

The division between a deregulated public sphere and hyper-regularized private sphere is, however, surely unconvincing. For me, this is really but a variant of the idea of big institutions dominating individual lives, such as we find in the Frankfurt School's concept of the 'totally administered society' or Habermas' thesis of an 'inner colonization of the lifeworld' by technical systems. Perhaps the most interesting development in social theory in this context has been around the idea of individualization, an idea elaborated by the German sociologist Ulrich Beck in his recent books *Risk Society* (1992), *Ecological Politics in the Age of Risk* (1994), *The Normal Chaos of Love* (1995) and *The Reinvention of Politics* (1997). Beck's argument, bluntly stated, is that contemporary society is marked by reflexive individual decision making in a context of growing uncertainty, risk and hazard. At once stripped of its traditions and scarred by all kinds of menacing global risks, contemporary culture radicalizes individual decision making and individual initiative. 'Certainties', says Beck (1997), 'have fragmented into questions which are now spinning around in people's heads.' By this I take Beck to mean that the very definition of social co-ordinates, ranging from love and sex through marriage and family to politics and democracy, are up for grabs, with new modes of life being worked out, arranged and justified. Quite spectacular individual opportunities arise in this respect, as decisions (sometimes undecidable or painfully ambiguous ones) lead to further questions, dilemmas, problems.

Before anyone concludes that all this is little more than some manic upgrading of the narcissistic illusions of the ego at the level of theory, let me point out that Beck is not suggesting that individualization processes produce unfettered autonomy. On the contrary, individualization presupposes the internalization of social regulations, laws and precepts. Thus the very social conditions which encourage individualization (such as de-traditionalization and internationally mobile capital) produce new, unintended consequences (such as psychic fragmentation and the privatization of public, moral issues). But the other side of opportunity is more than simply danger in post-traditional society. It is *risk* says Beck, and risk on an astonishing global scale. In an age of commodified multiple choice, instrumental rationality, and genetic, chemical and nuclear technoscience, there is a diminishing protection of social life – we live today in an 'uninsured society'. Whereas expert knowledge was once imagined to offer a sense of security from external risks, today science, technology and industry are seen as deeply intertwined with the very origins of global risk. Global awareness of menacing risks are routinely discussed, interrogated, criticized, made use of, and agonized over. How can anyone know, for example, what possible effects the nuclear meltdown at Chernobyl might have on human bodies 50 years from now? And what, precisely, might be the long-term effects of global warming, psychologically, ecologically and politically?

These are important questions, and experts disagree about the answers. Politically speaking, however, it is near impossible to predict the likely scenarios, energizing and catastrophic, arising from global interconnectedness. The critical point that Beck makes is that risk management and risk avoidance are constitutive of personal and cultural life today, if only for the reason that we are confronted by hazards and risks that previous generations didn't have to face – we live with risk on a global scale. After all no one can 'opt-out', says Beck, from the consequences of ecological catastrophe or nuclear disaster.

But there are important political limits to the sort of reflexive risk calculation that Beck claims late modernity has ushered into existence. Perhaps most significantly, what gets displaced here are some of the more pernicious effects of deregulation upon social reflexivity. In a deregulated, market-driven society, significant constraints impinge upon our capacities for risk monitoring and risk calculation. Of key importance here is the *privatization of risk*. Today, risk is increasingly 'dumped' into the individualized world of acting subjects; risk is presented as a series of technical problems to be individually coped with and reacted to through individual effort. More and more, our cultural know-how is shaped by scientifically pre-selected and pre-defined risks. But rather than acknowledge the hiatus between global processes of risk production which are largely beyond the control of their victims and the denial of risk in the public sphere, we are returned to the dumping of risk at an individual level, a dumping which can be connected with the individualization and subpoliticization of civic concerns, of which more shortly.

New Paths of Citizenship

Let me, at this point, extend the preceding discussion by focusing on the new paths – at once personal and political – of citizenship created by the institutional influences of globalization, mass media and new communication technologies, modernity and postmodernization. A systematic account of citizenship in an age of reflexive risk and postmodernization might be elaborated as follows:

Context	Modes	Sites
Subjectivity	Subject/self relation, as mediated by conscious/unconscious dualism	Psyche, body, identity, differentiation
Intersubjectivity	Self/other relation, as mediated by boundary maintenance of identity/ difference	Association, relationship, emotional literacy
Subpolitics	Communal points of opening/closure	Civic discourse, disruption, reproduction
Globality	Global/local nexus	Mass media UN, social movements Trans-disciplinarity

In the realm of modes and sites, there are many points of overlap – such that it makes little sense to attempt to define any axiomatic neatness here. Nonetheless, we can identify these categories in summary form:

1   The self-construction, self-elaboration, self-staging and self-revision of the *subject as citizen* is a new mode of arranging life strategies. What is at issue here is not the traditional connection of welfare policies and national solidarity as a means of confronting the social inequalities of late capitalism, but rather the reflexive scanning of the subject at those nodal points in which identity, biography, citizenship, social networks and administrative systems are looped. This may of course, and it often does, take the form of the individual as citizen in the frame of welfare systems (i.e., unemployment and health benefits). The important point today, however, is that involvement in welfare systems constitutes individuals as *at once subject to sub-systems of administration and regulation, and also bearers of individual rights.*

> Most social welfare rights are individual rights. Families cannot lay claim to them, only individuals, more exactly, working individuals (or those who are unemployed but willing to work). Participation in the material protections and benefits of the welfare state presupposes labour participation in the greatest majority of cases...All these requirements which do not command anything, but call upon the individual kindly to constitute himself or herself as an individual, to plan, understand, design and act – or to suffer the consequences which will be considered self-inflicted in case of failure. (Beck, 1997: 97)

'Individualization' in this context might be taken to mean 'do-it-yourself citizen-ship', as various governmental and collective agencies – including the education system, welfare networks and the labour market – compel people to devise new ways of life and interaction. In these circumstances, the personal or subjective dimensions of citizenship are raised to the second power. Questions and issues surrounding self-identity, sexuality, gender, the body, as well as the relationship between human beings and nature, become political in a new sense: today's world is becoming increasingly reflexive in terms of the problematization of human subjectivity, and crucially this raises matters concerning both economic and cultural resources for the development and expansion of citizenship.

Indeed, much recent social theory has concentrated on the suffering and frailty of the human body as a basis for human rights and civic concern (Clarke, 1996; Morris, 1996; Turner, 1993, 1997). Such attempts to place citizenship studies in the wider context of a sociology of self and body reflect an individualization of culture to the degree that there is a questioning of the traditional division between private and public, and in particular a questioning of the personal/political vicissitudes in which civics are experienced and embodied. This type of individualization of citizenship demands a thorough-going revision of the groundwork of what counts as community and solidarity, and thus presumes high levels of autonomy and self-reflection – capacities which, due to the insidious influence of commodification and techno-science, are more and more under threat.

2   The language of citizenship is framed, reproduced and redefined through intersubjective involvement in the socio-political field, those spaces in which self and Other embrace and define boundaries of identity and difference. Citizenship, in this sense, liberates us from the prison-house of self-referentiality, and becomes a primary social-historical site for explorations in both solidarity and subordination.

The prime theorist of intersubjectivity in social theory is Habermas. Against the backdrop of the Frankfurt School's Weberian antimodernism, Habermas' innovation was his introduction of the distinction between 'lifeworld' and 'systems reproduction' in the context of an intersubjective theory of communication. Instrumentalization – the colonization of the lifeworld by systems logic – is Habermas' version of Horkheimer and Adorno's 'dialectic of enlightenment'; but, crucially, he is also able to unpack the more progressive, democratic advances of modernity. Habermas sees political conflict and ambivalence as central to the world of late modernity, and it is here that issues about citizenship and civic intervention arise. However, partly for reasons associated with his interpretation of Freud and psychoanalysis, and partly for reasons associated with his privileging of methodological concerns over more substantive issues, Habermas' theory of intersubjectivity is a highly idealized one – concerned as it is with the justification of certain universal norms. Many commentators have criticized Habermas' intersubjective realm for its purely cognitive, linguistic and formalistic bent, while others have pointed out that it reinstates rationalistic oppositions between reason and unreason, subject and object, knower and known, active and passive, and so forth (Benhabib, 1992; Elliott, 1999; Whitebook, 1995).

The complexities of these debates are not my central concern here. Rather than trace these out, what I want to note is that both the Habermasian theory of intersubjectivity, as well as attempts to develop a post-Habermasian account of intersubjective contexts (see Benjamin, 1998), are important for analysing the shifting, differentiated components of citizenship, culture and society. For inter-subjectivity, in both its Habermasian and post-Habermasian varieties, signifies the subject-to-subject context in which individuals and groups live with, work through and manage the uncertainties and anxieties of contemporary civics.

The intersubjective underpinnings of citizenship, with its constant cognitive and affective interchanges among individuals and groups, is at the heart of processes of individualization. In the Habermasian frame of intersubjective soli-darity, strategies tend to be project-orientated, with clearly defined forms of policy regulation, political territoriality, collective goals, as well as a strict normal-ization of the behaviours and boundaries considered appropriate to civil society. In this frame, the language of citizenship functions through forms of inclusion and exclusion, usually through the institutional domain of the nation-state. In particular, various minority groups – such as aboriginal groups in the white-settler societies of Australia, New Zealand, Canada and the United States – are excluded and subordinated in modernist patterns of citizenship; and there is no doubt that the idea of assimilation has been one of the most brutal ways of destroying aboriginal cultures. Such repressive types of citizenship definition, however, are increasingly subject to postmodern critique. In the post-Habermasian frame of intersubjective solidarity, strategies tend to be more fluid, revisable and self-questioning. In the case of excluded aboriginal groups and cultural minori-ties, the postmodern critique of modernist citizenship focuses squarely on the pernicious influence of ethnocentrism, evolutionism, sexism and colonialism in collective decision making or community activities.

The civil condition so deeply socialized and disciplined in modernist and post-modernist cultural politics can be defined as attitudes of mind with varying degrees of openness and reflectiveness. Oakeshott's (1991) discussion of what he calls 'intelligent relationship' has certain parallels with modernist encodings of civic expression – civil association, Oakeshott says, 'is not organic, evolutionary, teleological, functional or syndromic relationship but an understood relationship of intelligent agents'. In other words, modernist prescriptions of civic engage-ment emerge from purposive, procedural, instrumental rationalities, with tight and strictly circumscribed limits for defining the common political interest. By contrast, postmodernity reconstitutes and recontextualizes the community spirit, at once enlarging the very definition of the political (via deconstructing binary divisions of private/public, centre/periphery, real/imagined) and narrowing genuine interest in politics (through privatization, deregulation and socio-cultural frag-mentation). What Susie Orbach (1994) has termed 'emotional literacy' is perhaps a key intersubjective resource in the postmodern framing of regional, local, national and supra-national civic communications. 'Emotional literacy', writes Orbach (1994), 'is about hearing another's distress without being impelled to smother their feelings; about allowing the complexity of emotional responses to coexist with commandeering them to simplified categories of good and bad; about finding a way to accept the differences between us without resorting to prejudice or emotional fundamentalism. Emotional literacy is the call for a new agenda in which we restructure our institutions to accommodate and enhance our emotional, social and civic selves.' In other words, emotional literacy is both condition and outcome of postmodern responses to citizenship.

3   Entry to and exit from communities is regulated in many different ways, and are based not just on gender, race, and class but also age, nation, region, empire and colony. All in all, the new spirit of community is one based on strategic flexibility in negotiating multiple forms of oppression, and such utopian civics implicitly reject modernist modes of thinking in favour of postmodernist cultural politics. That is to say, politics breaks open beyond the formal institutional domain (witness the breakdown of solidarity forging through local government, trade unions, etc.) into zones of subpolitics and subpolicy (Beck), the politiciza-tion of social relations and institutional structures previously treated as *un*political. 'Subpolitics', writes Beck (1997: 103), 'is distinguished from politics in that (a) agents outside the political or corporatist system are also allowed on the stage of social design and (b) not only social and collective agents, but individuals as well compete with the latter and each other for the emerging power to shape poli-tics.' This ranges from 'single issue' actions involving local initiatives or health precautions to 'planetary issue' actions involving global warming or the deple-tion of the ozone layer.

What matters from the vantage point of citizenship, in particular, are the com-munal points of opening and closure in the fabrication of relations of power that the realm of subpolitics now constitutes. As Bauman (1995: 274–5) writes of the more fleeting, transitory citizenship practices of the postmodern:

> Like other events, such collective causes burst into attention for a brief moment only to fade out to make room for other preoccupations…Very seldom do such 'single issues' manifest or enhance the sentiment of moral responsibility for common welfare. Much more often they mobilize sentiments against, not for; against closing down a school or a mine here rather than elsewhere, against a bypass or a rail link, against a Romany camp or travelers' convoy, against a dumping ground for toxic waste. What they would wish to achieve is not so much making the shared world nicer and more habitable, but redistributing its less prepossessing aspects: dumping the awkward and unpleasant parts of it in the neighbours' back-yard. They divide more than they unite.

Bauman's citizenry of subpolitics appears as almost apolitical – no sooner consti-tuted as collective project than divided, no sooner focused than fragmented. Yet the disruption and disordering of institutionalized political space is perhaps more energizing and associative than Bauman's account recognizes; after all, the civic inhabiting of 'other spaces' – the margins and crevices of the social system – can be seen, as many postcolonial, postfeminist and postmodern critics have argued, as vital to alternative critical imaginaries. But what Bauman does bring to our attention is an underlining of the fragmentation of the civic imagination; he high-lights the immense difficulties in exploring thought, and also passion (which is distinct from excitement), in the 'shared world'.

There are also other reasons why a decline in shared public commitments and solidarity forging occurs in these conditions. Much has recently been written about various global flows, principally economic and financial in character, but the impor-tance of immigration and tourist flows is also increasingly important to grasping the changing dimensions of citizenship. One of the most crucial implications arising from the massive global flows of tourists, according to John Urry, lies in its restructuring of peoples' conceptions of home, and with that the relationship between the home society and other societies. 'Citizenship rights', says Urry (1995: 165) 'increasingly involve claims to consume other cultures and places throughout the world. A modern person is one who is able to exercise those rights and who conceives of him or herself as a consumer of other cultures and places.' If, as Urry contends, citizenship in the postmodern world is more a matter of consumption than of rights and duties, then this might be said to shatter once and for all the reciprocity of rights against, and duties towards, the political community that the liberal-democratic conception of citizenship is based upon. Yet it is unlikely that things are so cut and dried. For if people in some robustly entrepreneurial nations have been able to consolidate some travel and tourist gains as rights, it is also the case that such people are themselves transformed as citizens in the process. That is, how people define themselves as citizens is increasingly bound up with, and constructed with reference to, the changing world of space and place into which an increasing number of societies are being thrust. This is a point not lost of governments either, as the shift from taxation of income to consumption begins to take hold everywhere. This is why consumerist notions of citizenship demand more critical attention than they have otherwise attracted. The critique of the consumerist citizen as the negative index of modernist citizenship is surely lacking in critical depth, since it allows one to reject the development of postmodernity as intrinsically repressive or oppressive. This is not to say that the privatization and deregulation of governmental and state agencies has not carried devastating consequences for the boundedness of communities and community spirit. Clearly, it has (see Elliott, forthcoming). Politics is today less and less defined in relation to notions such as 'the public interest' or 'common interests' than ever before; but the reasons for this have a good deal more to do with far-reaching upheavals in the social, economic and political organization of world society than current rhetoric about civic apathy.

4   Behind these interlockings of subjectivity, intersubjectivity and subpolitics lies the assumption that citizenship needs to be comprehended from the vantage point of a global perspective, or global paradigm, in the social sciences and humanities. And behind this, in turn, lies the current upsurge of interest in social theory about the collusion between globalization and regionalization, or processes of global-systemic power and rupture. While these issues are of core importance to grasping the reinvention of citizenship at the current social-historical juncture, there can be little doubt that students of civil society have too easily imagined a simplisitic binary opposition between globalization and its Others (difference, particularity, region, specificity). Yet what is clear is that there is an increasing interdependence between these domains in contemporary social life, such that neat conceptual distinctions between globality and locality become increasingly forced and implausible. As Roland Robertson (1992: 52–53) explains the need to overcome such simple opposites: 'The distinction between the global and the local is becoming very complex and problematic, to the extent that we should now perhaps speak in such terms as the global institutionalization of the life-world and the localization of globality.' As concerns citizenry, we might well say that globalization is always experienced (and constructed) from highly local

situations, just as we might also speak of the global production of the local concerns of citizens. Nobody of course has ever witnessed a globality, in the sense of having directly seen global warming or the depletion of the ozone layer. Rather, people are likely to find themselves in situations where, in order to make sense of the risks surrounding the pollution of the earth's atmosphere or of a limited nuclear exchange, the scientific-technical knowledge of experts is drawn upon and deployed in order to set about confronting and transforming the local/global environment. This, after all, is how radicals came to urge the imperative to think globally and act locally.

The point, anyway, is that globalization implies a radicalization of citizenship, primarily because it brings into focus problems, risks and hazards which are operating at a great distance from the individual; this is the global compression of risks and responsibilities to which the trans-disciplinarity of globality (Robertson) is a response, at the level of the academy certainly, but also from time to time in public debate. Understanding the globalization of citizenship opens up interesting avenues for examining why, in conditions of postmodernization, civil, cultural and political dilemmas are at once rendered omnipresent and ordinary, overwhelmingly catastrophic and genuinely common. Much has been written on how a sense of social or cultural crisis today is being rapidly replaced by the more postmodern blend of cynicism and distance, local spaces in which global risk environments are conjured into their opposite, or at least stripped of their power to shock and disturb. Giddens (1991: 184) argues that today 'crisis becomes normalized'. Crisis becomes 'normal' in the sense that high-consequence environmental, economic and military risks pervade the fabric of everyday life, either experienced directly or via the mass media.

More deeply, the postmodern thrust of civics and citizenship today is altered because it is increasingly evident that the meaning of 'political community' involves a complex, contradictory blending of regional, national and global domains. Gender politics, ecology, homosexual rights, the rights of children against parents or the state, AIDS – civic rights today may arise from various interlockings of regional and global struggles, but the final court of appeal is increasingly centred on the world stage (such as United Nations' legislative enactments of civil and human rights). As Held (1995: 281) explains: 'The political space for a cosmopolitan model of democracy…is being made by numerous trans-national movements, agencies and institutional initiatives pursuing greater coordination and accountability of those forces which determine the use of the globe's resources, and which set the rules governing trans-national public life.' To this it might be added, trans-national civic life is being invented, which itself is a reinvention of the politics of citizenship.

Conclusion

In this chapter I have sought to examine, mostly in broad stokes, some current dilemmas facing the social theory of citizenship. I have primarily concentrated upon the complicated relationship between modernity, postmodernization and the reinvention of citizenship, and have examined in particular the altered global conditions of citizenship formation. In noting the institutional settings which underpin the constitution and reproduction of modern and postmodern citizenship, namely the nation-state and globalization, I have attempted to show how some of these sociological concerns might be more satisfactorily analysed in the frame of both personal and political life strategies. I then set out, in a strictly tentative and provisional manner, a range of issues concerning contemporary civic politics. These new paths of citizenship were divided into four key areas: (1) the individualization of citizenship; (2) the intersubjective framing of regional, local, national and supra-national civic communications; (3) the reinvention of citizenship within altered contexts of subpolitics; and, (4) the radicalization of citizenship in terms of the interlacing of globalization and regionalization. My argument throughout has been that the foregoing issues are of the utmost importance to the analysis of citizenship in contemporary social theory.

References

Bauman, Z. (1991) *Intimations of Postmodernity*. London: Routledge.
Bauman, Z. (1992) *Mortality, Immortality and Other Life Strategies*. Cambridge: Polity.
Bauman, Z. (1995) *Life in Fragments*. Oxford: Blackwell.
Bauman, Z. (1997) *Postmodernity and its Discontents*. Cambridge: Polity.
Beck, U. (1992) *Risk Society*. London: Sage.
Beck, U. (1994) *Ecological Politics in the Age of Risk*. Cambridge: Polity.
Beck, U. and Beck-Gernsheim, E. (1995) *The Normal Chaos of Love*. Cambridge: Polity.
Beck, U. (1997) *The Reinvention of Politics*. Cambridge: Polity.
Benhabib, S. (1992) *Situating the Self*. Cambridge: Polity.
Benjamin, J. (1995) *Like Subjects, Love Objects*. New Haven: Yale University Press.
Benjamin, J. (1998) *Shadow of the Other*. New York: Routledge.
Bollas, C. (1995) *Cracking Up*. London: Routledge.
Castoriadis, C. (1997) *The Castoriadis Reader*. Oxford: Blackwell.
Clarke, P.B. (1996) *Deep Citizenship*. London: Pluto Press.
Elliott, A. (1996) *Subject to Ourselves: Social Theory, Psychoanalysis and Postmodernity*. Cambridge: Polity.
Elliott, A. (1999) *Social Theory and Psychoanalysis in Transition* (2nd edn). London: Free Association Books.
Elliott, A. (forthcoming) 'The Psychic Costs of Privatization', *Free Associations*. London: Free Association Books.
Freud, S. (1930) *Civilization and its Discontents*. London: Hogarth.
Freud, S. (1921) *Beyond the Pleasure Principle*. London: Hogarth
Giddens, A. (1991) *Modernity and Self-Identity*. Cambridge: Polity.
Giddens, A. (1992) *The Transformation of Intimacy*. Cambridge: Polity.
Giddens, A. (1996) *In Defence of Sociology*. Cambridge: Polity.
Held, D. (1995) *Democracy and the Global Order*. Cambridge: Polity.
Kristeva, J. (1991) *Strangers To Ourselves*. London: Harvester Wheatsheaf.
Kristeva, J. (1995) 'Psychoanalysis in Times of Distress', in S. Shamdasani and M. Munchow (eds), *Speculations after Freud: Psychoanalysis, Philosophy and Culture*. London: Routledge.
Lacan, J. (1977) *Ecrits*. London: Routledge.
Lasch, C. (1984) *The Minimal Self*. New York: Norton.
Lyotard, J.-F. (1988) *Reecrire la Modernite*. Paris: Lille.
Marshall, T.H. (1973) *Class, Citizenship and Social Development*. Westport: Greenwood Press.
Morris, D.B. (1996) 'About Suffering: Voice, Genre and Moral Community', *Daedalus*, 125: 25–45.
Oakeshott, M. (1991) *On Human Conduct*. Oxford: Clarendon.

Orbach, S. (1994) *What's Really Going On Here? Making Sense of our Emotional Lives*. London: Virago.

Robertson, R. (1992) *Globalization: Social Theory and Global Culture*. London: Sage.

Turner, B.S. (1993) 'Contemporary Problems in the Theory of Citizenship', in B.S. Turner, *Citizenship and Social Theory*. London: Sage.

Turner, B.S. (1997) 'A Neo-Hobbesian Theory of Human Rights: A Reply to Malcolm Waters', *Sociology*, 31 (3): 565–571.

Urry, J. (1995) *Consuming Places*. London: Routledge.

Whitebook, J. (1995) *Perversion and Utopia*. Cambridge: MIT.

5

PSYCHOANALYSIS, IDENTITY AND CITIZENSHIP

Stephen Frosh

Upon what is citizenship based? In discussions about rights and responsibilities, obligations and entitlements, belonging and participation, a set of questions keeps insisting: how does one imagine oneself in connection with a community, a culture or a nation? What is it that allows one to feel part of a social order, able to take up 'citizenship', neither excluded nor excluding oneself? What emotions and fantasies insert themselves into the process of being so that citizenship is not an abstract notion, another fashionable academic category about to dissolve, but instead contains something material and 'real' inside it? If the concept of citizenship is to be more than a simple totting up of rights and duties, it needs to embrace this space of feeling and fantasy, this realm of the subjective, of what might properly be termed the *investments* which human subjects accrue towards their social world. 'Cultural' citizenship has as much to do with these investments, emotional and irrational as they may be, as it has to do with the formal question of who is allowed to do, or has access to, what. To be a citizen, one not only has to formally belong somewhere; one has also to feel that this belonging is real.

These demands bear on the nature of theory building in the area of 'cultural citizenship'. If one wants to know, 'How does it feel to be a subject?', a theory is required which engages with subjectivity, which can encompass the multiple and potentially contradictory lines of connection between what one believes oneself to be and where one places oneself in relation to others – as individuals, or as a social order. More specifically, if citizenship theory is to do more than describe abstract patterns of rights and responsibilities (and hence to avoid falling into the destructive trap of imposing a virtual world onto real human subjects, as economists have so loudly done), then it has to engage with the specificity of the relationships between subjects and their communities, with all the wilful, unexpected, irrational and sometimes even uncanny phenomena so produced. How can this be achieved without some notion of psychological *autonomy*, some recognition of the existence of a sphere of emotional activity connected to, but always out of step with, external events? That is to say, in the actual world of real human subjects, what one feels about belonging or exclusion, participation or isolation, may only be loosely coupled with the 'objective' conditions of rights, duties and cultural opportunities.

Speaking in this language immediately produces an engagement with psychoanalysis, as the discipline dealing with the eccentric, the erratic and the excessive – with all that is 'out of step' with the apparent rationality of social circumstances.

Psychoanalysis, recognizing the gap between what people have and what they experience, has developed a language and set of concepts that attempt to do justice to the complexity of the 'inside' of the psyche, to the mental contents that constitute each of us as subjects in the dual sense of 'agents' of our actions and 'subject to' the workings of the unconscious. It is legitimately called into action, therefore, when what is demanded is a theory that can make sense of the subjective determinants or impact of a set of phenomena – the 'meaning' of an event for people, its resonance or its threat. If, for example, a country explodes into internecine warfare, if cultural cohesion is demonstrated through 'ethnic cleansing' (that is, genocide) and vicious aggression over apparently trivial land claims, it is unlikely that the explanation for this will be found solely (which is not to say that it will not be found at all) in political and social history or economic advantage. Something else is bound to be operating here, some excessive factor which reverberates subjectively for people, into which their fears and desires are channelled, generating and sustaining the blood-letting and mutual persecution. This is a good example of what is meant by *excess*: the desperate and rigid self-defining of whole communities in terms of 'nationality' and the demonizing of almost identical other communities; the desperate clinging onto some notion of identity bearing small relation to any real attribute of the individual or group, but nevertheless enormously powerful as an organizing principle for people's lives. Without social, economic and political analysis, it would be impossible to understand the context and effects of phenomena such as these; but without the addition of an investigation of subjectivity and the unconscious, the social explanations fail to give an account of what drives people on, when no objective, rational interests are perceivable.

The language of the previous paragraph should provide a pointer to the exact terrain of psychoanalysis' potential influence on all attempts to theorize social phenomena, cultural citizenship included. As psychoanalysis attests in the clinical sphere, there is always something excessive about psychic functioning; this is, indeed, the precise nature and definition of the unconscious. Social events build on this and exploit it and may also provide some of its contents. But just as 'ideology' can no longer be reduced to false consciousness, but is seen, following Althusser, as a medium through which the social is articulated and experienced, so the psychological dimension cannot be mapped unproblematically onto the social: always, something extra remains. This does not, of course, mean that there is no relationship between the social and the psychological; in fact, one major contribution of psychoanalytically informed social theorists has been to demonstrate how much the structure of the individual psyche is infiltrated by the structure of society. However, it does suggest that a very specific conceptual apparatus is required to spell out the psychic attributes that interdigitate with the social; purely social categories will not suffice. While there might be a range of possible languages for delivering this account, including those of literary and cultural criticism, psychoanalysis is the most elaborate and the only one that takes fantasy as its prime object, irrespective of the products or actual content of the fantasy in question, removed from all aesthetic considerations, and from moral judgement or remonstrance.

Narrowing this down still further to the question of what makes for a person's investment in culture, the focus on fantasy means that we are not here dealing even with subjectivity as a whole but with a specific psychological function. Loosely put, this is the connection between the dreams and nightmares of the mind and social activity. In individual psychoanalysis, the object of study is the unconscious, explored through its penetration of consciousness and its capacity to twist and turn every trick of being. 'Subject to' the unconscious, the analysand finds her or his own subjectivity riven with excess, with that which cannot be pinned down or controlled. Away from the couch, going through our everyday lives, we are dominated by fantasy; it keeps us moving, it trips us up. To take the most obvious example, sexuality is more vision than deed, taking its form from, and providing its enjoyment by, the investment of the imagination in the act. Indeed, as is testified to by the ubiquity of pornography, most of the work of sexuality takes place in the mind, willed to some extent, but beyond control much of the time. Writ large, into the social, the fantasy structures of society produce imaginary worlds in which we all have our very material existence. Cornelius Castoriadis (1995: 28), exploring the virtuosity of unconscious productivity, comments on, 'The autonomization of the imagination, which is no longer enslaved to functionality…There is unlimited, unmasterable representational flux, representational spontaneity without any assignable end….' Society offers a container for this, imposing structure and constraint upon the radical wildness of the imagination, but also (and here is its 'ideological' practice in the traditional sense) marginalizing it so that it reappears only as individual pathology or, under some conditions, social explosion.

> [Through] this social fabrication of the individual, the institution subjugates the singular imagination of the subject and, as a general rule, lets it manifest itself only through dreaming, phantasying, transgression, illness. (Castoriadis, 1995: 29)

Individual versus Society

Despite the claim here that psychoanalysis has a significant role to play in the articulation of a theory of cultural citizenship, it has to be admitted that its encounters with social theory have not always been very well focused. Freud had a notoriously negative and in some respects crude view of the relationship between the individual and society. For protection and out of fear, serving the rule of the reality principle as it works to curb unconscious impulses, individuals form together in groups: civilization is built out of this, as a necessary but nonetheless repressive agency. Civilization thus has a containing function; it is,

> the whole sum of the achievements and the regulations which distinguish our lives from those of our animal ancestors and which serve two purposes – namely to protect men against nature and to adjust their mutual relations. (Freud, 1930: 278)

Civilization is thus a way of controlling individual passion in the interests of social survival; it is therefore opposed to the individual subject even though it acts to protect and support the maintenance of personal as well as group life – after all, where would the individual be without social constraints on aggression or sexual expression? Freud's story about individual development is to a considerable extent premised on this notion of the necessary opposition between individual desire and social control, with the Oedipus complex being the best known and most power-fully articulated account of how these controls come to be thoroughly internalized and entwined in our deepest psychic layers. From outside comes the constraint, building a fortress against incestuous desire by utilizing the energic capacities of the subject – the boy's aggression towards his father, for example, which is projected and then reabsorbed as fear of the father's castrating anger, institutional-izing the social taboo on incest as a structure within the mind. The individual's desire, turned outwards, threatens to blow the whole social enterprise apart; yet without the social, the individual cannot live. So, Freud argues that civilization has to exist, antagonistic towards the individual, yet acting in her or his best interests.

This model of individual opposed to society continues to excite psychoanalysts (and others) in various ways, with the Lacanian idea that some kind of alienation occurs as the subject becomes incorporated into the symbolic order being just one further, related, powerful example. To some extent at least, this means that citizen-ship can only be a compromise, a balance between what one might 'truly' desire (to explode all possible constraints) and the limits of what can be allowed if life is to go on. Interestingly, whereas the Freudian image of individual-social tension was quite influential amongst prominent social theorists in the past – with the Frankfurt School being the major example (e.g. Marcuse, 1955) – some recent writers have turned to alternative models of the individual-social relationship offered by other psychoanalytic schools, notably those connected to the British object-relations tradition. For example, Winnicott's (1958) idea that there might be specifiable conditions for 'good enough mothering' that lay the foundations for secure self-hood and hence for healthy development and relationships, has been taken up by Anthony Giddens in several recent publications dealing with the necessary bases for constructive social relations – a crucial mode of discus-sion of citizenship. Elliott (1994: 71) provides a summary account of Giddens' position here:

> Drawing on the object-relational theories of Winnicott and Erikson, Giddens argues that the forging of personal trust is a central element in the structuring of self-identity as well as the essential basis for a constructive involvement with the broader institutional contexts of modernity. Trust, in Giddens' view, is a basic mechanism for handling the demands and dangers of everyday social life, for establishing what he terms 'ontologi-cal security'. It is because an individual learns a sense of trust in other people that feel-ings of inner trustworthiness come to predominate over anxiety. Trust established between self and others is fundamental to creative, ongoing human relations; and it is what enables individuals to achieve a practical engagement with the open nature of modern social life.

The social contract arises out of the interpersonal encounter between self and other, which under suitable conditions allows the subject to feel confident about the ongoing support and predictability to be found in the world. In a relatively optimistic formulation, Giddens thus suggests that it is possible for the individual to negotiate contemporary ambiguities (which he regards as the basis of the 'risk' culture) if her or his self has been formed out of a nexus of trust and support.

Opposition between individual and society no longer looks unavoidable; rather, its existence is a sign of the failure to provide a suitable foundation for a positive social identity.

Michael Rustin, over many publications, has also employed the object-relational perspective, this time with the sharper edge offered by Kleinian theory, to argue that it is possible to conceive of positive individual-social encounters (Rustin, 1991). His basic point is that Kleinian theory acknowledges the destructive potential to be found in each individual subject (one can hardly go further along this route than the positing of a 'death instinct') but goes on to specify the conditions under which this destructiveness can be managed and indeed put to creative, reparative uses. The infant, threatened with engulfment by the overwhelming power of its own aggression, projects its feelings into the maternal 'object'; her capacity to withstand these fantastic assaults and to remain loving and accepting allows the infant to build up a capacity for integration and toleration of ambivalent impulses. Out of this, a less paranoid view of the world emerges, in which objects are regarded as potentially integrated yet also ambiguous, and in which responsibility is taken for one's actions, so producing feelings of guilt and loss, but also establishing an urge towards linkage. The crucial point here is that the external world, while it has the potential to be experienced by the infant as hostile and persecutory, can also become containing and benevolent, and that under those conditions one might imagine a mode of citizenship which is constructive rather than oppositional. Rustin (1995: 226) summarizes the contribution of this British 'school' of psychoanalysis, in opposition to what he regards as the 'negativity' of the French Lacanian tradition, as follows.

> The idea of the 'negative' focuses attention on the inherent limits of human self-understanding and the inherent distortions and falsifications involved in representation...By contrast, the object relations and Kleinian traditions postulate a 'positive' core of ideas about human nature and its more benign forms of development...The first tradition is above all adapted to the unending investigation of the inauthentic, idealized and self-regarding aspects of human consciousness. The second tradition regards psychoanalytic investigation not only as a method of recognition of illusions and self-deceptions, but also as a source of grounded understanding of 'authentic' states of feeling and object relations, conceived as the foundation of creative forms of life.

A familiar dichotomy emerges here, between theories based on *lack* and those based on plenitude. In the former, desire emerges as a gap in what can be obtained: we wish only for what we cannot have, and all beliefs in fulfilment are wishful, 'inauthentic' or narcissistic – 'imaginary' in the pejorative sense. Society is in essence alienating, a structure into which the subject is propelled, losing itself on the way. By contrast, the 'positive' theories speculate that there may be conditions of satisfaction for the subject, even if they are hard to construct. Some societies, some institutional contexts, might have integrating effects; 'citizenship' there could mean something worthwhile.

Fantasies of Enjoyment

Following up this divergence in psychoanalytic theory, one of the many dimensions along which Kleinian thought is differentiated from Freudian, concerns the basic operational structures of the mind. The theoretical treatment of fantasy brings this point into focus. Whereas Freud, and Lacan after him, describes fantasy as occurring in the space between the wish and the lost object, so that it is always a substitute for reality, Kleinians present it ('phantasy') as simply what the mind does. 'Phantasy is not merely an escape from reality, but a constant and unavoidable accompaniment of real experiences, constantly interacting with them' (Segal, 1973: 14). In addition to the constructive operations of the perceptual apparatus, attested to by the researches of cognitive psychologists, whereby we build up pictures of the world on a moment-by-moment basis through our expectations and active grasping of part perceptions to make them whole, Kleinian psychoanalysis asserts that unconscious fantasies are constantly playing in our minds. Nothing is 'only' real; it all connects with other thoughts and ideas, other wishes or dreams, other anxieties. And this is true of material objects and of cultural concerns, in political as well as in individual life.

The (Lacanian) Slovenian cultural critic, Slavoj Zizek communicates this idea exactly, in a piece on Eastern Europe published shortly after the demise of the Soviet Union and the collapse of Yugoslavia, in which he articulates the way fantasy might govern the relationship of individuals and collectives to themselves and others. Writing about the new nationalism to be found operating so particularly virulently in ex-Yugoslavia, he employs the notion of 'enjoyment' in a shocking and unexpected way, to convey the emotional investment that might be sucked into any symbolic position. Indeed, the argument runs that it is only through use of this notion of enjoyment that the power of these apparently ('rationally' speaking) arbitrary categories of self- and social-definition can be understood.

> To explain this unexpected turn [the self-destructive new nationalism of the ex-communist states], we have to rethink the most elementary notions about national identification – and here, psychoanalysis can be of help. The element that holds together a given community cannot be reduced to the point of symbolic communication: the bond linking its members always implies a shared relationship to a Thing, towards Enjoyment incarnated. This relationship towards a Thing, structured by means of fantasies, is what is at stake when we speak of the menace to our 'way of life' presented by the Other; it is what is threatened when, for example, a white Englishman is panicked because of the growing presence of 'aliens'. It is this eruption of 'Enjoyment' which explains what is happening in the East.... (Zizek, 1990: 51–52)

Rustin (1995: 235) comments about the stress on fantasy identifications in this piece, that Zizek's 'argument, consistent with Freud, is that such phenomena need to be acknowledged as substantive dimensions of any actual political process'. More precisely, accounts of social phenomena which neglect detailed examination of the investment ('enjoyment') of fantasy, will remain abstracted from the activities of the people – seen as individuals or collectives – who are involved. In a slightly later publication, by which time the Bosnian war had taken full hold, Zizek spells out the complex relationship between fantasies of survival and destruction, which have the effect of perpetuating the fear of the Other in the very moment in which that Other is attacked and destroyed. Arguing that 'hatred is not limited to the "actual properties" of its object' but is instead targeted at what the other represents in fantasy, he comments that 'the more we destroy the object in reality, the more powerfully its sublime kernel rises before us' (Zizek, 1994: 78).

> This paradox, which has already emerged apropos the Jews in Nazi Germany (the more they were ruthlessly exterminated, the more horrifying were the dimensions acquired by those who remained), can be perceived today apropos of Muslims in Bosnia: the more they are slaughtered and starved out, the more powerful is the danger of 'Muslim fundamentalism' in Serbian eyes. Our relationship to this traumatic real kernel of surplus enjoyment that 'bothers us' in the Other is structured in fantasies (about the Other's omnipotence, about 'their' strange sexual practices, etc.). In this precise sense, war is always also a war of fantasies. (Zizek, 1994: 78)

What is excessive is what the Other signifies. This cannot be explained solely in terms of ordinary war aims, or personal or political interests, nor can it necessarily be articulated by the protagonists. It can, however, be observed or deduced from observations: what, if there is no element of fantasy involved, can explain the frenzy, the willingness to demolish the self as well as the Other, and the escalating hatred so evident on the contemporary political scene? Whether the language employed here is derived from Klein (paranoid-schizoid functioning, the term given to the state of mind characterized by intense projection of destructive fantasies into the outside world, which is then experienced as persecutory) or Lacan or elsewhere, something has to be said about this excess, this astonishing psychic energy which leaves rationality staggering behind.

Developing still further the connection between fantasy investments and social meanings, Jacqueline Rose argues that fantasy should be 'at the heart of our political vocabulary' and comments,

> There is a common assumption that fantasy has tended to be excluded from the political rhetoric of the left because it is not serious, not material, too flighty and hence not worth bothering about. My starting premise works the other way round. Like blood, fantasy is thicker than water, all too solid – *contra* another of fantasy's more familiar glosses as ungrounded supposition, lacking in foundation, not solid *enough*. (Rose, 1996: 5)

Like Zizek, Rose identifies the material nature of fantasy, the way its processes as well as its effects can be seen. Moreover, the issue is not just one of 'acknowledging' fantasy, taking it into account when piecing together a full picture of an event: Rose states that it should be 'at the heart of our political vocabulary'. It is the fantasy that fuels the politics, as well as the other way around; indeed, it may be that it is the former even more than the latter.

Postmodern Identities

Returning to the issues involved in cultural citizenship, many of the concerns over the interlacing of social and personal fantasies can be seen at work in the contemporary fascination with questions of identity. In the 1950s and 1960s, the major interest of politically oriented psychoanalysts and theorists of psychoanalysis was in the politics of social class ('Freudo-Marxism'). Included in this was an honourable tradition of work on prejudice, anti-semitism and fascism, work which has had a lasting impact in arguing for the importance of unconscious as well as socio-political elements in these phenomena (for example, Adorno et al., 1950; Fanon, 1952). More recently, however, some new critical forces have come into play which make problematic the positions taken by the classic radical Freudians. These have their origins in what has come to be called the 'identity politics' of the last 20 years, which have questioned the grand narratives of oppression and liberation put forward by previous generations on the political left, and which have argued for the centrality of specific configurations of power and resistance to be found in different, often fluid forms in a range of individuals, groups and situations. The most powerful discourses here surround feminism, gay and lesbian politics, and the black and anti-racist movements, all of which either dispute or supplement the economic and class-based analyses of inequality which previously dominated the scene. The idea of a monolithic state as the source of all power, to be opposed through alliances of workers brokered by their shared class interests, has given way in the face of theoretical developments (notably by Foucault) and the articulating consciousness of women, black people and gay and lesbian groups as they recast themselves as political agents. The task for political and social theory here is to find a way of comprehending this new phenomenon without falling back into reductive, economistic explanations that miss the point of identity politics altogether. For psychoanalysis, the problem is to find a way of theorizing unconscious investments in wildly divergent patterns of being, which can be fragmented and contradictory and which cut across the traditional fault lines of class, sexuality, 'race' and gender. In a way, this is a golden opportunity, for the new identity politics is explicitly organized around patterns of identification and personal investment which are recognizably multiple and unstable, with visible contradictions in individuals' personal locations (witness the multiple identity positions contained, for example, in the complex location of an individual as a white lesbian woman or a black heterosexual man). Moreover, there is a newly focused understanding of the constructive nature of the process undertaken socially and personally as people find their place in an identity group-ing and explore the understanding of themselves and the social order which this can bring. In principle, therefore, psychoanalysis is well attuned to the needs of the time: as politics becomes more concerned with subjectivity, it more than ever needs a language in which to talk about the interrelationships between conscious-ness, fantasy and social positioning. Psychoanalysis could, again in principle, supply such a language; it could make sense of the complex business of creating and re-creating 'identities' and of filling these out with content, as well as explor-ing the intense investments which people hold in them, and the deep aggression to which they often (for example, as racism or homophobia) give rise.

The new identity politics is related to a further term, that of postmodernism. This is certainly an arena in which psychoanalysis has had a voice; indeed, a con-siderable portion of the language of postmodernism has been borrowed from psychoanalysis, again because of its concern with subjectivity and the influence of the fracturing of the modern world on personal status and consciousness (see Frosh, 1991). Anthony Elliott comments,

> Psychoanalysis has made significant contributions to these theoretical debates on modern
> and postmodern identity, providing methods of analysis for thinking through the connec-
> tions between these cultural trends and new patterns of self-organization. In these debates,
> psychoanalysis has been used to trace the fragile and precarious structures of psychic inte-
> riority engendered by the cultural conditions of our late modern age. (Elliott, 1994: 7–8)

Postmodernism stresses the fragmentary nature of social being, its lack of cohesion and direction, and the way discourses arise out of this fragmentary existence
to organize consciousness. That is to say, the postmodernist vision is one in which
stable absolutes cease to exist, even as a possibility, and in their place come a
swirling multiplicity of subject-positions, fluid in their nature, destabilizing and at
times interchangeable, relativistic and reactive. Out of these, certain structuring
lines of being are constructed through symbolic procedures, so that the categories
of identity can be held onto. Race, gender and class are amongst the most powerful
of such categories, because the social order as a whole employs them as organizing principles, but they are not absolute, either in their meaning or in their
constitution. How they are invested in by people and what they come to mean in
practice, are complex questions demanding analysis of the way social categories
and personal structures of desire interweave.

   In the context of this unpredictable flux of identifications and subject-positions,
it becomes clearer how citizenship itself is constituted in part as a set of fantasy
relationships in which individual subjects and their communities are reciprocally
entwined. The discourse of 'rights and responsibilities' is related to this as a set
of transactions and rules for engagement, but it is neither superior nor reducible
to the fantasy level: what one is, is in large part what one can imagine oneself to
be. Turner's (1990) two 'dimensions' model of citizenship – public/private and
active/passive – also offers considerable space for psychological readings and
points to the complex intersections of identities which is characteristic of this
area. Nevertheless, the intensity of personal investments to be found in experiences of citizenship requires something more than the mapping of a space for
conceptualization. It requires an actual drawing out of the passionate if often
incoherent wishes and anxieties that drive life along. One of the things which
psychoanalytic investigation can offer here, when it does not succumb to its own
normative tendencies, is a powerful means for displaying the contradictory and
ambivalent positions to be found underlying even what appear to be the most
secure foundations for identity.

Fundamentalist Citizens

To close this argument with an example, take one of the more urgent and astrin-
gent contemporary instances of identity politics: religious fundamentalism.
Fundamentalism, particularly in its militant or evangelical forms, has leapt on the
scene as an object of fascination and often of threat, raising the question of where
its potency and attractiveness come from. Clearly, there are major issues here
concerned with imperialism, economic marginalization and power, and the fate
of resistance struggles around the world. But there is also an additional set of
questions connected with what Zizek might refer to as the 'enjoyment' associated

with fundamentalism – the emotional charge that connects it to its subjects, making them feel that here they have roots, here they are genuinely 'citizens' with something to call their own. Some element of the fundamentalist project is not reducible to economic or political analysis; rather, it acts as a mobilizing force, an excess, out of which the excitement and perhaps the terror of fundamentalism is born.

Amongst all the many aspects of fundamentalism which might be examined in this light, one which stands out in terms of its symbolic significance as well as its political visibility is its gender politics. It has often been pointed out (see Sahgal and Yuval-Davis, 1992) that fundamentalist cultures are fascinated by the question of the position of women, and that most of their mechanisms of social control are directed at women, who represent the measure of the community's cohesion. Women are the property not only of the individual man, their father or husband, but of the community; in important ways, they are what power acts upon. Injunctions concerning modesty apply predominantly to women, whose very existence threatens, through the power of sensuality, to make the fundamentalist edifice crumble. Women's voices should not be heard, ostensibly because they are a distraction away from God-given religious observances; women are impure as well as seductive, so they cannot be in holy places with men; women must be hidden, must keep out of the light. Structurally speaking, it is clear that the 'woman' functions as a signifier passed around in the system, making it work. The letter of the law applies to her, and through her the wheels of the system are oiled. Even more obviously, it does not need a full-blown Foucauldian analysis to reveal that in this machinery of repression there is fascination with sex, with its disruptive, energic capabilities, with its offer of something other than absolute obedience. Psychodynamically and social-symbolically, women represent an Otherness in the heart of fundamentalism, a necessary but contaminating germ. The fundamentalist order's purity is reasserted with each repudiation of this Otherness, with each masking of the desire associated with femininity. However, the act of repression, the attempt to silence sexuality, also draws attention to it as a disruptive potential, a source of excitement; as the tension so produced is never resolved, it continues to feed the frenzy.

The discourse being drawn upon here is the familiar one of bodily, worldly, feminine temptation ranged against masculine spirituality. Desexualizing women purifies the community, locating temptation and sexual excitement outside it, leaving the field clear for fantasies of the ideal. Regulating women symbolically actually regulates the generative power of the community as a whole. Nevertheless, to keep the spirit alive, the success of the regulation must never be complete; woman remains present as more than an irritant; she also, perhaps literally, embodies that which is desired but never allowed.

Building on this description, it is apparent that the fundamentalist control of femininity links with its broader repudiation of modernity (or, rather, some aspects of modernity, because its alliance with technology is very strong) as a way of keeping difference at bay. Rather than exploring the multiple identities offered by the contemporary environment, fundamentalism silences alternative voices, closing down people's ability to imagine themselves into the position of another. Fundamentalism trades on the prohibition of this kind of sympathetic imagination, replacing it with the stereotyped, arid imaginary of heaven and hell, permitted and unclean, good and evil. Under contemporary circumstances, this narrowing of vision can be appealingly reassuring. As a response to the complexity of the modern world, 'them versus us' is intellectually infantile but emotionally compelling, refreshingly easy to hold onto when the alternative is a dizzying awareness of rootlessness, disruption and fragmentation. Again in psychoanalytic terms, it is a narcissistic retreat in which everything is made 'same'. The deep appeal of this is that the fantasy of complete salvation need never be relinquished; that is, it preserves the imaginary idea that the challenges as well as the horrors of the world need never be faced, but can be wished away. Psychoanalytically, this is a regressive impulse, a return to the fantasized oneness with the prenatal mother, whose function it is to stop anything nasty and contentious coming into the womb.

In the context of a global social order teetering on the edge of collapse, with fragmentation and disruption of identity always staring one in the eye, fundamentalism thus offers a way of staying in one piece, of riding this whirlwind of dissolution by disowning it, projecting it outside. Its narcissistic energy is based on omnipotent fantasies and on the denial of Otherness, the disavowal of legitimate contradiction and alternative ways of being. It offers solace to lost souls, ways of succeeding in a world where the forces seem ranged against one, an easily accessible terrain of meaning and value, translated into the language of 'purity' and truth. Most of all, if one can accede to its regulating force, it offers release from the pain of uncertainty. In gender terms, it is as if the awesome power of the punitive father is used as a protection against the persecutory inner world, creating a 'maternal' space of community and security. That this maternal space is preserved only by energetic and often vicious policing is part of its appeal, because the effectiveness of the policing attests to the continuing vigour of the father – and hence of the structure itself. Battling to keep the community pure, the fundamentalist 'father' may use the utmost brutality against enemies from without and within. The more belligerent and aggressive this symbolic/real father becomes, the stronger does the fundamentalist movement feel. What this is built on is in some ways an old-fashioned Oedipal challenge, albeit reforged in the context of new modes of political and religious authority. But what this account also suggests is that the extremity of fundamentalist violence is based on a flight from the complexity of both 'mother' and 'father', each being posited as pure and simple and strong. The mother is desexualized, her only role that of preserving everything as the same; the father is made monolithic, non-nurturing, his role – enacted with striking efficacy by so many fundamentalist leaders – to police the boundary so that nothing alien comes in. The tremendous excitement and power of this way of being cannot be denied: it rests upon narcissistic and omnipotent fantasies present in most people, but enhanced of course by political and economic circumstances making the movements historically viable.

The language of rights and responsibilities has a bearing on all this, but the question of how one finds a place in a fundamentalist culture clearly could not be exhausted thereby. As I have suggested in this sketch, the emotional energy which infuses fundamentalism is essential to it. 'Citizenship' in this regard is not just a matter of taking up one's allotted place, although it does require that set of regulated behaviours. It is also a matter of investing oneself in the emotional complex of the social order and its institutions, enjoying its successes, imagining its future progress, projecting away its anxieties, closing down the alternatives. Not all systems are like this – that is the point of fundamentalism's difference and why it is such a good example of the fantasy dimension of citizenship. It shows much more clearly than most other structures just how crucial a certain kind of imaginary is to finding and moulding the subject's relationship with culture and community. But while fundamentalism may be an extreme example, the point it illustrates is a general one: without a process of fantasy investment, there is no cultural (or any other) citizenship at all.

Acknowledgement

Some of the material in this chapter was first published in S. Frosh (1997) *For and Against Psychoanalysis*, London: Routledge.

References

Adorno, T., Frenkel-Brunswik, E., Levinson, D. and Sandford, R. (1950) *The Authoritarian Personality*. New York: Norton, 1982.

Castoriadis, C. (1995) 'Logic, Imagination, Reflection', in A. Elliott and S. Frosh (eds), *Psychoanalysis in Contexts*. London: Routledge.

Elliott, A. (1994) *Psychoanalytic Theory: An Introduction*. Oxford: Blackwell.

Fanon, F. (1952) *Black Skin, White Masks*. London: Pluto Press, 1986.

Freud, S. (1930) 'Civilization and its Discontents', in S. Freud, *Civilization, Society and Religion*. Harmondsworth: Penguin, 1985.

Frosh, S. (1991) *Identity Crisis*. London: Macmillan.

Marcuse, H. (1955) *Eros and Civilization*. Boston: Beacon Press, 1966.

Rose, J. (1996) *States of Fantasy*. Oxford: Clarendon Press.

Rustin, M. (1991) *The Good Society and the Inner World*. London: Verso.

Rustin, M. (1995) 'Lacan, Klein and Politics', in A. Elliott and S. Frosh (eds), *Psychoanalysis in Contexts*. London: Routledge.

Sahgal, G. and Yuval-Davis, N. (eds) (1992) *Refusing Holy Orders: Women and Fundamentalism in Britain*. London: Virago.

Segal, H. (1973) *Introduction to the Work of Melanie Klein*. London: Hogarth Press.

Turner, B. (1990) 'Outline of a Theory of Citizenship', *Sociology*, 24: 189–218.

Winnicott, D. (1958) *Through Paediatrics to Psychoanalysis*. London: Hogarth Press.

Zizek, S. (1990) 'East European Republics of Gilead', *New Left Review*, 183: 50–62.

Zizek, S. (1994) *The Metastases of Enjoyment*. London: Verso.

6

CITIZENSHIP, POPULAR CULTURE AND EUROPE

Maurice Roche

This chapter aims to respond to two of the main challenges which animate this book in general. First, there is the fact that academic interests in the study of culture and of citizenship have tended to develop in isolation from each other and thus there is the challenge to see what can be gained from exploring their interconnections. Secondly, there is the fact that late twentieth century processes of globalization provide a common context and set of animating problems in the two spheres of culture and citizenship, and thus there is the challenge to explore the interconnections in relation to this context of globalization. The view taken in this chapter is that in the medium- and long-term globalization processes in the twenty-first century will increasingly require and produce complex trans-national regulation and governance systems, that an important level in such systems will be 'world regions' (Gamble and Payne, 1996; Roche, 1992a: Ch. 8), and that the European Union (EU) as currently the most advanced of these systems is an important model and harbinger of future 'post-national' developments (Roche, 1987, 1992a: Ch. 8, 1996; Roche and van Berkel, 1997).

Given this background this chapter aims to consider something of the nature of 'European culture', 'European citizenship' and relevant Europeanization processes as contemporary EU policy themes and problems, exploring some of their actual and potential interconnections and mutual implications. It looks at examples from the world of 'mass' or 'popular' culture rather than from the beaten tracks of 'high' or elite culture. In particular it looks at Europeanization processes and issues in relation to two cultural institution/cultural industry complexes which are structurally important in contemporary societies and their economies but which are too often overlooked as such, namely those of sport (see also Roche, 1998), which is a primary focus in this chapter, and also tourism, which is discussed more briefly (see also Roche, 1992b, 2000).

A caveat should perhaps be entered here. Evidently the meanings of and interconnections between the concepts of 'culture' and 'citizenship' and other related and relevant concepts such as 'collective identity' are intrinsically complex matters when considered at the level of the nation-states and national societies. This is not least because of the periodically changing cultural composition of national societies in the twentieth century due to flows of international migration. Contemporary Western national societies are struggling to redefine themselves as 'multi-cultural'. This process has important if often unclear implications for current and future concepts and popular experiences of culture, citizenship and identity in such societies. Equally evidently these problems of complexity are multiplied and taken to a new order of magnitude when considering the experiences of contemporary European nation-states, both in their number and diversity and also in their aspirations to integration within the trans-national polity of the European Union. The fact that the European Union is very much a long-term project in the relatively early stages of construction means that it is continually changing and thus presents analysis with the additional problem of attempting to track a 'moving target'. For these reasons it is not realistic in a chapter such as this to attempt to give a comprehensive account of the many connections, disjunctions and developments relating to 'culture', 'citizenship' and 'identity' across contemporary Europe and of the theoretical issues they throw up. In recognition of this the discussion aims to provide a preliminary review of some aspects of the current situation in Europe in the popular cultural fields of sport in particular, and also, in passing, tourism. This is prefaced by a brief outline of some relevant analytic aspects of the relationships between culture, identity and citizenship.

The chapter is divided into three main sections each of which raises issues about the relationship between culture and citizenship in a European context. The first section briefly introduces some concepts and debates relevant to understanding the mutual implications of culture and citizenship and their significance in the emergence of a European level of societal organization in the late twentieth century. The second section discusses the development of European Union cultural policy as a process of 'official' Europeanization. It briefly considers tourism in particular as an area where official and popular forms of Europeanization might be said to be operating. The third section focuses on the popular cultural form of sport, in particular spectator sport and media sport, in relation to the development of Europeanization and also some EU policy responses to this.

Citizenship, Culture and Europe – Themes and Issues

The view taken in this chapter about the circuits of mutual implications which exist between culture, identity and citizenship, while too complex to be mapped in detail, can be indicated in outline in this section. Common culture is often taken to be the basis for collective (ethnic and national) identity, which in turn is often taken to be the basis (via nationality) for citizenship. The social history and sociology of the rise of national societies in modernity often operates with this line of analysis, exploring the influence of common values, common myths and symbols, collective memories and traditions, a common language and so on.[1] This analysis tends to be more weighted towards 'heritage' and the 'common past' rather than to the 'common future', or indeed even than to the 'common present'. It is evidently easier to apply this analysis in the case of nation-states, national identities and national forms of citizenship than it is in the case of the European Union.

Many of the allegedly common values, myths, symbols, memories and traditions supporting national identities and citizenships can be argued to be contested and/or artificial 'inventions' and 'imaginings' (Anderson, 1991; Hobsbawm, 1984). Nonetheless, in the form of tradition and heritage, they usually have some kind of commonly recognized standing and social reality within national cultures. The common (vernacular, official and writtten) language characteristic of nations is lacking in Europe, although increasingly a de facto 'lingua franca' does seem to be taking hold across Europe, namely English.[2] In general national-type traditions are evidently lacking, or only present in weak and unconvincing ways, at the trans-national European level. This makes the concept of a common 'European identity', and thus allegedly also the concept of a common 'European citizenship', difficult to conceptualize, experience and communicate.[3]

However the perspective guiding this chapter is that too much significance can be attributed to heritage, memory and 'the common past' when conceptualizing culture and collective identity in modernity. Societies based on immigration, most notably the USA, or on acts of revolution, notably France and (in its day) the USSR, or more generally societies organized around science-based technological production and/or risk-taking capitalist markets necessarily locate and explore their collective identities in terms of their common presents and futures rather than their pasts.

Following this line of analysis, in the following section we will consider the idea that conceptualizations of common culture which are more present and future oriented, such as those expressed in terms of the metaphors of 'ground' and 'space', are more relevant to understanding contemporary and emerging possibilities for European citizenship than is the banal fact of the European Union's evident lack of a nation-state type tradition and heritage.[4] Furthermore these models of culture help to open out the concept of citizenship, to reconnect it directly to cultural processes and to 'civil society', and to disconnect it from dependency on morally highly questionable notions of collective identity such as those involved in ethnically based (and potentially 'ethnically pure' and 'ethnically cleansable') conceptions of nationality. To explore these issues we will first consider some aspects of the sociology of citizenship in modernity.

Conceptualizing Culture in the Sociology of Citizenship – 'Ground' and 'Space'

The field of the sociology of modern citizenship has tended to be restricted to exploring the three spheres of citizens' rights originally mapped out, in the early post-war period, by the British sociologist T.H. Marshall, namely the spheres of civil, political and social (welfare) rights and responsibilities. Marshall, in so far as he worked with any concept of culture at all, appeared to take the existence of a common and dominant national culture very much for granted as a relatively unproblematic background for his analysis, and to assume that cultural rights were implicit in civil and social rights.

T.H. Marshall[5] began his famous lecture with a consideration of his namesake, the economist Alfred Marshall, and his implicit sociological view of class and inequality. Alfred Marshall accepted the legitimacy of quantitative or economic inequality, but condemned qualitative or cultural inequality in respect of 'a qualitative assessment of life as a whole in terms of the essential elements in civilization or culture'. T.H. Marshall called this an implicitly but effectively 'sociological hypothesis' in Alfred Marshall's views. T.H. Marshall seemed to share this hypothesis in his observation that there is a 'unified civilization which makes social inequalities acceptable...' (Marshall, 1992: 47). He explicated the hypothesis in terms of 'the claim of all to enjoy (the conditions of a 'civilized' person's/gentleman's life MR)'. This 'claim of all', according to T.H. Marshall, 'is a claim to be admitted to a share in the social heritage, which in turn means a claim to be accepted as full members of the society, that is, as citizens'. This view 'postulates that there is a kind of basic human equality associated with the concept of full human membership of a community – or, as I should say, of citizenship...'. In the development of modern forms of society since the eighteenth century Marshall believes that, 'the basic human equality of membership...has been enriched with new substance and invested with a formidable array of rights. ...It has been clearly identified with the status of citizenship.' Thus Marshall's view seems to be that common national cultures or 'civilizations' have evolved in societies in the modern period to which all members of those societies have an equal claim. The satisfaction of this basic claim to cultural membership and inclusion is more or less compatible with a certain range of class-based cultural diversity and also with meritocratic social inequalities. In terms of this analysis, then, we can say that there is a 'common ground' or cultural basis to citizenship.

These sorts of 'common ground' assumptions are also to be found in other notable post-war British social and cultural analysts such as Raymond Williams and A.H. Halsey. From an anthropological perspective, traditionally concerned with relatively simple, small scale, self-reliant and self-reproducing communities, the concept of 'culture' can be defined in terms of the whole 'way of life' of the community, 'the common culture' which generates the common collective identity of societal members and which reflects 'the common condition' of their life together. The 'national culture' concept present in the work of T.H. Marshall, Williams, Halsey and many others could be said to take this anthropological 'common culture' and 'way of life' concept up to the level of the large-scale complex modern society. Functionalist anthropology and sociology from Emile Durkheim to Talcott Parsons has also operated with comparable assumptions, and so too have more contemporary definers and defenders of the concept of national societies (for instance Gellner, 1983 and Smith, 1995). Such nationally oriented, even ethnically oriented, assumptions about the cultural underpinnings or 'grounds' of citizenship, have seen a revival in recent years and are important elements in contemporary debates about the relationship between nation-states and the European Union. Even critical (or so-called 'Left') British sociology, when it addresses the prospects for and problems of the European Union, can take positions which can appear to attribute great, and to my view unwarranted, longevity and/or normative value to the nation-state form of social organization in modernity (Anderson, 1996; Mann, 1993). However these sorts of assumptions are surely becoming increasingly untenable in the context of late twentieth century Western history, at least in those national societies in the European world region.

The historical and irreversible facts of large-scale labour and asylum migrations in the twentieth century have led to an internal fragmentation of national cultures in European societies. This, at the very least, requires that these nations, periodically and profoundly, re-identify, make explicit and reaffirm their traditional 'common cultures'. More realistically it also requires them to consider developing their conception of their 'common cultures' to recognize the new 'common conditions' and 'ways of life' produced by culturalism, pluralism, co-existence and hybridization. It requires them to rethink their 'common ground' and to recognize new forms of it. Thus, within the contemporary sociology of citizenship, calls have been made for the need to develop clear conceptualizations of cultural rights in respect of such matters as the citizens' rights of access to cultural resources and competences to take part in the common culture, including access to information and the media, and at the same time rights to multi-cultural education, ethnic minority rights and cultural pluralism (Turner, 1994). In addition, as we will consider in this chapter, perhaps the realm of 'common conditions' and of the cultural interaction and communication relating to those conditions has now begun to shift decisively beyond the level of the nation-state, particularly so for the European nation-states given the process of European-level integration they have been exploring for two generations since the early post-war period. Perhaps the cultural 'grounds of membership and of citizenship' have begun to shift ineluctably to incorporate a substantial and growing European dimension.

To grasp this shift it is helpul to add to the interpretation of the conception of culture as a 'way of life' which is provided by the metaphor of a 'common ground', the perspective offered by an alternative metaphor, namely that of a 'common space', or more pointedly a 'common arena'. The space/arena metaphor is the model implied when economists stress the importance of 'markets' and when political theorists stress the importance of the role of 'civil society' in defining the nature of modern societies. Culture, then, as a dimension of the common space or arena, is connected with, although not wholly reducible to, processes of production and consumption, and with processes of struggle to achieve interests and power, which go on within the space/arena. Culture is the dimension of the social space/arena in which communication, mediation and in particular symbolism, is performed in pursuit of economic, political or intrinsic (moral or aesthetic) interests.

From a sociological perspective concerned with the highly complex, large scale, interdependent and self-transforming social systems of modernity, culture can be seen as a relatively distinctive and differentiated sphere. In this perspective culture is the sphere in which, in ideal typical terms, the dominant forms of rationalization and instrumentalism operative in the modern (capitalist) economy and (democratic) polity are largely disconnected and collective actions are engaged in for largely intrinsic and/or symbolic reasons. Examples of institutions concerned with these sorts of attitudes would typically be said to include the institutions of education, religion, sport, science, public service news media, each of which have at some time or another involved well-known claims to be domains free from politics and economics. However in modern societies evidently politics and economy cannot be kept out of any area and, for good or ill, penetrate all. So it is important to recognize that the sphere of culture is often a contested sphere in which institutions of intrinsic and symbolic action and rationality exist in a dialectic with cultural industries (cultural production and management, and cultural consumption) and cultural policy domains (cultural policy-making, regulation and implementation) which can undermine, colonize or control cultural institutions.

From the perspective of this chapter the culture–citizenship relationship can be seen either in terms of the metaphor of 'ground' as the 'common ground' of citizenship, or in terms of the metaphor of 'space', as the common space/arena for citizens' interactions and communications. Nation-state based societies, undoubtedly currently retain a traditional priority in providing people with much of their experience of this cultural ground and space. Nonetheless they do not monopolize and exhaust this experience, and indeed they are inexorably losing influence within the emergence of wider trans-national forms of common ground and common space. This is particularly so for the European nation-states, in terms of the slow but relentless emergence of a European level of cultural experience, participation and communication available to their citizens. This level is being formed by a variety of types of 'Europeanization' processes principally those of official EU cultural policy-making (see below) and of popular cultural consumerism (see below). It offers a different, trans-national and multi-dimensional cultural ground and space in which new possibilities for the exercise of social identity, membership and citizenship beyond and below the level of the nation-state are likely to become increasingly visible and possible as we move into the twenty-first century.

Europe: Problems of Culture and Citizenship

Clearly there are problems in defining what the identity and boundaries of Europe and its culture are. This is particularly so given the continuing enlargement of the European Union and the likely future continuation of this to include the Eastern European nations up to but excluding Russia, and possibly also Turkey with its strong Islamic character. The historical and 'high cultural' heritage Europe (of Greece, Rome, mediaeval Christendom, Renaissance, Enlightenment, industrialization, democratization etc.) is complex, ambiguous and open to interpretation (Delanty, 1995; Garcia, 1993, 1997). Nonetheless EU policy makers claim that a distinctive 'European' 'heritage' and set of values exists and that there is a distinctive modern 'European model' social and socio-economic policy (EC, 1995, 1996a). From this view, then, common 'European' cultural traditions and forms exist. This in turn raises relevant and interconnected policy questions – on the one hand how to promote and develop this common culture and on the other hand how to secure equal access to it and possibilities for participation in it to all as a matter of the *cultural* rights of EU citizenship.

The current state of the European Union and its institutions, even for 'Europhiles', is fundamentally flawed and in need of major structural development (Roche, 1997). On the economic front the Single Market project launched in 1992 remains radically incomplete until Economic and Monetary Union

(EMU), including a single currency, has been established around the turn of the century, and also as long as national labour market structures and traditions continue to block the development of massive and fluid pan-European labour mobility on the same continental scale as that long established in the USA (Delors Report, 1993). On the political front there is the well-known and long-criticized 'democratic deficit' in relation to the powers of Europe's citizens to control EU level policy-making (as against the inter-governmental Council of member-state ministers), which also has the dimensions of a 'legitimacy deficit' (Garcia, 1993) and a 'constitutional deficit' (Roche, 1997) which corrode and undermine EU institutions and policies in the eyes of Europe's publics. In addition, for many observers there is a serious 'social deficit' (Begg and Nectoux, 1995; Roche and van Berkel, 1997) associated with the attempt to construct a unified EU market in advance of the construction of a unified EU work, income and welfare regime. Further, while the political and economic logic of the European Union seems to move member states inescapably towards the achievement of a more integrated federal type 'United States of Europe' some time in the early twenty-first century, this is currently seen as highly controversial and to be resisted by nationalists, 'Europhobes' and 'Eurosceptics' in many of the member states, not least, of course, Britain.

These political, economic and social developments and controversies carry over into the spheres of 'citizenship' and 'culture', and they can either be directly expressed in terms of 'citizenship' and 'culture', or they can be seen as containing analogies for comparable themes and problems in these spheres. Thus the various deficits can be expressed as deficits of citizenship and rights. They can also be explained in terms of the strength of national cultures and their associated public spheres and collective identities, as against the 'cultural deficit' of the weakness or absence of European level popular culture, public sphere and collective identity.

However, the problems involved in understanding the nature and interconnections, the contradictions and trends, in cultural politics, policy making and citizenship in Europe evidently do not stop there. Between the continuing and indeed resurgent strength of nationalists' claims for nation-state cultures and identities on the one hand and EU policy makers' claims and hopes for some sort of homogeneous European culture and identity on the other, there are the challenges of (i) the various long-standing and resurgent sub-national ethnic, regional and urban/local cultures across Europe (e.g. Scots, Bretons, Flemish, Basques, Catalonians, Corsicans, North and South Italians, Sicillians etc.) and (ii) the various cosmopolitan, diaspora and multi-cultural social mixtures in cities and nations across Europe. These phenomena require an acceptance and valuation of human rights to cultural difference and diversity at a fundamental level in the constitution of modern nations and supra-national systems such as the EU. In particular they require that whatever else 'the European model' of a 'common culture', 'common values', etc. may or may not be claimed to be it must emphatically be pluralist and multi-cultural – a framework for co-existence, and for the recognition and respect of difference – and it must emphatically oppose all forms of racism and cultural discrimination.[6]

In the light of this discussion the idea that 'culture' can be taken for granted, whether in its national form, as T.H. Marshall and his followers in the sociology of citizenship tended to do, or in its trans-national forms, is evidently untenable in the late twentieth century historical context, and will be increasingly so as we move into the twenty-first century. Processes of globalization and of the construction of influential trans-national political fields and public spheres, of which the European Union is the leading example require us to go beyond this kind of thinking. In idealistic and futuristic vein Jürgen Habermas,[7] for instance, while acknowledging the current priority of nation-states and national public cultures, envisages a future Europe as a republican political multi-culture: 'In a future Federal Republic of European States, the same legal principles would...have to be interpreted from the vantage point of different national traditions and histories.' 'In the future...differentiation could occur in a European culture between a common political culture and the branching national traditions of art and literature, historiography, philosophy etc.'. 'Particularist anchorages of this sort would in no way impair the universalist meaning of popular sovereignty and human rights.' Furthermore he argues that 'a European constitutional patriotism would have to grow from different interpretations, which the same universalistic rights and constitutional principles enjoy by receiving their place in the context of different national histories'. Thus he suggests that 'our task is less to reassure ourselves of our common origins in the European Middle Ages than to develop a new political self-confidence commensurate with the role of Europe in the world of the twenty-first century'.

However, as Habermas himself well recognizes, there is evidently very much to be done to turn this ideal future Europe into something approaching reality. Current versions of EU citizens' civil, political and social rights all remain defective in important ways[8] and there is a lot of room and need for political development in respect of trans-national European cultural rights, minorities' rights in particular (Garcia, 1993, 1997). Currently within the EU, anomalous forms of partial citizenship for some ethnic minorities exist (e.g. the 'denizenship' of settled Turkish migrants in Germany), and 'anti-social' racist and extreme nationalist politico–cultural movements are beginning to gain legitimacy and some elements of power (e.g. in France and Germany).[9] It is worth bearing in mind that in any future twenty-first century quasi-federal or more fully federal EU *all* nations and their 'ethnic national' communities will effectively have the status of minorities. They will thus all be in as much need of legal recognition and protection as 'minorities' currently are within nation-states. It is in the light of this unavoidable fact of Europe's cultural and political diversity within a common territory, a common socio-economic space and a common constitutional framework, that the reality of a common and shared European 'public sphere', culture and identity will be developed in the twenty-first century.

Culture, Europeanization and Policy

In this section we first consider some general conceptualizations of European common culture and processes of Europeanization. We then briefly outline the development of 'culture' as a theme in European Community/European Union policy. This provides some context for a consideration of official and popular Europeanization in two areas of popular culture, namely tourism and sport. Tourism is considered briefly later in this section, and sport is considered more substantially in the following main section of the chapter.

The development of the European Community, and now Union, in the post-war period has tended to be driven by governments and political elites, with occasional (although, since Maastricht 1992, increasing) exercises in political consultation with mass publics and legitimation of these processes by means of referenda. The development has also often appeared to be mainly driven by economic and political logics and interests identified by elites and disconnected from the experiences of ordinary people in Europe. However the view taken in this chapter is that it is important to recognize the degree to which the late twentieth century Europeanization politically driven integration process responds to and derives from real-world dynamics in common conditions faced by the peoples of Europe and not just by political and economic elites. These common conditions may sometimes be obscured or misrepresented in public and media debates conducted within traditional nation-state terms of reference, and in which the politics of nationalism can sometimes play a dominating role. The common conditions within and between European societies and their peoples have at least what can be called politico-military and neo-economic dimensions. The view taken in this chapter is that these two dimensions generate the socio-historical basis and the normative political imperative for the further development of what might be called a distinctive 'European public culture'.

The politico-military dimension relates to collective understandings of the past and the present, and it provides something of a European-level 'common ground' for contemporary Europeans. The dimension relates to the popularly remembered and understood inherent flaws and limits of purely nation-state based, nationalistic and authoritarian conceptions of domestic and international politics. The common politico-military condition faced by all nations in Europe in the twentieth century is that of the absolute vulnerability, in a small sub-continent, of armies and civilian populations to complete destruction under the technological conditions of modern 'total' war, and their common history, experiences and memories of this (thus their shared and common culture) in the two 'World' wars in particular and to a certain extent also in the Cold war period. In terms of this politico-military dimension the development of the EC/EU has been the form taken by absolute, profound and imperative need, recognized both by political elites and also by mass publics, for peaceful co-existence and co-operation between nations and peoples in Europe deriving from their common historical (spatio-cultural) conditions of existence, whatever their more apparent (and more superficial) linguistic or other differences.

It may be that the grassroots politics connected with this politico-military dimension has long remained relatively undeveloped, but its existence and potential within and between European national societies and publics contributes to a sense in which 'Europe' is (wants to be, has to be) at least a distinctive kind of world regional 'civil society', whatever is or is not achieved in the name of the proto-federalist EU project in the contemporary period.

The 'neo-economic' dimension relates to collective understandings of the present and the future, and it provides something of a European-level 'common space' for contemporary Europeans. The dimension refers to the contemporary phase of 'Europeanization' of ordinary people's economic and environmental experiences in European societies in the 1990s. The EU's Single Market project which, after decades gestating began to be constructed in earnest from 1992, and its single currency project which began to be put in place from 1999 onwards, are important elements in the long-term construction of Europe in the twenty-first century as a trans-national 'economic space' (for instance see 'Agenda 2000', EC, 1997) As the official policy rhetoric originally developed by EC President Jacques Delors from the mid-1980s to the early 1990s presents it, this aims to be a 'Europe without frontiers' in terms of the free movement of goods and services, of information and the media, and of people (whether tourists, business travellers or labour migrants) around a (by then) truly 'common market' (for instance see the Delors Report, EC, 1993). Partly as a result of the important European-level economic institution building, and partly as a result of the European 'world-regional' effects of general trends towards internationalization and globalization in production and marketing European people's identities as consumers in particular, and also to a certain extent as workers, are becoming significantly dis-embedded from national economic cultures and 'Europeanized'.

The fact that 'Europe' means something to mass publics in each of the European nations, together with the different things it may mean to different groups and nations, are matters which are currently being constructed through such popular cultural practices as shopping and touring, and to a lesser extent watching television. Through such everyday and popular cultural practices as these, and not (only) by the 'top-down' impositions of elite policy makers in the EU system, a new Europe is being constructed as both a trans-national region and also as a meta-cultural space containing a rich diversity of cultures ('heritages', local cultures, national styles etc.) and a massive potential for creative cultural hybridization (evident in the central zones of its main cities and tourist resorts). In addition the growth of environmental consciousness and politics, which is connected with the rise of consumer culture and a public recognition of its costs in all Western nations in the late twentieth century, has encouraged people in European societies to become aware of Europe as a common environmental space, a common homeland, as well as a common cultural space, in both senses a 'place' as well as a 'space'.

The increasing development of common European transport infrastructures, particularly high speed train systems, is one of a number of contemporary developments which tend to promote these notions of Europe as a common place/space. Accelerating the growth and popularity of trans-national intra-European travel carries obvious implications for the further development of popular touristic consumerist recognitions of and attitudes towards Europe. It also carries the potential for promoting awareness of and debate about Europe as an environment at risk and as needing conservation and sustainable development.

The popular cultural sphere in Europe can be said to include sport, tourism, the media, as well as education and science. My perspective is that these spheres are becoming subject to a long-term process of Europeanization, under the impact of the development of European-level trends in these institutions, industries and policy spheres. To fully substantiate this perspective a comprehensive account of each of them would be needed both in aggregate (cross-nationally, across each of the EU member states), and also at the EU level. However, as we have already indicated, since this kind of comprehensive account is not appropriate for a chapter we will instead focus on sport culture, and discuss some elements of EU level trends and policy developments in relation to it.

To introduce this discussion we will first briefly consider some background issues in the development of official EU-level approaches to culture and heritage in general and to popular culture in particular, illustrating the latter with reference to the field of tourism.

European Integration and Cultural Policy

It would be wrong to characterize the cultural policy of the European Union, outside of the higher education and vocational training spheres where it is probably most developed, as having very much coherence, penetration and influence at this stage in the development of European integration. However a basis has been laid and a start made in a number of areas. The EU first formally gave itself authority to act in the sphere of culture in the 1992 Maastricht Treaty of Union adding to this only marginally in the 1997 Amsterdam Treaty.[10] The cultural article of the 1992 Treaty is stated in very general terms and, among other things, gives the Union the new obligation to promote 'the common cultural heritage' and also the obligation to 'contribute to the flowering of the cultures of the Member States while respecting their national and regional diversity'.

However it should be noted that the EC/EU's activities in the field of culture have been ongoing in various ways since the mid-1980s. The growth of EC/EU interests and powers in the two spheres of culture and citizenship, given their politically sensitive character and given also financial constraints, has so far been fairly limited. But nonetheless a beginning has been made in a number of areas on long-term processes of 'official' cultural Europeanization. The stirrings of policy in these areas has been connected with the recognition by the Commission in the 1980s of the 'legitimacy' deficit and the need for information and propaganda around Europe's publics of the nature, role and future of the EU independent of the member states' varying governmental and media versions of the European idea. The EC/EU's conceptions of European-level culture and citizenship, and its approaches to them as policy domains have tended to be developed in step with each other, with some discursive connections made at each stage. This was so in the 1992 Maastricht Treaty which, besides the new authority in the sphere of culture, also first formally created the legal category of 'citizen of the European Union', albeit at this stage with few substantive rights.[11] It has also characterized the recent revision of the Maastricht Treaty in the 1997 Amsterdam Treaty which gives the EU some formal authority in the area of sport for the first time as well as adding significantly to the legal substance of European citizenship.[12]

This link, or at least parallel, between the development of EC/EU policy for culture (including sport) and citizenship was also evident in the Commission's first main foray into the cultural policy field in 1985 with the Addonino Report 'A People's Europe.'[13] This report recognized the need for a popular cultural strategy to promote the EC and the cause of 'Europeanization' and its relevance for people's everyday lives if the long and difficult process of European integration, particularly the creation of the Single Market which Commission President Jacques Delors had begun promoting in the mid-1980s, was to be regarded as legitimate and popular around Europe's publics. The report recognized the problems at the time of national 'red tape' blocking EC citizens' abilities to move around Europe as tourists, or for work and settlement. It proposed EC passports, driving licences, emergency health cards, border signs and flags as tangible, popular and everyday indicators of EC identity and also the promotion of sport, tourism and an EC TV channel to get the European message across. However in 1990, while implying the affirmative, the Commission was moved to ask itself: 'A flag, a passport, an anthem, are these just silly gimmicks or the symbols of the banding together of peoples committed to democracy and peace?'[14] Whether or not these sorts of things are 'silly gimmicks' certainly the recognition, in the mid-1980s, that the EC needed to be involved in the popular cultural fields of sport and tourism was realistic, even far-sighted. As we suggest below these have developed a decade later, both with and without EC encouragement, into major institutions and industries in which important processes of cultural Europeanization have begun to take root.

Also in 1985 the Commission began to roll out some initial practical vehicles of 'official' Europeanization. For instance the 'European City of Culture' event cycle was created. In 1985 Athens was the first city awarded this event, and notable successors include Glasgow 1990 and Madrid 1992. This has broadened in recent years in the concept of a Commission-backed programme of 'millennium' festivals and events celebrating the European idea in nine European cities in the year 2000.[15] Also in 1985 the Commission first began to define a 'European cultural area' in the field of the media and in terms of its regulation of the media in Europe.[16] In 1991 the Commission produced the 'TV without frontiers' Directive. This involved programme quotas to protect European-based programming against non-European (particularly American) programming, and it also provided for the free 'movement' of TV broadcasting within the EU. This Directive and related EU competition policy approaches to the operation of media companies are particularly important in relation to the kind of participation and rights related to TV sport events, and we will consider this again later (in the final main section).

Citizenship in general, and European citizenship in particular has long been a prominent theme in the Commission's internal policy discourse, its approach to public communications about and legitimation of the EU integration process and its publicity discourse in general. This has been particularly true in the 1990s and also characterizes its approach to its cultural policy initiatives in this period. For instance in 1996 the President of the Commission Jacques Santer launched a publicity campaign to popularize the European Union on the theme of 'Citizens

First'. This was aimed at raising EU citizens' awareness about the opportunities available to them in the Single Market, and about their economic, consumer and social rights, and has had a significant take-up.

In the field of education the EU continues to have little power and authority when compared to member state governments. Various pilot projects are being explored at the secondary level, particularly involving the development of information technology networks between European schools. In addition, in its first venture into the controversial area of 'political education' in schools the Commission is supporting a project to promote the idea of Europe and European citizenship involving the holding of 'mock' elections to the European Parliament in secondary schools across Europe in the year 1999 (Morrell, 1996). The picture is more substantial in the higher education sector where successive and influential research and development 'framework' programmes and also the Erasmus/ Socrates student exchange and access programmes between institutions across Europe carry the Europeanization message, albeit in a relatively elite cultural sphere.

In the economically important popular cultural area of tourism the EU has also begun to develop a policy role related to the single market project, but also related to the attempt to promote European heritage and identity. Without delving into the detail of EU policies and Europeanization processes in this field it is worth briefly considering some of the rationales motivating them before we move on to our main focus on sport.[17] In 'Tourism, Europe and Identity' John Urry (1995) argues that 'current debates about the changing nature of "Europe" cannot be undertaken without relating them to the possible transformations of social identity that mass mobility brings about' (Urry, 1995: 163), particularly so given the prominent role of Europe in what is the world's largest and fastest growing international/global economic sector. In terms of the connection between social identities and 'imagined communities', long testified to in the construction of the nation-state in modernity, Urry raises the question of the implications of the growth of international tourism for 'the multiple forms of identity within Europe' (1995: 166). Tourism is an important dimension of modern (and indeed 'postmodern') cultural economies, popular cultural practices and identity formation. It is also an important dimension of the field of contemporary cultural policy, whether such policy is exercised at the nation level (e.g. Hall and Jenkins, 1995), at the sub-national (e.g. urban) levels (e.g. Roche, 1992), or as we will consider in this section, at the trans-national (here, European) level.

In spite of all this, tourism might be thought to be of only marginal interest when we conceive of the nature of modern citizenship and contemporary changes in citizenship. However, as Urry suggests, 'the right to travel has become a marker of citizenship' (1995: 165). Although Urry does not develop this implication in this paper, clearly this kind of right – the freedom to move, to exit one's nation and re-enter it – can be understood to be a basic ethico-political right of citizenship both in liberal and democratic nations and also in the 'global citizenship' of human rights. Urry himself emphasizes more the connection between tourism, citizenship and consumerism. Thus he notes that 'citizenship rights increasingly involve claims to consume other cultures and places throughout the world' (1995: 165). In addition, as will be noted in the discussion of European tourism policy, tourism can also relate to citizenship seen from the perspective of employment, and thus as relating to citizens as 'workers' as well as citizens as 'consumers'. So tourism has a important claim to make not only on the analysis of culture, and here on the Europeanization of some aspects of tourism policy making, but more generally on the analysis of citizenship in some of its main aspects (political, economic and cultural), and on the long-term possibilities for the development of further Europeanization in these broader terms.

Urry suggests that 'mass mobility is probably one of the main factors that will determine whether a European identity will emerge' (1995: 170). The seasonal migrations of Europe's masses from the wealthier North to the relatively poorer South – together with European-level promotion and regulation of culture in general, this industry in particular within the Single Market project – are indeed likely to be potentially powerful vehicles of cultural Europeanization in the early twenty-first century. However equally powerful and parallel trends are at work in another particular sphere of contemporary popular culture, namely sport. In the following section we can look at some of the Europeanization dynamics currently at work in the sphere of sport, particularly spectator sport and media sport.

Sport and Cultural Europeanization

Marx's legendary dictum that 'religion is the opium of the people' needs to be modified to apply to the ostensibly non-religious culture of late twentieth century society in which the mass of people not only claim to be disinterested in religion but also have virtually open access to the 'opium' of a vast range of mood-altering legal and illegal drugs. In this context perhaps it is more appropriate to observe that 'sport is the religion of the people' providing apparently secular, but from a sociological perspective, quasi-religious experiences such as those of sacredness and transcendence, communal ritual and symbolism, and collective drama and emotionality. Sport is an important sector of popular culture in modern societies both as a quasi-religious institution and also an industry. Particularly in its professional, spectatorial and media sport forms, as sport industry, it provides one of the few significant arenas where collective identities, from the local to the national can be publicly symbolized and emotionally expressed (Roche, 1998). Sport's calendars and cycles of controlled contests provide rich experiences and forms of participation for mass audiences. Major sport events have compelling dramatic, ceremonial and festive dimensions both as 'live events' in the cathedral-like structures of modern stadia and also as 'media-events', that is as a distinct, compelling and commercially important genre of television programming (Roche and Arundel, 1998).

Modern sport has been increasingly globalized since the late nineteenth century, a process driven by, among other factors, the ideological agendas of European empires (Guttman, 1994), the internationalist mission and values of the Olympic movement (Houlihan, 1994) and the globalization of consumer markets and the global reach of television (Roche, 1998; Whannel, 1992). However it is worth noting, even allowing for the powerful influence of American commercial and media sport models, that modern sport has a special relationship with Europe's cultures and identities. The cultural institutions of modern sport in most of its forms were largely created in Europe. This was most notably the case in nineteenth century England where many modern games and the ideology of 'amateurism' were created and also in late nineteenth century and early twentieth century France where the Olympic movement and the international dimension of many sports was cultivated. The development of international sport in the late nineteenth century and early twentieth century evidently provided a potent focus for the cultural mobilization of the new urban middle classes and industrial working classes around the idea of nationalism and national identity (Hobsbawm, 1984). However it also helped construct elements of a popular international awareness and helped give some form to ordinary people's conceptions of and interests in the social world beyond the nation-state (Houlihan, 1994; Roche, 2000). In spite of the development of European-level governing bodies and sports industry markets and corporations the development of European Community/ Union integration in the post-war and late twentieth century periods has had little explicit connection with sport until relatively recently.

It is true to say that the concept of mass sport participation among the publics of Europe's nations, for health and other such reasons, the 'sport for all' policy, was developed and promoted as a form of state cultural policy, in the post-war period by a European-level organization, namely the Council of Europe. However 'sport for all' policies, leaving aside the question of how successful they were (Roche, 1994), were not publicly perceived as being connected with Europe or anything much outside of the nation and locality in which they were practised. As we have seen the European Commission's Addonino Report in 1985, among other things, noted that, at least in principle, European identity might be promoted if international sports were ever to recognize teams representing the 'European Community'. In practice the only significant sport in which something like this has developed is golf, in the form of the prestigious annual Ryder Cup competition between representative teams from the USA and a set of European nations. Compared with the long-standing use of representative international sport to promote national identities, the multi-national and trans-national European Union has not really attempted to cultivate sport in any comparable way as a vehicle for the development and popularization of a 'European' identity. Indeed sport was not explicitly mentioned at all in European Community treaties up to and including the important Maastricht Treaty of Union in 1992.

However in the post-Maastricht period this situation has begun to change in some significant ways (for an overview see Houlihan, 1994: Ch. 4). The European Union in its 1997 Amsterdam Treaty for the first time explicitly and formally recognized 'the social significance of sport, in particular its role in forging identity and bringing people together'. The Treaty implies that there may well be occasions involving the various policy-making bodies of the Union (i.e. the Council of Ministers, the Court of Justice, the Parliament, the Commission) when 'important questions affecting sport are at issue'. And it 'calls on' those bodies 'to listen to sports associations' and to seek their views on those issues (Duff, 1997: 87). What the 'important questions' referred to here are is not made clear, and so it might be tempting to view this enigma as indicating empty rhetoric. This would be a mistake. What has become clear in recent years is the beginning of the impact of the EU's trans-national Single Market project on the sports industries, the media industries, and thus the 'sports media' industries, of its member states. The EU, through acts of both commission and omission, of both de-regulation and re-regulation, is beginning to reshape the market conditions, the cultural space and the common interests, in terms of which spectator sport and media sport is being produced and consumed. It is thereby beginning to affect the exercise of European citizens' rights in the fields of both cultural industry employment and cultural consumption, and also more generally in what is effectively an emerging European-level popular cultural sphere operating within and across national boundaries in the Union. Whether intentionally or more likely as an unintended consequence of the construction of the Single Market a process of popular cultural Europeanization has been set in motion in the fields of spectator sport and media sport, and this is most clearly visible in the most popular sport across Europe, namely professional soccer. Three points need to be made to illustrate this process of Europeanization.

First, there is the issue of the impact of Europeanization on citizens' employment rights in the industry of professional sport in the member states of the European Union. Professional football clubs in most European countries had traditionally claimed the power to control the careers of players associated with them even if they were at the end of their contracts by charging other clubs transfer fees for them. In 1995 the European Court of Justice, petitioned by the player Marc Bosman, ruled that this power was illegal and an infringement on the free movement of labour in the Single Market. Henceforth all players in professional football and other similar sports would have the legally enforceable right against their employing club to a free transfer to another club on the expiry of the period of their contract with the employing club. In more recent cases players' rights to a free transfer prior to the expiry of their contract, on the basis of the player giving some specifiable period of notice and working it out, have been considered by the Court (Donegan, 1997).

Secondly there is the issue of the Europeanization of spectators' 'consumption' of the spectacle of professional football, in particular the identities of football teams and the character of the leagues in which they compete. The Bosman ruling, together with the new high levels of income from the sale of rights to the television coverage of games has led to a transformation in the composition of teams towards a new European-oriented cosmopolitanism. The great city clubs and their teams in the leading national leagues around Europe (the Italian, German and English leagues for instance) were traditionally composed at least of fellow nationals and often of locally developed players. In a real way they were connected with the identities of the communities in which their fans lived. They are now increasingly composed of multi-national mixtures of 'star' players bought on the international football player labour market. The objective connections between clubs and communities have now been significantly undermined. Ironically (and surprisingly, given the capacity of football fans in all countries for myopic parochialism), the symbolic identifications of local fans with these new cosmopolitanized clubs and of the clubs with their host cities seem to have often intensified in spite of this.

This is partly because there has begun to be a decisive shift in the character of the leagues in which these clubs compete. From competing in national leagues, and thus representing the locality to the nation, the leading clubs are now in addition committed to competing in competitions such as UEFA's Champions League. These are effectively European-level 'super-leagues' in which clubs represent both their locality and also their nation on 'the European stage'. As such they thereby carry higher status and more complex and intense symbolic identifications both for their local fans and also for the wider football culture of a given nation. National-level leagues often dating from the late nineteenth century have a traditional status and standing for national publics which the European-level competitions, developed in the post-war period, could never match. They continue to have great importance for national football fans. However we are now seeing the beginnings of a major challenge to the standing of the national leagues, namely the evolution of a popularly identifiable and perceivedly high status European level of football organization inhabited by increasingly familiar 'European', if still 'foreign', clubs. The main stimulus for this development, and the cultural industry which makes these processes of Europeanization technically possible, is of course the influence of commercial television. So we should now finally consider the possibility that a process of Europeanization of citizens' rights to cultural participation is beginning to get under way in the sphere of citizens' rights to 'consume' media sport.

'Media sport' as a cultural form, and 'television sport' as a particular TV programming genre,[18] have long been seen as important to the construction of national cultural identity,[19] and thus as requiring full access by national publics. This access has traditionally been provided, in America and Europe in the post-war period, through different mixes of commercial and state-based broadcasting. The importance of the TV sport genre to the health, indeed the very survival of commercial TV networks has been particularly clear in the USA. Since the 1960s the competition between the big three networks for the TV rights to sport events seen as of national significance, such as major league baseball, American football and the Olympic games, has been increasingly intense over the years. It has been less well appreciated in European countries with state-based TV stations, such as the BBC in Britain, which have traditionally had relatively inexpensive and uncontested access to the broadcasting of such sports and events, and also where public access to 'key' sport events via TV may also have been protected in law (as in the case of Britain's 'listed events').

With the advent of satellite and cable TV in Europe since the 1980s and with the simultaneous weakening of the previously central role of state-based broadcasting there has been a greater recognition of the importance of TV sport. On the one hand commercial TV recognizes the capacity of media sport to 'capture' massive and/or committed audiences with class and consumption profiles attractive to advertisers and sponsors. On the other hand public service TV recognizes the capacity of media sport to provide opportunities for cultural inclusion and for bringing national and international publics together in the sharing of calendars of common events, and of sharable experiences in a common (mediated) space and time – a common and recurrent national and international public culture in an increasingly fragmented and changing world.[20] State-based and commercially based versions of wide-access terrestrial 'free to view' TV were competitive with each other, but they could also be compatible. They could even be complementary, in terms of sharing the broadcasting of a given year's major sport events. However the advent of satellite and cable TV systems in the 1980s and their market penetration and growth in the 1990s has begun to shift the balance decisively and inexorably in favour of commercial television. This has raised major regulatory problems in relation to public access for all forms of programming, but in particular for sport TV.

These systems, and the further technological development they promise through digitalization in the late 1990s, have enabled, and will increasingly enable, commercial TV to make profits by processes of 'intensification' of products and markets in ways notably different from, and additional to, the processes of 'extensification' involved in traditional 'broadcasting' to a wide audience. The process of extending mass market penetration in the British and European market, of course, continues in parallel with intensification, as satellite TV in particular attempts to use its buying power to control exclusive rights to attractive major sport events in order to sell receiver dishes. However, in the new generation of digitalized systems profitability is made viable, to a greater extent than ever before, by attracting special interest audiences. These audiences are willing to pay for access to channels specializing in intensive single-genre programming (pay-TV), and indeed are willing to go further and to pay extra fees, in addition, for one-off events, so-called 'pay-per-view' (PPV). It is estimated that there is a very strong latent demand for PPV in Britain and Europe more generally. In Britain this latent demand is estimated to be a massive extra £2.5 billion annually in potential consumer expenditure across all programming genres but particularly on sport programming (Gratton, 1997). In Europe generally it is estimated to be of the order of $23 billion by the year 2000 (Short, 1996). To feed the bottomless programming needs of these systems, and in order to reap the profits that are available through both extension and also intensification processes, TV companies (Murdoch's in particular as we will discuss in a moment) have risked taking on heavy debt exposure in order buy up exclusive rights to the transmission of many key national and world level sport events, because of their strategic importance and profitability. This can be most clearly seen in recent years in the case of Rupert Murdoch's media companies' use of national and international spectator sport in their drive to dominate national and international media markets, which we can now consider as a case in a little more detail, both in general and also in terms of the implications of this case for the European sport media 'space', and embryonic popular cultural rights to 'TV sport for all' within this space.

Rupert Murdoch has always seen media sport as a key element in his corporate strategies and increasingly so in recent years as his companies have begun to create an international media network with truly global reach. For him they have always been a leading programming genre, along with films[21] and live news.[22] These three genres, with media sport prominent among them, are of great value to Murdoch in his efforts to enter and dominate national, international and global press and TV markets. Media sport in particular allows him to create profitable new synergies within his media complex between his press and TV companies, and more broadly between his media companies in general on the one hand, and the wider global corporate market-place of advertising and sport sponsorship on the other.

Murdoch's sport-led corporate strategies have been evident over a number of decades in his various media operations around the world – since the 1970s in Australia and Britain, since the 1980s in the USA, and in the 1990s in continental Europe and Asia.[23] Within Murdoch's complex global network of press, TV and other types of media companies his specifically television-oriented companies and interests, which have been most involved in developing his media sports-led global corporate strategy, include the following: Fox TV in the USA, Star TV in Asia and China, Channel 7 in Australia, as well as BSkyB in Britain and Europe, and, in Germany, the Vox and Kirsch media companies in which he has stakes.

Murdoch has a long-proven ability to read and play media-cultural markets, and to take risks in order to dominate them (Horsman, 1997; Shawcross, 1992). Currently, for instance, the revolutionary new digital generation of massive capacity multi-channel and interactive TV systems, in both satellite and terrestrial versions, is being introduced in Britain and more broadly in Europe. The British terrestrial versions of digital TV, in which Murdoch has a significant stake, together with Murdoch's own satellite version of digital TV broadcasting to Britain and Europe rolled out in 1998. This in turn will provide for a much greater development of PPV in sport than already exists, for instance through single club-based channels, and also in other TV programme areas.

However, in a European context, it is worth noting that, at least in principle, there are certain constraints on Murdoch's room for manouevre in relation to British and European sport. On the one hand there are also competitive constraints on Sky. Sky, unlike the BBC, is not a member of the European Broadcasting Union (EBU). This alliance of EU nations' 'public service' broadcasters has been very effective in gaining European transmission rights to global mega-events such as the Olympics and soccer World Cups, and also the prestigious European Nations soccer competition. However there is currently some doubt about its 'cartel'-type role in the EU broadcasting sphere given the EU's Single Market project and anti-cartel competition policy, which may give Sky greater room for manoeuvre in future (Henderson, 1996; Short, 1996).

On the other hand there are regulatory constraints. These include the UK's 'listed events' legislation which requires key national and international level sport events deemed to be of national significance to be provided on a free and widely available basis in the UK via traditional terrestrial broadcasters such as the BBC or ITV. There are versions of this kind of 'listed events' protection in other European countries' media legislation. 'Listed events' legislation could be said to be a media version of 'sport for all' policy, i.e. 'TV sport spectatorship for all' – a version of the cultural rights of national citizenship. In Britain the number of these listed events protected for 'free to view' TV or in other relevant ways was increased by the New Labour government in 1998. Some other European countries have similar media regulation, and currently there is some prospect of this kind of legislation being supported and complemented by EU-level media legislation.

The stategic use of sport, in the form of 'flagship' media sport programming by international media corporations such as Murdoch's stable of companies evidently can have a number of destabilizing effects in relation to the organization and identities of nationally or regionally based sports, and the communities from which they traditionally drew their support (see also Rowe, 1996). On the one hand the intervention of TV on this scale destabilizes traditional relationships between organizers, players and fans within sports. Important new flows of income are injected into sport governing bodies and their clubs, rendering them dependent on TV income rather than gate-receipts from fans and spectators, and leading to inflation and instability in the labour market for players (Bale and Maguire, 1994). On the other hand TV's intervention destabilizes the public's access to nationally significant sport events by effectively privatizing them. In the late 1990s, particularly in Europe in sports like soccer and rugby, we are seeing the development of complex power struggles over both of these issues, involving media companies, representative governments, sport organizations and fans. These struggles are complicated also by the trans-national character of some of the leading media companies, in particular Rupert Murdoch's stable of companies, and also of the system of governance emerging within the European Union (EU) as a result of the attempt both to create and to regulate the Single Market.

In 1996 the European Parliament called on the European Commission 'to work for the granting of transmission rights for big sports programmes to free television channels' (EP, 1996). In response the European Union Commissioner for competition policy, Karel van Miert, recognized a responsibility to monitor, and if necessary control, the growth of exclusive TV rights arrangements in Europe (Henderson, 1996; Short, 1996). In effect these struggles over access to media sport can be said to contribute to the development of new national and 'post-national' conceptions of cultural identity (Morley and Robbins, 1995) and 'cultural citizenship' and the rights of such citizenship in the contemporary period (O'Keefe, 1998; Roche, 2000; Rowe, 1996).

Conclusion

In this chapter we have considered the mutual implications of the concepts of 'culture' and 'citizenship' in the context of contemporary European integration. T.H. Marshall's well-known analysis of citizenship as a three dimensional complex and of the historical emergence of this complex in modern national societies tends to marginalize the sphere of culture and cultural rights by taking it for granted as the traditional communal ground of societal membership. The long-term post-war developments of (i) a 'common market' between the European nations, and (ii) more recently the emergence of elements of a more institutionalized trans-national polity in the form of the European Union and its Single Market and single currency projects in the post-Maastricht period, carry important long-term implications for citizenship and its analysis.

These developments challenge the Marshallian analysis in various ways, not least in terms of its prioritization of the national level, its evolutionary assumptions and also its taken-for-granted version of the relevance of culture to citizenship. The latter is a particular weakness in the European context where the diversity of national cultures is evident and also where the construction of a trans-national level of cultural and rights of access to and inclusion in it will necessarily involve a new balance between the mono-culture of an emerging European legal constitution and sphere of governance on the one hand, and the de facto multi-cultures of Europe's national, ethnic, regional and immigrant cultural diversity on the other. Unlike national forms of citizenship the formal features of 'European citizenship' are currently relatively minimal and the (potentially substantial) de facto rights and forms of citizenship being constructed through the process of social and economic integration are dependent for their development and realization on institutions which remain weak and defective in many important respects.

Further, except at elite levels, there is currently very little in the European Union comparable to the 'public spheres' which exist at the national level within the member states. In addition, outside of the perceptions of elite groups and perhaps also some of the Christian churches, there is little explicit awareness of a common cultural heritage. So in each of these respects the bases for the development of a European dimension to individuals' and collectivities' sense of identity, versions of a European identity, do not currently appear to be very substantial. Nevertheless the discussion in this chapter suggests that the processes of integration and Europeanization at work within and between the member states of the European Union are long-term, effectively irreversible and will in time have profound impacts on the experience of citizenship and cultural participation in European societies, developing a fully fledged trans-national public culture at once competitive with and complementary to those of the nation-states.

It was suggested that these processes can usefully be conceptualized in terms of the development of popular understandings of Europe as a 'common ground' and a 'common space'. The 'common ground' metaphor relates less to backward-looking elite versions of history as 'heritage' and more to public understandings of history in terms of commonalities in the present situation and future possibilities facing everybody in societies located in the European 'world region' in the context of the range of influences exerted by various forms of globalization, not least economic and environmental forms. The 'common space' metaphor refers to the implications of the European Community's/European Union's long-standing efforts to build a 'common/Single Market' with a common currency and legally sanctionable freedom of movement for goods, information and people beyond the regulation of the nation-state. The common 'economic space' which is beginning to be constructed at the European level carries implications ('top-down') for the conceptualization and development of cultural policy and ('bottom-up') for people as workers, consumers and citizens. To illustrate some of these implications some of the currently undeveloped forms of cultural policy in the European Union were reviewed, and Europeanization processes particularly for consumers in the two popular cultural areas and industries of sport and also, albeit more briefly, tourism were considered.

It may be that an inclusionary and forward-looking conception of contemporary European culture and, relatedly, a demand for citizen's rights to 'European culture for all' has not yet begun to be articulated. But this chapter suggests that if it is ever to be articulated it is likely to be so, initially at least, in popular cultural consumerist fields such as sport, the media and tourism. As we have seen, even the unlikely looking field of 'media sport' might present some important and interesting challenges for the development of a politics of cultural citizenship and collective identity, of 'common ground' and 'common space', in the new Europe as we enter the twenty-first century.

Notes

This chapter owes much to the sociability and research community provided by friends in Sheffield University. In this context I would like to thank Nick Stevenson for many useful conversations and comments on the themes of this chapter and of this book in general. In addition I would also like to thank Jackie Harrison (Journalism Studies) and Lorna Woods (Law) for their ideas and encouragement in our ongoing conversations about European citizenship, cultural policy and media regulation (see for instance, Harrison and Woods, 1998). It should be said, of course, that they have no responsibility for any inaccuracies or weaknesses in the chapter.

1. See References for studies by Anderson, 1996; Gellner, 1983; Hobsbawm, 1984; Mosse, 1975; Smith, 1995; and Spillman, 1997.

2. Thanks to David Marquand for this observation and the irony it contains.

3. See References for studies by Delanty, 1995; Garcia, 1993, 1997; Meehan, 1993; Roche and van Berkel, 1997; Rosas and Antola, 1995.

4. See Anthony Smith's comments on 'Pan-Europeanism' and European 'super-nationalism', in Smith, 1995: Ch. 5.

5. See Marshall, 1992. All quotes in this paragraph are taken from pp. 6–7, unless otherwise indicated.

6. For relevant discussions of this necessarily pluralist and 'post-national' character and imperative of the EU and its implications for politics and citizenship see References for studies by Habermas, 1994; Meehan, 1993; Tassin, 1992; and Weiner, 1996.

7. See Habermas, 1994. The quotations in this paragraph are from pp. 27/8 and pp. 33/4.

8. See Roche, 1992a: Ch. 8, 1997 and generally Roche and van Berkel, 1997. Also Rosas and Antola, 1995; Meehan, 1993; and Spencer, 1995.

9. Brubaker, 1992: Faist, 1995; Modood and Werbner, 1997; Wrench and Solomos, 1993.

10. See EC, 1992a: Title IX, Article 128; Duff, 1997: Amended Article 128 (4); for commentary see Church and Phinnemore, 1994: 203.

11. The main rights listed in the Maastricht Treaty as possessed by a European Union citizen in the narrowly conceived Article 8 of the Maastricht Treaty are as follows: (i) freedom of movement and residence within the EU; (ii) rights to vote and stand for election as a candidate in local and European (but not national) elections in whatever member state of the EU the EU citizen happens to reside; (iii) rights when outside the EU, to protection by the diplomatic authorities of any EU member state; (iv) rights to petition the European Parliament and of access to the European Ombudsman.

12. The Amsterdam Treaty adds to the legal substance of EU citizens' rights for instance by formally declaring that the basis of the Union lies in fundamental human rights (as defined in the European Convention on Human Rights, Rome 1950), fundamental social rights (as defined in the European Social Charter, Turin, 1961, and as developed in the Community's own Charter of Social Rights 1989) (Duff, 1997: 3) and practical employment-related social rights (Articles 117–120, Duff, 1997: 66–71).

13. Addonino Report, 1985, see References.

14. Quoted in Roche, 1996: 201.

15. For studies of urban cultural policy and urban leisure policy in a comparative European and EU-level context see Bianchini and Parkinson, 1993 and Henry et al., 1993 respectively.

16. EC, 1984, Church and Phinnemore, 1994: 204; also Harrison and Woods, 1998; Morley and Robins, 1995; Schlesinger, 1991, 1997.

17. For instance MacCannell, 1976; Urry, 1990. On comparative EU member-state tourism and also EU-level tourism see Davidson, 1992 and Berg et al., 1995; also Henry et al., 1993 and Bianchini and Parkinson, 1993. On EC policy to tourism relevant culture and leisure industries at a local level see EC, 1996b; also Williams, 1997.

18. For instance Goldlust, 1987; Real, 1996; Rowe, 1996; Wenner, 1989; Whannel, 1992.

19. For instance Blain et al., 1993; Chandler, 1988; Hargreaves, 1986, Ch. 7.

20. See Dayan and Katz, 1992; Real, 1996; Roche 2000, Ch. 6.

21. From his USA Fox company's (ex-'Twentieth Century Fox') archives and current production, and from partners like the Disney corporation.

22. Currently only from his USA Fox News and European Sky News operations, having failed in his bid to buy up the global cable TV news market leader company CNN in 1994.

23. See Herman and McChesney, 1997: Ch. 3; Horsman, 1997; Shawcross, 1992; Tunstall and Palmer, 1991.

References

Addonino Report (1985) 'A People's Europe' (Parts I and II). Bulletin of the European Communities, Supplement 7185. Luxembourg: EC.

Anderson, B. (1991) *Imagined Communities*. London: Verso.

Anderson, P. (1996) 'The Europe to Come', *London Review of Books*, 25 January.

Bale, J. and Maguire, J. (eds) *The Global Sports Arena*. London: Frank Cass.

Begg, I. and Nectoux, F. (1995) 'Social Protection and Economic Union', *Journal of European Social Policy*, 5 (1): 29–42.

Berg, L. van den, Borg, J. van der and Meer, J. van der (1995) *Urban Tourism: Performance and Strategies in Eight European Cities*. Aldershot: Avebury.

Bianchini, F. and Parkinson, M. (eds) (1993) *Cultural Policy and Urban Regeneration: The West European Experience*. Manchester: Manchester University Press.

Blain, N., Boyle, R. and O'Donnell, H. (eds) (1993) *Sport and National Identity in the European Media*. Leicester: Leicester University Press.

Blumler, J. (ed.) (1992) *Television and the Public Interest: Vulnerable Values in West European Broadcasting*. London: Sage.

Brubaker, R. (1992) *Citizenship and Nationhood in France and Germany*. London: Harvard University Press.

Chandler, J. (1988) *Television and National Sport: The United States and Britain*. Urbana: University of Illinois Press.

Church, C. and Phinnemore, D. (1994) *European Union and the European Community: A Handbook and Commentary on the Post-Maastricht Treaties*. London: Harvester/Wheatsheaf.

Davidson, R. (1992) *Tourism in Europe*. London: Pitman.

Dayan, D. and Katz, E. (1992) *Media Events*. London: Harvard University Press.

Delanty, G. (1995) *Inventing Europe: Idea, Identity, Reality*. London: Macmillan.

Delors Report (1993) see EC, 1993.

Donegan, L. (1997) 'Honor for a Career Cut Short', *The Guardian*, 3 June.

Duff, A. (ed.) (1997) *The Treaty of Amsterdam*. London: Federal Trust.

EC (European Commission) (1984) *Television without frontiers*. Brussels: EC.

EC (1992a) Treaty on European Union. Luxembourg: EC Publications.

EC (1992b) New Prospects for Community Cultural Action, COM (92) 149. Brussels: EC.

EC (1993) *Growth, Competitiveness, Employment* (The Delors Report). Luxembourg: EC.

EC (1995) *Intergovernmental Conference 1996: Commission Report for the Reflection Group*. Luxembourg: EC.

EC (1996a) Intergovernmental Conference 1996: Commission Opinion – Reinforcing Political Union and Preparing for Enlargement. Luxembourg: EC.

EC (1996b) 'Promotion of Local Employment Initiatives in the Context of Regional Development', discussion paper. Brussels: EC.

EC (1997) *Agenda 2000 – Volume 1: For a Stronger and Wider Europe*, DOC/97/6. Strasbourg: EC.

EP (European Parliament) (1996) 'TV – Challenge to Satellite Sport Monopoly', *EP News* 4. European Parliament: Brussels.

Faist, T. (1995) *Social Citizenship for Whom?* Aldershot: Avebury.

Gamble, A. and Payne, A. (eds) (1996) *Regionalism and World Order*. London: Macmillan.

Garcia, S. (1993) 'Europe's Fragmented Identities and the Frontiers of Citizenship', in S. Garcia, (ed.), *European Identity and the Search for Legitimacy*. London: Pinter Publishers, Ch. 1.

Garcia, S. (1997) 'European Union Identity and Citizenship: Some Challenges', in M. Roche and R. van Berkel (eds), *European Citizenship and Social Exclusion*. Aldershot: Ashgate.

Gellner, E. (1983) *Nations and Nationalism*. Oxford: Blackwell.

Goldlust, J. (1987) *Playing for Keeps: Sport, the Media and Society*. Melbourne: Longman Cheshire.

Gratton, C. (1997) 'The Economic and Social Significance of Sport', unpublished paper. Leisure Industries Research Centre, Sheffield Hallam University, Sheffield.

Guttman, A. (1994) *Games and Empire*. New York: Columbia University Press.

Habermas, J. (1994) 'Citizenship and National Identity', in B. van Steenbergen, (ed.), *The Condition of Citizenship*. London: Sage.

Hall, C.M. and Jenkins, J. (1995) *Tourism and Public Policy*. London: Routledge.

Hargreaves, J. (1986) *Sports, Power and Culture*. Cambridge: Polity.

Harrison, J. and Woods, L. (1998) 'European Broadcasting Policy: Towards a European Culture', unpublished UACES 1998 conference paper (available from the authors). Sheffield: Sheffield University.

Henderson, J. (1996) 'Behind the Screen', *The Observer*, 27 Nov.

Henry, I., Bramham, P., Mommaas, H. and Poel, H. van der (eds) (1993) *Leisure Policies in Europe*. Wallingford, Oxon: CAB International.

Herman, E. and McChesney, R. (1997) *The Global Media*. London: Cassell.

Hobsbawm, E. (1984) 'Mass-Producing Traditions: Europe, 1870–1914', in E. Hobsbawm and T. Ranger (eds), *The Invention of Tradition*. Cambridge: Cambridge University Press, Ch. 7.

Horsman, M. (1997) *Sky High*. London: Orion.

Houlihan, B. (1994) *Sport and International Politics*. London: Harvester/Wheatsheaf.

MacCannell, D. (1976) *The Tourist: A New Theory of the Leisure Class*. London: Macmillan.

Mann, M. (1993) 'Nation-States in Europe and Other Continents: Diversifying, Developing, Not Dying', *Daedelus*, 122 (3): 115–140.

Marshall, T.H. (1992) 'Citizenship and Social Class', in T.H. Marshall, and T. Bottomore (eds), *Citizenship and Social Class*. London: Pluto.

Meehan, E. (1993) *Citizenship and the European Community*. London: Sage.

Modood, T. and Werbner, P. (eds) (1997) *The Politics of Multiculturalism in the New Europe*. London: Zed Books.

Morley, D. and Robins, K. (1995) *Spaces of Identity: Global Media, Electronic Landscapes and Cultural Boundaries*. London: Routledge.

Morrell, F. (1996) 'Citizenship, Barbarism and Exclusion'. London: Federal Trust.

Mosse, G. (1975) *The Nationalisation of the Masses: Political Symbolism and Mass Movements in Germany*. New York: Howard Fertig.

O'Keefe, R. (1998) 'The "Right to take part in cultural life" under Article 15 of the ICESCR', *International and Comparative Law Quarterly*, 47, October: 904–923.

Real, M. (1996) *Exploring Media Culture*. London: Sage.

Roche, M. (1987) 'Citizenship, Social Theory and Social Change', *Theory and Society*, 16: 363–399.

Roche, M. (1992a) *Rethinking Citizenship*. Cambridge: Polity.

Roche, M. (1992b) 'Mega-Events and Micro-Modernization: On the Sociology of the New Urban Tourism', *British Journal of Sociology*, 43 (4): 563–600.

Roche, M. (1992c) 'Mega-Event Planning and Citizenship' *Vrijetijd en Samenleving (Leisure and Society)*, 10 (4): 47–67.

Roche, M. (1994) 'Mega-Events and Urban Policy', *Annals of Tourism Research*, 21 (1): 1–19.

Roche, M. (1996) 'Citizenship and Modernity', *British Journal of Sociology*. 6 (4): 715–733.

Roche, M. (1997) 'Citizenship and Exclusion: Reconstructing the European Union', in M. Roche and R. van Berkel (eds), *European Citizenship and Social Exclusion*. Aldershot: Ashgate.

Roche, M. (ed.) (1998) *Sport, Popular Culture and Identity*. Aachen: Meyer and Meyer Verlag.

Roche, M. (2000) *Mega-Events and Modernity: Olympics and Worlds Fairs in the Construction of Public Culture*. London: Routledge.

Roche, M. and Arundel, J. (1998) 'Media Sport and Local Identity', in M. Roche (ed.), *Sport, Popular Culture and Identity*. Aachen: Meyer and Meyer Verlag.

Roche, M. and van Berkel, R. (eds) (1997) *European Citizenship and Social Exclusion*. Aldershot: Ashgate.

Rosas, A. and Antola, E. (eds) (1995) *A Citizens' Europe*. London: Sage.

Rowe, D. (1996) 'The Global Love-Match: Sport and Television', *Media, Culture and Society,* 18: 565–582.

Schlesinger, P. (1991) *Media, State and Nation*. London: Sage.

Schlesinger, P. (1997) 'From Cultural Defence to Political Culture: Media Politics and Collective Identity in the European Union', *Media, Culture and Society*, 19: 369–391.

Shawcross, W. (1992) *Rupert Murdoch: Ringmaster of the Information Circus*. London: Pan Books.

Short, D. (1996) 'TV Contenders get a New Referee', *The European*, 25 July.

Smith, A. (1995) *Nations and Nationalism in a Global Era*. Cambridge: Polity.

Spencer, M. (1995) *States of Injustice*. London: Pluto Press.

Spillman, L. (1997) *Nation and Commemoration: Creating National Identities in the United States and Australia*. Cambridge: Cambridge University Press.

Tassin, E. (1992) 'Europe: A Political Community?' in C. Mouffe (ed.), *Dimensions of Radical Democracy*. London: Verso, Ch. 8.

Tunstall, J. and Palmer, M. (1991) *Media Moguls*. London: Routledge.

Turner, B. (1994) 'Postmodern Culture/Modern Citizens', in B. van Steenbergen (ed.) *The Condition of Citizenship*. London: Sage.

Urry, J. (1990) *The Tourist Gaze*. London: Sage.

Urry, J. (1995) 'Tourism, Europe and Identity', in J. Urry, *Consuming Places*. London: Routledge, Ch. 11.

Weiner, A. (1996) 'Making Sense of the New Geography of Citizenship', unpublished conference paper. Florence: European University Institute.

Wenner, L. (ed.) (1989) *Media, Sports and Society*. London: Sage.

Whannel, G. (1992) *Fields in Vision: Television Sport and Cultural Transformation*. London: Routledge.

Williams, C. (1997) *Consumer Services and Economic Development*. London: Routledge.

Wrench, J. and Solomos, J. (eds) (1993) *Racism and Migration in Western Europe*. Oxford: Berg.

7

CULTURAL CITIZENSHIP AND URBAN GOVERNANCE IN WESTERN EUROPE

Jude Bloomfield and Franco Bianchini

The Political Context of Debates over Citizenship

The concept of citizenship has acquired renewed salience and popularity in the last twenty years in response to the demise of the post-war political and social settlement and sustained theoretical and political attack on equality and the means of achieving it through the welfare state. The social fragmentation and marginalization, brought about by the economic restructuring of the 1970s and 1980s, and the growth of cultural pluralism, resulting from global migration and communication flows have thrown in doubt the capacity of the state to satisfy the diverse range of needs and demands for participation.

Novel protagonists of citizenship emerged in the new left libertarian movements which arose after 1968. The student and protest movements against the Vietnam War spawned more enduring movements that were not only against specific forms of oppression but for a transformation of social relationships in everyday life. The feminist and environmental movements, community action and squatters groups, anti-racist and solidarity movements enacted a new relationship between the individual and collective through participation in person in a collective endeavour without surrendering individual autonomy. The movements were a loose voluntary form of association without binding rules, heirarchy or professional bureaucracy. Their practice was social and cultural, as well as political, encompassing self-help and practical support, celebration and artistic expression as well as mobilization and direct action (Melucci, 1989; Touraine, 1981). They extended political contestation to new spheres such as health, the environment and urban life, to the intimacy of the home and private life. What had been self-enclosed and internally regulated spheres – of firms operating in the market, of state regulated and social institutions such as hospitals, schools, universities, cultural and planning bodies – came under public scrutiny and challenge for their exclusive structures of power (Habermas, 1986; Offe, 1987).

The organized left in power at local level in Western Europe was forced to confront the critique of Greens and feminists of industrialism, powerful producer lobbies, state centralist bureaucracy and professional hierarchies. Its renewed interest in citizenship has sought to adapt its traditional welfarist concerns with collective provision and universal access to the diversification of demands, interests and forms of participation. But it reacted to the debate on equality and difference in the ideological context of neo-conservative ascendancy and so sought, often uncritically, to appropriate the latter's political vocabulary of individual freedom and choice. At the same time, it resisted the tightening of the fiscal noose by central government which encroached on local autonomy.

In the case of the Right, its use of the language of citizenship has been a response to growing public anxiety about the social consequences – such as decaying housing estates, long-term and youth unemployment, poverty, and the growth of crime – of the increasingly deregulated, and internationally integrated, model of capitalist economic development pursued in Western Europe. In Britain, civic conservatives, associated with the Social Market Foundation, reasserted the link between the free market and social institutions in which culture plays a central role. They have responded to growing social and cultural diversity by proposing restricted access to welfare entitlements according to a set of moral criteria which differentiate between the deserving and undeserving poor: widows over New Age travellers, the unemployed actively seeking work over the drug addict and petty criminal, in the name of reinforcing 'the shared values of the community' (Willetts, 1994: 41–43). They developed a concept of active citizenship for an elite of volunteers, to take over the running of a range of local public bodies as private responsibilities (Hurd, 1988). More generally, a widespread rhetoric of the citizen as an apolitical private consumer has accompanied a strong ideological reassertion of national and family virtues.

Strongly influenced by American writers, a new centre-left have also taken up communitarian themes of individual responsibility – duties over rights, within a framework of traditional ties of family and community (Blair, 1995). These institutions are portrayed as internally homogeneous and harmonious, and therefore, what constitutes a family or a community and who has membership is taken as uncontentious. As a result, the distinctive interests of women, or children or diverse 'others' have been scripted out. Civil society is conceived as a sphere of rooted kinship, tradition and social stability which the atomization of market individualism is tearing asunder. Therefore, communitarians look to the state to reinforce social discipline and prescribe moral values, ostracizing or punishing 'undesirables' and dissenters. This trend threatens to ostracize and criminalize ethnic minority subcultures which are linked to the street and mass gatherings of young people with potential for recreational drug-taking or civil disobedience. More widely, the new poor are labelled as an 'under class' to be dealt with, rather than accorded the dignity and agency which social and cultural citizenship confers.

Theories of Citizenship and Concepts of Culture

Cultural Rights as Extended Social Rights

Social citizenship as a strategy to reduce class inequalities and create equal opportunities was legitimated politically as a means to secure effective exercise of self-determination by all citizens. T.H. Marshall justified the expansion of citizenship to comprise social rights to guarantee a level of welfare and education which would enable working class people to lead a 'civilized life'. This meant that they would be able to make informed choices, and thus realize their civil and political rights (Marshall and Bottomore, 1992). Marshall's tripartite division in citizenship between civil rights, (habeas corpus – security and property of the person, freedom of thought, beliefs, association), political rights (to vote and stand for office) and social rights (particularly to education and welfare) can be extended further to encompass cultural rights.

Cultural citizenship has been presented as a response both to the emergence of cultural pluralism from global migratory and communication flows and to the simultaneous demise of the welfare state as a national regulatory system. This perspective takes for granted that citizenship claims which involve social redistribution are obsolescent (Pakulski, 1997). In part, this is a one-sided reading of new social movements which are not only cultural – defending different ways of life and value systems – but also social and political – attacking unequal distributions and unaccountable powers. However, it also overlooks other features of the new international division of labour which is encompassed by 'globalization'. Culture itself has become a key form of capital – at the leading edge of the global economy in media and telecommunications, with cultural industries and services like tourism, as growth sectors of national and local economies. The reorientation of production to symbolic, rather than material, goods in the advanced capitalist countries has also exerted a strong cultural impact on more traditional sectors, through communications, product innovation and system design. Cultural capital has become a key determinant in the skilling of the labour force – enlarging the stratum of 'symbolic analysts' and cultural producers, and therefore, also in the class location and market opportunities of social actors (Bourdieu, 1977, 1984; Lash and Urry, 1994). The possession and redistribution of cultural capital, which hinges primarily, though not solely, on educational attainment, has become crucial to countering inequality.

The right to culture was implicitly recognized by Marshall when he referred to education and self-improvement. This was understood as a duty of the citizen to raise the level of civilization of the society:

> It was increasingly recognized as the nineteenth century wore on, that political democracy needed an educated electorate and that scientific manufacture needed educated workers and technicians. The duty to improve and civilize oneself is therefore a social duty, and not merely a personal one, because the social health of society depends upon the civilization of its members. And a community that enforces this duty has begun to realize that its culture is an organic unity and its civilization a national heritage. (Marshall and Bottomore, 1992: 16)

This conception of culture presumed a social obligation on the part of workers to seek self-improvement, by actively acquiring scientific and critical competences, thus raising labour productivity and the overall cultural level of society. However, it unproblematically assumed that the culture in which workers participated was inherited and given, that they would not leave their mark on it, and shape it in turn. Despite Marshall's requirement that the working class participate, the conception remained of a homogeneous, national culture, handed down by intellectual elites.

Following Marshall's logic in recognizing the enhanced socio-economic importance of culture as capital, we can start by defining cultural rights under modern conditions as equal access to the cultural literacy, critical competences and public cultural goods which would enable equal opportunity to participate in cultural – as well as economic and political – life. However, we would also have to recognize that participation in culture itself has diversified in practice and thus problematized and recast cultural theory and policy.

Challenging Cultural Hegemony – from Counter Culture to Cultural Pluralism

The monolithic and elite conception of culture, assumed as the groundwork of social citizenship, became subject to explicit challenge in practice from the cultural politics of the new social movements. These movements forged new collective identities – oriented to self-actualization through active participation, and to experimenting with new structures and forms of association. This spawned a rediscovery in cultural and political sociology of concepts of cultural dominance and subordination, of popular culture, commercially driven, mass reproduced culture and its differential appropriation in subcultures. It reintroduced culture as a field of contested power and domination through the translation and absorption of Althusser's concept of ideology as the lived relation of the imaginary and of cultural reproduction through ideological state apparatuses (Althusser, 1971) and through Gramsci's more articulated political concept of hegemony in which culture is a contested site of political dominance and legitimation, not only as high culture but as popular culture and common-sense (Gramsci, 1971). Popular culture was defined by class and its corporate, rather than national hegemonic character, embodying concrete, lived relationships, less abstract and value laden than highbrow culture. The Gramscian conception of hegemony highlighted the transformative potential of intervention in popular culture and the reach of the dominant culture, and, at the same time, its limits. However the dominant/ popular culture dichotomy was overtaken by the study of mass culture – from which popular culture could no longer be separated. Based on mass consumption and media spectacle, mass culture had been disparaged as the ultimate capitalist incorporation of the masses through commodification of leisure and 'free time'. However, in his rediscovery of Benjamin, Enzensberger argued the democratic potential of the mass media and mass reproducible, elecronic art forms in demystifying and decommodifying high art forms, and thus dislodging the sacred position of the art object as a rare commodity (Enzensberger, 1974). He focused on the capacity for transforming the restrictive capitalist control of the media to enable interactive feedback, critical response and collective self-organization – which has subsequently stimulated thinking on the potential of electronic democracy (see Bryan Turner's contribution to this book).

The analysis of subcultures situated them in the generational conflict within class cultures and the access of its youthful protagonists to mass culture and consumption. Working class and lower middle class youth became social actors with a margin of autonomy (free time and disposable income) for collective self-expression, where culture was viewed as a live performance. *Bricolage*, the anthropological term coined by Clarke, Hebdige and others, for the selection, appropriation and meaningful assemblage of material symbols and practices – such as dress, music, hairstyle, slang, social and territorial aggregation – explained how the subculture was constituted to differentiate the group both from its elders and outsiders, to gain greater control over its environment (Clarke et al., 1975; Hebdige, 1979).

Some writers have developed the material analysis of subcultures to show how they interrelate to the wider economy, and how some subcultural stylists themselves manage to become cultural producers and entrepreneurs (McRobbie, 1989). Sarah Thornton has applied Bourdieu's concept of cultural capital further to this field as 'subcultural capital'. The aspect which is particularly significant for a political strategy of cultural citizenship is the recognition of informal know-how – what Thornton defines as 'hipness' in relation to club cultures (Thornton, 1995). These could be more aptly defined as the skills and networks acquired autonomously of institutions, not directly from formal training or education. Without romanticizing their oppositional and critical value, they embody, nevertheless, the creative capacity of young people in an unalienated form. The recognition of the creativity in subcultures transforms the perception of their subjects from passive recipients to active producers, challenging a traditional premise of cultural policy. This has a policy implication of harnessing subcultural creativity to the local cultural economy by developing the potential of socially marginalized groups. Rather than treating them as a problem, facilitating their self-expression and autonomy would be integral to any solution.

Analysis has varied as to the degree of resistance, explicit political opposition and life solutions that subcultures offer, according to the perspective adopted: a pluralist, and subsequently postmodern view of the proliferation of scenes and identities (Irwin, 1970); or Marxist-Weberian syntheses of structured power relations and reproduction of class and status through cultural distinctions (for an overview see Gelder and Thornton, 1997). There is also an implicit tension between Bourdieu's structural analysis of culture as capital, and the open-ended formation of culture in a democratic public sphere, where diversity cannot be read solely as representing differential locations within the social heirarchy, but as representing plural possibilities. In their symbolic nature, cultural forms remain ambivalent in meaning, and open to diverse interpretation and appropriation within different social milieux. This tension can perhaps be resolved by recognizing that unequal cultural distribution, no less than unequal social distribution, inhibits freedom of individual and collective self-expression and development. Therefore, a cultural politics for deepening democracy has to embody both dimensions – of redistribution to overcome structural limitations and pluralist recognition. However, recognition of the multiple cultural practices and processes within a society seems to have left the communitarian understanding of culture untouched.

In the liberal-communitarian debate, the theoretical challenge to the conception of a homogeneous national culture has come to the fore only on the grounds of ethnic, not class or social, exclusivity. An assumption of cultural homogeneity in the liberal theory of distributive justice has been unearthed. In the theory, primary goods are the necessary means to self-fulfilment, that is, the rights, resources, 'opportunities and powers' required to fulfil one's desires and life aims (Rawls, 1973: 62, 90–95). Kymlicka argues that because the theory took for granted a single, unified culture in each political community, i.e. that societies were mono-ethnic, cultural belonging was overlooked as a primary good. Thus, if cultural belonging is seen as a primary good, cultural rights have to be grounded not only in equal opportunity but also in recognition of different cultural communities (Kymlicka, 1989: 165–166). However, this raises further problems of the conception of culture.

Conflicting Conceptions of Culture

Belonging to a specific cultural community presumes that culture is hermetically sealed in distinctive communities, to which each person belongs, and to one alone. There is an attempt to geneticize culture as though it were ascriptive like skin colour: 'One cannot choose to belong. One belongs because of who one is' (Kymlicka, 1995a: 84). The cultural conception here is close to a communitarian one of idealized and naturalized social relationships. According to this argument, those who are born into a culture which enjoys low social esteem should not suffer the stigma and disadvantage which it brings. But this refers very much to inherited culture, the language, myths and fairy tales we are socialized into as children, rather than the culture we acquire self-consciously through education, and the selective incorporation of new influences and rejection of some older elements which forms part of growing up. It implies a purely ethnic reading of minorities whose other sources of culture are not recognized as it is assumed that skin colour or place of origin determine all aspects of your culture.

Here culture is defined as an impervious and integral whole, exclusively tied to a defined group of people and territory. Kymlicka's societal culture has only room for one language and history – but this takes for granted the mythological narrative of the nation as a pre-given cultural unity. As contemporary analysis of nationalism has shown, the state and its agencies construct and disseminate national identity, through the army, public administration and primary school; invent traditions which historicize and legitimize the power of the state and suppress alternative cultures and languages which act as potential rivals (Gellner, 1983; Hobsbawm and Ranger, 1983; Weber, 1977). This conception of culture has no way of recognizing the persistence and proliferation of subcultures: linguistic, class-based, regional, ethnic, sexual which contest the monopoly status of the dominant culture.

In an age of intense cultural interaction, where global cultural diffusion and transfers permeate national cultural boundaries, the territorial defence of cultural purity becomes increasingly untenable and anachronistic. The French Right attempted to protect the purity of the national culture in the 1993 Loi Toubon, named after the then French Minister of Culture, Jacques Toubon. This law tried to purge American slang from the French language and limit the use of English in state administration and large private sector firms. However, it made the government appear like an archaic cultural border police. Cultural identities are becoming deterritorialized, detached from any specific territorial location and of multifarious origins, contrary to Michael Walzer's assertion that 'the distinctiveness of cultures and groups depends upon closure and, without it, cannot be conceived as a stable feature of human life' (Walzer, 1983: 39). Alongside the reciprocal interaction of global, national, sub-national and subcultural elements, a defensive reterritorialization and racialization of identities is taking place on a micro scale (Castells, 1994: 27; Turner, 1993). Exclusive, territorial claims with tribal and racial overtones vie with a civic identity of place as the common meeting place of differences.

The debate over cultural rights has been locked into the presumption that culture is rooted in territory, and has been dominated by the question of group rights, generalizing the situation of aboriginal peoples who were forcibly deprived of their ancient lands on which their culture depends (Kymlicka, 1995a). These conditions do not pertain for diasporic cultures and most multi-cultural societies in the modern world and the attempt to address their claims for equality or recognition within such a framework fails to identify the core discrimination they face. If the existence of multiple cultures is taken seriously, citizenship of a democratic state has to be detached from exclusive cultural belonging. Citizenship thus rests on residence not roots. Clearly democratic states do actively uphold a dominant culture, but it cannot be normatively justified (Bader, 1996) and is publicly contested in its discriminatory effects – in cultural representations of ethnic minorities, history teaching in schools, public commemorations.

While it is not legitimate for a democratic state to promote a dominant culture as it infringes the rights of cultural minorities, the position of cultural minorities cannot be resolved conceptually by treating their cultures as exclusive and pure in turn, attaching to them a notional territorial community or group belonging e.g. as unhyphenated Asian or West Indian. These attempts to ensure the survival of cultures by separating them off, relocating them somewhere else other than where they are actually taking place, thus reconfirms their marginality to that society. Leaving aside the problematic use of state power to enforce the survival of a culture (Hannerz, 1996; Kymlicka, 1995a; Taylor, 1994: 51–61), this bypasses the real problem for multiple cultural groups living in the same society – of the pluralistic transformation of the dominant culture – beyond a notion of incorporation and the equalization of cultural capital, cultural opportunities and life chances in advanced capitalist societies.

Cultural Recognition and Multi-culturalism

The liberal and communitarian positions converge in accepting the importance of self-respect and social esteem to the individual's development. The marginalization of a minority group's heritage and history causes shame and belittlement which deprive its members of power and self-esteem (Kymlicka, 1989: 167–168; Rawls, 1973: 440–446). The recognition of diverse cultures and ways of life as equally worthy of respect – where they accord that right to others – is not only seen as compatible with universal rights but as necessary to their fulfilment (Rawls, 1973: 442; Taylor, 1994: 38).

However, there are provisos which we would add. Cultures can only claim equal rights, recognition and respect in so far as they are freely constituted and do not impose their way of life on others. There is no virtue in diversity per se if cultures are based on racial or male supremacism or other forms of domination. The erosion of social citizenship in the Anglo-American – and Australian – context with the demise of welfare provision and attempts to delegitimize universality, is too readily assumed to be justified on both pragmatic grounds and in the name of 'difference'. However, there is no simple move from the politics of redistribution to the politics of recognition as though the one replaces the other, as Pakulski argues (1997) or as though they are in simple opposition (see critique in Fraser, 1995a, 1995b). Furthermore, cultural recognition involves not only non-discrimination, respect for cultural differences and freedom of cultural practice, but also the pluralistic revision of the dominant public culture and education system. In this context, the defence of the cultural forms derived from member-ship of a minority community is not a substitute for access and participation in shaping the culture as a whole.

Cultural pluralism raises theoretical and practical difficulties. For while it is important to recognize cultural minorities both because they face real discrimi-nation and deprivation and because cultural diversity based on rights is a virtue of a pluralist society, this has to avoid essentializing the cultural community. Faced with external racist dangers and material disadvantage, for purposes of political mobilization there is pressure from within an oppressed minority to present a unified identity to the outside world – what Calhoun calls 'in-group essentialism' – and to suppress internal differences and dissent (Calhoun, 1994: 26–7). Corporate multi-culturalism harbours the danger of entrenching a singular representation of a community that is itself pluralistic and thus excluding discor-dant voices, particularly of women and younger people. While all cultures which respect the rights of other cultures have a right to recognition, they cannot be shut off and denied the opportunity to interact with, and influence the mainstream, or be influenced, in turn, by other cultures. Cultural recognition must also offer opportunities to renew a culture as well as to preserve it. Otherwise it condemns minority cultures to the margins, in the defensive quest for purism, while depriv-ing the mainstream culture of both the creative interaction and friction which generates innovation and cross-fertilization.

Gerd Baumann's work on South Asians in Britain shows how this 'commu-nity' moves between an ethnic discourse of self as the Asian other, as a minority defined by origin – which Baumann (1997) defines as the dominant discourse, and a discourse of various politically and culturally constructed selves in relation to non-ethnic others – which he refers to as a 'demotic' discourse, i.e. of the people. It is significant that they inescapably use both demotic and dominant discourses, faced both with defence of themselves and specific cultural practices for which they suffer disadvantage and racism in the society, while, at the same time, living and interacting with other cultures and forming political alliances and cross-ethnic allegiances within the larger culture.

Inter-culturalism

Only with a conception of culture as a composite, a 'bricolage', whose diverse elements, through interaction, critical selection and appropriation, converge to produce new forms, can culture be viewed as a living process, not an endangered species in a museum. This approach entails a necessary revisionism – but not arbitrary eclecticism. It does not imply raiding the 'other' as an exotic accoutrement to the cosmopolitan identity of a global cultural consumer as has been rather glibly portrayed by Waldron (Waldron, 1996; for a critique of this approach see Jordan and Weedon, 1995). The process can be psychologically unsettling and seen as a threat to the purity of an identity – national or ethnic, particularly in times of rapid social change which is not easily understood, but all cultures are adaptive and in more or less permanent transition. Cultural meanings undergo transformation through interaction and when transferred from one context to another. The Muslim headscarf over which conflicts have flared up in France and Germany is not, as Kymlicka argues, a chadour, the full cloak and headcover worn in traditional and authoritarian Islamic societies (Kymlicka, 1995a). The headscarf is worn by Muslim women in non-Western societies that have evolved less restrictive symbols of religious and cultural affiliation. In Western societies, therefore, it already represents an adaptation to modernity, apart from the multifarious and secular meanings it takes on in negotiations between Muslim girls, the state, their schools and families (Gaspard and Khosrokhavar, 1995).

Inter-culturality has historically occurred in the most manifest way in border zones where cultural mixing has been most pronounced (Nederveen Pieterse, 1994). However, it may be most linguistically evident in those particular sites but it is a process that occurs spontaneously between all specific cultures, whether they are territorially bounded and situated or not. This process is intensified or speeded up in periods of mass migration or cultural transfer where the culture 'carried' to the new context is inevitably transformed in the process, and the culture 'left behind' remains fixed in the memory. When it is returned to after many years, it too has changed, sometimes unrecognizably. The process of transformation is systematically denied by nation-state narratives which fix cultures to boundaries and therefore believe them to be impermeable.

Furthermore national narratives deny the effect that deregulation of broadcasting and the internationalization of all forms of communication have had in desynchronizing the national community, disconnecting it from shared moments, common themes and issues, thus fragmenting the national public. There is an incoherence in propagating attachment to the national culture when its contours are no longer discernible as a discrete entity, but the effect is to foster mental closure. For self-reflexivity, involved in comparing and relativizing your own culture, is implicit in inter-culturality – but this does not mean rejecting the one or surrendering wholesale to the other as though they were exclusive (Hannerz, 1990). The capacity to gain autonomy from your own culture, open yourself to other cultures, take and incorporate into your own symbolic repertoire selective elements creates, what Hannerz defines as, the 'decontextualized cultural capital' of cosmopolitans. Though this is treated as though it were the attribute of a small elite, it is an integral part of everyday life – interacting with 'others' through trans-national trade flows of products, cultural artifacts and services which we consume, and through the global communications networks that filter music, images, ideas into our contemporary mental worlds. The foreign and the local combine all the time to form hybrids whether in historically absorbed forms of culture, now signified as 'national', such as Italian pasta that Marco Polo brought back from China, or the combination of low Saxon, courtly French, American slang and many other influences, that we call English, or in the contemporary mass cultural forms of Banghra rock or Islamic rap (Baumann, 1997; Soysal, 1996).

Thus cultural literacy has to be rethought, not only in pluralistic, but also in inter-cultural terms. Inter-cultural literacy is based on the capacity not only to interpret your own culture but other cultures, and to engage in a creative process of interaction, transformation and fusion. Consequently the cultural content of education cannot aim to impart a set of values, specific to any one culture, but rather critical skills – of comparison, evaluation of meaning and adequacy of means.

Participation and Cultural Representation

In advanced capitalist societies, with multiple cultures where there is no agreement on values, there is, however, a shared polity and procedures to make claims and pursue conflicts whether these result in agreement or agreement to differ. A civic identity, which does not privilege any particular culture, but rather the city as a meeting place of cultures, of exchange, is a prerequisite for cultural pluralism in the public sphere, not on the basis of corporate representation of fixed ethnicized collectivities but on the basis of universal rights and republican citizenship.

A republican conception of citizenship is premised on the active mobilization and participation of citizens in realizing their rights. The degree to which rights will be effective depends on the capacity of citizens to come together, formulate their demands collectively and organize a public presence (Habermas, 1994: 113). The articulation of a collective identity as a group facilitates the political mobilization of those without a voice. Identity can become a 'symbolic tool' in mobilizing claims to substantive rights or resources (Bourdieu, 1992; Soysal, 1996). In a republican view of citizenship, it is incumbent on the public authorities to solicit active participation, particularly of those poorly represented and weakly organized (Habermas, 1994). They can stimulate collective organization by creating political opportunity structures in the cultural field – such as through publicly accountable devolved funding and self-managed projects. But to draw in those who are poor in organizational resources and knowledge of how to use political institutions, training in civic competences is required. This facilitates collective self-organization and representation in the public sphere, enabling previously unorganized groups to gain access to the local media, to bring initiatives to fruition in projects for the city. Cultural rights thus come to be oriented to equal opportunity to participate in the society as a whole and to engage with the public culture, and, in the process, transform it.

Passive Citizenship and the Right to Consume

An alternative, restricted conception of citizenship developed in reaction to a broad, participatory one. Neo-liberal theorists attacked the moral basis of redistribution and thus the public sphere, arguing that taxation is theft of lawfully expended labour, falsely appropriated by the state, in violation of individual property rights. In this view, property rights are sovereign and unfettered and the state coercive in forcing people to work part of the time to pay for others, rather than to acquire more for themselves (Nozick, 1974). This view confines the legitimate action of the state to upholding property, enforcing contract and defending sovereignty. There is no conception of public goods, necessary to the realization of individual rights, with the exception of security. But this is conceived in purely military terms, without regard to the wider social conditions of security in a society, such as low levels of poverty and fear.

Monetarist and overload theorists argued on efficiency grounds for the reduction of the public sphere and the level of public expenditure, and on moral grounds against escalating tax pressures derived from the increasing benefits to interest groups whose costs are off-loaded onto the whole of society (Bacon and Eltis, 1976; Brittan, 1975; Friedman, 1976). Civil society was reconceived in reductionist terms, stressing the rational choice of the individual as a consumer in economic and, likewise, political exchange. Politics was redefined as a market, based on narrow self-interest, without ethical or social dimensions. This regressive reinterpretation went against the trend towards the democratic expansion of citizenship since the eighteenth century, which had progressively detached rights from economic status, enlarging their spread and scope. The political effect was to redefine citizenship in passive terms for the majority of people as consumers with minimal rights of political participation. This was achieved, not primarily through restricting voting rights as in the past, but by removing more and more competences from the political domain, so that decisions are increasingly taken outside of any form of public accountability.

This conception of citizenship has come to be presented as a right to consume without regard to questions of unequal market access and distribution. Cultural goods and services have increasingly been viewed as commodities like any others, entitlement to which is dependent on market choice and opportunities. This conception has had a far wider effect than merely on its neo-conservative adherents, redefining and diminishing the scope for cultural intervention and impinging on the claims made to cultural goods and services. These are often formulated in terms of a right to consume or consumer choice rather than equalizing access to cultural life, freedom of expression and pluralist representation in the public realm. So claims for cultural rights are being legitimated, not on democratic, but on market, grounds, and they are treated as such, as merely new forms of consumer demand.

The Locus of Citizenship

Overlapping and Multilayered Sovereignty

The insistence on citizenship as a system of rights and claims on the normative and regulative capacities of the state – to equalize, on the one hand, the resources required for self-determination, and on the other, access to the public realm – focuses attention on the political level at which these claims and entitlements can become effective. It is often taken for granted that the national level is still the dominant framework of political reference and regulation. As Preuss, among others, has argued, citizenship rights are rights to membership of a bounded community and therefore, to inclusion in a particular polity (Brubaker, 1992; Preuss, 1995). Thus, citizenship rights are analytically distinct from human rights which are not dependent on state membership or bounded by territory but are attached to the person, regardless of nationality or place of residence. However, these rights are only respected to the degree they are recognized by the specific state within which the person resides or finds him/herself. Nevertheless the recognition of culture as an explicit right has significantly come at international, rather than national level.

Claims for cultural rights, recognition and resources are thus directed at different levels, and agencies, and those made to the national state often make use of international law – the UN Declaration on Rights of Persons belonging to National or Ethnic, Religious and Linguistic Minorities 1993 and Article 27 of the United Nations International Covenant of Civil and Political Rights 1996 (Waldron, 1995) – to legitimate their case. Appeals for recognition of minority identity and cultural rights also refer to express commitments of European bodies such as the Conference on Security and Co-operation in Europe's Declaration on the Rights of National Minorities of 1991 and the Council of Europe's European Charter for Regional and Minority Languages 1992 (Kymlicka, 1995a). However, the attention of our study is particularly focused on the city, which has evolved as a key locus for cultural policy and planning in reaction to the emergence of overlapping and multi-layered sovereignty.

Cities and Citizenship

The origins of the modern concept of citizenship are inextricably linked with cities and urban life since the times of the emergence of citizenship as cultural and political membership of the Greek *polis*. The city embodied freedom – as the saying derived from the medieval communes 'Stadt Luft macht frei' ('City air is liberating') testifies (Park, 1925). Michael Ignatieff reiterates the point in a contemporary context: 'to talk about being a citizen is to talk about cities. It is in the city that we live as civic beings: it is the urban environment that provides us with the minute by minute sense that we belong or do not belong to something called political society' (Ignatieff, 1990). The words themselves 'citizen', Bürger, citoyen, cittadino, ciudadano, bear the etymological mark of the tie between the concept of citizen and the city. Yet curiously this has often been overlooked in contemporary debate about cities. The debate on 'urban regeneration', for example, has tended to focus mainly on cities as physical and economic entities. It has generally underplayed the ties between citizens and the city as an artifact, symbolic space, repository of memory and shared meanings, local political system and social ecology with particular networks and dynamics.

The Conceptions of Citizenship in Urban Cultural Policy

West European cultural policies since the end of the Second World War have embodied these different conceptions of culture and citizenship. However subsequent conceptions have not replaced preceding ones but rather been grafted on, producing sometimes contradictory justifications for urban cultural intervention. The history of urban cultural policy making in liberal democracies in Western Europe, since the mid-1940s can be divided into three broad phases, reflecting the different conceptions of citizenship outlined earlier. The dominant conception which lasted from the end of the war until the late 1960s was that of social citizenship. In the second phase from the late 1960s to the mid-1980s, the more innovative and radical notion of emancipatory citizenship emerged in many cities alongside social citizenship. In the third phase, from the mid-1980s to the present day, many city authorities, forced to respond to economic restructuring, growing inter-urban competition and fiscal pressures from neo-liberal central governments, assigned a secondary importance to both social and emancipatory citizenship. They prioritized the international image and locational attractiveness of the city to foreign firms, seeking short-term economic returns on cultural investment.

In the first two decades of the post-war period, one of the central justifications for cultural subsidy in West European countries was to provide cultural services as an extension of the welfare state (for Britain see Bennett, 1995). From the late 1940s till the late 1960s, city authorities tended to define culture in traditional, narrow terms, mainly as building based institutions of high culture, usually located in city centres, such as municipal theatres, opera houses, concert halls, museums and galleries (Bianchini and Landry, 1995: 6). Such cultural policies diluted the radical impulses and creative democratic potential of political debates and practical experiments such as those undertaken under the Popular Front government in France from 1936–39 (Rigby, 1991) and under the war-time government in Britain. These included the debates on popular education in France, as well as the activities of the Army Bureau of Current Affairs, of the Council for the Encouragement of Music and the Arts, and of the Workers' Educational Association in Britain.

These experiments had been based implicitly on the idea of cultural democracy in which people redefine the very meaning and concept of culture through active engagement in it. Especially after the onset of the Cold War in 1947, urban cultural policies adopted the less ambitious goal of the 'democratization of culture', based on the power of experts to define cultural value and the role of the state to 'civilize' the majority of people, by making culture more widely accessible to them. This was impelled by the belief, reinforced by the horror of the Second World War, that contact with the classical tradition of high art would strengthen democracy by elevating the moral sensibilities of ordinary people. Nevertheless, since work by professional artists was supported at the expense of arts in education and amateur cultural activities, this had the effect of widening the gap between artists and the mass public. The other shortcomings of urban cultural policies in these years were the paternalistic approach to the provision of cultural services, and the reinforcement of class distinctions through the gradual appropriation of subsidized high culture institutions by local bourgeois and professional elites.

The shift from the first to the second of the phases we have identified was brought about by socio-economic and political factors. There was a growth in cultural demand which arose, in part, from the general decline in working time, the increase in the proportion of disposable income spent on leisure activities and the higher levels of mass education and literacy. These changes themselves resulted from the unions' increasing bargaining power and the widening scope of demands at the end of the 1960s (from pay and hours to on-site healthcare and crèches and new educational opportunities – for example, the Italian campaign for 150 hours' paid leave for workers to undertake further education). Radical policy makers in the 1970s, like Hilmar Hoffmann in Frankfurt, responded to such growing public demand by formulating the notion of a citizens' entitlement to culture (Kultur für Alle). Pressure on local politicians was also exerted by organized social and political movements, which defied the traditional boundaries between culture and politics, and advocated autonomous, direct forms of action. Examples include the community media movement in Britain which encompassed radical film and video-makers, bookshops and magazines; the oral history projects, cultural 'cornershops' and other cultural initiatives at neighbourhood level developed by the Soziokultur movement in the Federal Republic of Germany and the youth movement of 1977 in Italy, which generated a network of free radio stations, alternative bookshops, radical magazines and performance venues.

Urban cultural policies during this phase placed a greater emphasis on the importance of popular participation in cultural activities as a means for social emancipation and community development. The definitions of 'culture' widened to include more contemporary and popular cultural forms such as electronic music, video, photography, comics and murals. A new infrastructure of neighbourhood cultural centres – combining adult education with youth and arts activities – emerged in many cities, especially in Germany. More funding was made available for artists to take their work into schools, hospitals, prisons and deprived neighbourhoods.

However, more traditional rationales for cultural funding were not abandoned. City governments were able both to expand subsidies for high arts institutions and to fund new forms of community and neighbourhood-based initiatives. To take just three examples: expenditure on culture by Italian municipalities grew from just over 300 billion lire in 1980 to 800 billion lire in 1984 (Bodo, 1988); in France per capita expenditure on cultural policy by the municipalities of cities with over 150,000 inhabitants grew, in real terms, from 601 FF in 1981 to 789 FF in 1984 and 905 FF in 1987 (*Développement culturel*, July 1989); and in England and Wales net revenue expenditure on 'arts support' by local authorities increased from about £20m in 1976–77 to just over £100m a decade later (Feist and Hutchison, 1990).

Municipal policy making in the cultural field acquired increasing autonomy with dedicated departments and higher quality personnel, primarily recruited from a more politicized generation of policy makers shaped by the experience of 1968 and the new forms of cultural politics.

Urban Cultural Policy for the Creation of a Civic Identity

The two main strategies for the implementation of emancipatory urban cultural policy objectives were interventions to create a common civic space and place identity, and to empower disadvantaged individuals and groups to express their voice, constitute themselves as self-conscious communities and make their presence felt in a revitalized public sphere. Many city governments, in the 1970s and early 1980s, developed new cultural policies to construct a form of city identity which could be shared by people from different neighbourhoods and belonging to diverse communities of interest. This was allied to the political objective of mobilizing people for purposes of ideological contestation and party legitimation.

Since the early 1970s, urban cultural policies in many West European countries have been an important element of strategies aimed at encouraging local citizens, particularly those resident in areas deprived of public amenities, to 'rediscover' and celebrate their cities. In response to the social traumas caused by de-industrialization and other processes of economic restructuring, growing socio-economic inequalities within cities, and increasing differentiation in urban life styles, policies on culture and leisure were used to counter alienation, encourage face-to-face interaction and promote community rebuilding. These initiatives were in many cases in reaction to the negative effects of functional zoning in post-war land use planning. They involved a revaluation of features of the pre-industrial city such as density, 'walkability' and the overlapping of social, cultural and economic uses. In an attempt to counteract trends towards social atomization – encouraged by the anonymity and isolation of suburban living and car culture – and the domesticization of cultural consumption, these policies aimed at reasserting the function of the city, and the city centre in particular, as a catalyst for public sociability for people of different ages, sex, social class, life style and ethnic origin.

The concept of cultural *animation* was particularly important in this context. Animation initiatives were used to help give life and meaning back to the use of time by the elderly and the unemployed, growing in numbers in most West European cities, and to revitalize 'dead' space, such as archaeological sites, derelict industrial buildings and office areas deserted at night. Arts festivals and other forms of cultural animation were combined with pedestrianization, traffic calming measures, the provision of better public transport in the evening and late at night, improvements in street lighting and community policing and urban design strategies to create new public spaces and make the city more attractive and 'legible'. These integrated strategies of the 1970s and early 1980s were found not only in cities controlled by the Left, such as Rome, Bologna, Lyons, Copenhagen and London, but also in Freiburg and Stuttgart (Bianchini, 1989; Bianchini and Bloomfield, 1996; TEST, 1988).

However, in terms of political mobilization, the most innovative and high-profile initiatives in Italy, France, West Germany and Britain were developed from the mid-1970s to the mid-1980s by Left-controlled local authorities which broke away from the tradition of assigning a relatively marginal and non-controversial role to cultural policy. The emergence of these initiatives, as suggested earlier, was related to the rise after 1968 of urban social movements – feminism, gay rights, the green movement, community action, ethnic minority activism and youth groups. In many cities, cultural policies were part of strategies developed by Left parties to respond to the decline of their traditional working-class constituencies and to establish a new political base encompassing the post-1968 urban social movements, the middle classes of the public and cultural sectors and young people disaffected by traditional party ideologies and organization. More generally, Left parties used cultural policy to link their distinctive style of governance to the strengthening of the city's function as a civic space, often in implicit or explicit juxtaposition to central government or local political opponents.

Urban Cultural Policy for Empowerment

The second strand of cultural policy for emancipatory citizenship developed by city authorities in the period between the late 1960s and mid-1980s, was to enable disadvantaged or marginalized social groups to have a visible cultural impact in the local public sphere. The recovery of a historic memory, which had been suppressed, had a significant impact in renegotiating the basis of inclusion in the civic sphere. In Hamburg under the cultural leadership of Tarnowski, the Social Democratic Senator for Culture in the state of Hamburg from 1978–83, the Jewish and Polish historic presence was made visible, through sign-posting and exhibitions, as part of the history of the city and of the rethinking of its current identity as unproblematically 'German'. A commitment to equalizing social opportunities through allocating financial and cultural resources to marginalized areas and deprived groups can itself be a powerful stimulus to collective self-organization and political mobilization. Such policies sought to address the class, gender and ethnic divisions in citizenship rights, particularly seeking to reverse the discrimination which ethnic minorities and women face. They also responded to a growing spatial divide in provision and generational tensions.

Decentralized forms of high quality, self-managed training have successfully capitalized on the informal skills and passions of youth, building bridges between amateurism and professionalism, to create channels linking subcultures and 'community arts' to the commercial sector. Initiatives of this kind are evident in the self-governing youth centres in Bologna, the 'Red Tape' municipal recording studios and rehearsal rooms – specifically targeted at unemployed youth – in Sheffield's 'Cultural Industries Quarter' and the Honigfabrik multi-media neighbourhood centre in Hamburg. All these initiatives aimed at reintegrating into the local economy geographically and socially marginalized young people whose skills and potential had often been overlooked by the professional cultural sector and formal training institutions.

These policies redefined the relationship between the local state and civil society, by recognizing the autonomy of cultural producers. In Bologna, the cultural *assessore*, Sandra Soster, gave 2–3 year rolling contracts to independent theatre groups to manage municipal theatres and handed over the running of the summer festival to outside organizers. The groups – usually co-operatives – had to submit a report and balance sheet at the end of each year (Bloomfield, 1993). In the case of Hamburg, the film-makers achieved a self-managed status in running the Hamburg Filmhaus and selecting the film projects to be funded.

Despite the success of some of the cultural policies implemented during the 'emancipatory' phase from the early 1970s, there was, in the mid-1980s, a clear shift away from equal opportunities and participation, towards economic development and urban regeneration priorities. The language of citizenship, of personal and community development, egalitarianism, social justice, neighbourhood decentralization and the socialization of urban space was gradually replaced by arguments reducing cultural policy to a function of urban economic and physical regeneration strategies.

The Phase of the 'Economic Turn'

A shift to the right in the political climate in most West European countries, and growing pressure on the financial resources of local government helped downgrade the earlier emphases on both social and emancipatory citizenship. Older moral and social rationales for urban cultural policy making were gradually abandoned, and new economic justifications emerged in many cities.

City decision makers perceived cultural policy as a valuable tool in attempting to diversify the local economic base, in response to the process of economic restructuring, the most spectacular manifestation of which was the crisis of traditional forms of manufacturing industry. Policy makers intervened in economic sectors – such as leisure, tourism, fashion, design, the media and other cultural industries – which they identified as expanding, in an attempt to compensate for jobs lost in traditional industrial and services sectors. A lively, cosmopolitan cultural life was increasingly seen as an ingredient of city marketing and international competitiveness strategies, designed to attract ostensibly mobile international capital and specialized personnel. The focus of urban cultural policy making shifted once more to city centres, which were seen as showcases for the local economy in emerging inter-urban competition, and as engines of economic growth. Peripheral neighbourhoods tended to suffer in this process in some cases, because city governments, in order to finance city centre-based cultural flagship projects cut expenditure on neighbourhood-based schools, libraries and other cultural services.

A rhetorical commitment to social and emancipatory citizenship was maintained however, in the cultural policy pronouncements of the majority of city authorities. Almost inevitably though, the commitment to the citizenship agendas furthered in the two previous historical phases, took second place. We would argue there was no conception of citizenship at all underpinning the urban cultural policies exclusively focused on international economic competitiveness. In so far as there was an underlying notion of the citizen in these market-oriented strategies, it was that of the depoliticized consumer.

The neo-conservative governments in Britain from 1979–97 succeeded, with echoes elsewhere in Europe, in implanting an enterprise management culture into the public sector (Bianchini and Schwengel, 1991; Clifford, 1993). Decentralized financial management has eroded uniform standards of service provision, intensified competition for resources between policy areas and undermined the co-ordination of policy across different departments on which successful civic cultural policies depend. On the other hand, decentralized decision making has opened up possibilities for establishing local partnerships and growth coalitions which could enhance civic life, though this depends far more than before on the organizational capacity of the weaker partners such as community groups or environmental organizations (Mayer, 1992).

The influence of the passive conception of citizenship was clearly discernible in the 'place marketing' strategies which were developed in the course of the last decade by many city authorities – including Left-controlled ones – to attract tourists, investors and skilled personnel ('Standortpolitik' in Hamburg, and its variants in Glasgow, Birmingham, Bilbao and elsewhere). One of the key concepts in city marketing was the nebulous notion of 'quality of life' of which cultural activities and facilities were viewed as important components. 'Quality of life' for policy makers was reduced to a set of discrete quantitative indicators to be used to enhance urban competitiveness. Since the later 1980s, research (for instance, Rogerson et al., 1987, 1989) has concentrated on measuring 'quality of life' through the use of opinion surveys and data on access to urban services and amenities – treating residents as passive consumers. Instead of considering quality of life as an objectifiable entity, it could be evaluated as the integral lived experience of residents of a city, the sum of social interactions which shape their participation in its public life. Such an anthropological approach would provide policy makers with valuable qualitative indicators (Bianchini and Landry, 1994). It is clear that this interpretation of 'quality of life' offers greater scope for the development of active citizenship. The projection of the city and its cultural life as a 'product' by place-marketing experts gave rise in many cases to conflicts. For example, Workers' City, a protest group in Glasgow, vociferously reacted against what they saw as the 'repackaging' of the city's image by urban policy makers for the 1990 European City of Culture celebrations (Boyle and Hughes, 1991).

The minimalist, passive notion of the citizen as private consumer has been supplemented by a concept of the active citizen, who, as a private individual, shoulders responsibilities once carried out by public authorities, but now devolved to private trusts, quangos and voluntary organizations. This formed part of the British Conservative government's centralizing strategy in the 1980s and 1990s to erode the autonomy of local government and replace statutory with voluntary, ad hoc accountability. The combination of passive citizenship for the majority as consumers, and active citizenship for the relative few, who are deemed sufficiently worthy and free enough to take part in decision making (so-called 'successful people' designated by Conservative Home Secretary, Douglas Hurd, in 1988) provided a rhetorical shield behind which an unprecedented degree of centralization of power at national level took place (Bianchini and Schwengel, 1991: 223–224; Crouch and Marquand, 1989).

Conclusions

In the urban context of the late 1990s of increasing social and economic polarization and exclusion, nobody seriously believes any longer in 'trickle down' but this does not automatically mean that citizenship in its emancipatory sense has returned to the policy agenda. The centre-left governments in Britain and Italy seem primarily concerned with containing social costs and reasserting social order, but their counterparts in France and now Germany are giving shape to a meaningful new agenda of social and European citizenship. In this context, what role can urban cultural policy play?

In order to enhance citizenship at the turn of the century, urban cultural policy will have to confront the destructive features of international competition which have distorted attempts at culturally led urban regeneration since the mid-1980s. The process of global detachment of capital from a specific local context, and its capacity to re-embed itself in alternative or rival localities has forced city authorities to compete with each other to attract investment. As a result broad and integrated socio-economic and cultural objectives have been sacrificed to narrow, short-term commercially driven ones. Property-led urban regeneration, with cultural policy in tow to prestige city-centre projects has proved harmful, in many ways, to civic development, and distorted cultural budgets overwhelmingly in favour of traditional, high-cost, high cultural institutions. Financial restrictions on local government have squeezed even further the margins for fostering production, experimentation and participatory projects. Yet such projects are the most effective in transforming human capital by imparting skills and the desire for learning, instilling confidence and building teamwork and inter-cultural understanding (Bianchini and Landry, 1995: 29–30).

Cross-sectoral partnerships can harness private, public and voluntary sector initiatives to civic goals. Each partner brings a different set of capacities and all can gain from combining their particular strengths, including business where it is committed to the local economy, a high quality workforce and an innovative environment (Moss Kantor, 1995). In contrast to a communitarian approach which assumes that a preconstituted consensus exists – which in fact communitarians construct through the criteria of selection of 'representatives of the community', which screens out alternative voices – we are advocating an open-ended system. This would be constructed through the self-organization of autonomous actors in civil society with the city offering training, and actively soliciting projects and ideas in all areas of urban policy. The model of the public competition and exhibition of proposals used for architecture and urban design could be extended to transport, economic development, social and cultural initiatives.

Cultural policies in many European cities during the phase of the 'economic turn' were successful in creating jobs in tourism, retailing and other consumer service industries. These jobs, however, were frequently low paid, part-time, deskilled, characterized by inadequate legal rights and poor working conditions. In the late 1990s, in order to address economic and social polarization and exclusion, cities have to develop production-oriented strategies aimed at creating skilled jobs in high value-added sectors of the local cultural economy such as design, fashion, film, TV and publishing. In the face of the erosion of commitment by large firms to specific places, some cities and regions have applied endogenous growth strategies which seek to maximize the resources under local control, diversify products and services, and exploit the locality's distinctive qualities and strengths. Such a strategy puts greatest value on the creative potential of human capital, since people are relatively tied to a specific place and their capacities often under-utilized. Therefore, training is a central feature of an embedding strategy, so that the city can produce and retain skilled people, and create a critical mass of small firms, skill clusters, cultural milieux which are attached to the city.

Civic cultural policies which seek to tap the unrealized potential in the city, have to address the socially disadvantaged and marginalized in a way that appeals to their talents and draws on their incipient skills. Cities have to take account of 'subcultural capital', of the dynamism in local youth cultures to tailor appropriate facilities, technical and financial support services. Training initiatives are most effective when based on their home territory, such as the well-used networks of cultural and youth centres with self-governing statutes in peripheral districts of Hamburg and Bologna.

Likewise, cultural policies to enhance citizenship have to counter the growing spatial polarization of cities, concentrated poverty in 'enforced communities' and no-go areas. There have been various attempts to bridge the growing divide between lively city centres and impoverished, inaccessible peripheries. One way of addressing conflicts in the spatial distribution of recreational provision is to locate new cultural facilities in neighbourhoods – such as the local parks, squares and artworks created by Barcelona City Council in the run-up to the Olympics (Borja, 1995). The establishment of neighbourhood-based facilities can effectively be combined with strategies aimed at democratizing access to city centre-based cultural provision. Integrated policies on public transport, pedestrianization, street lighting and policing, like those introduced by many European cities in the 1970s, retain their validity today. They could be highly effective if combined with strong outreach and educational programmes and imaginative marketing by the cultural institutions based in city centres.

The city authority, as an inclusive political space, cannot claim any longer to represent 'the community' as though it were singular rather than composite, in constructing a local civic identity and public sphere. Such a public sphere has to be both a multi-cultural and inter-cultural space, in which diverse voices can be heard, protagonists speak for themselves, control the representations of themselves to others, de- and reconstruct a common culture, as well as promulgate their own distinctive cultures. City government, as the authority closest to the citizen, which organizes and delivers services, has a crucial function in mobilizing the untapped talents and creative capacities of the unrepresented and disorganized, and enabling insertion into the local cultural economy. By providing civic training, it could stimulate a more effective public presence of marginalized groups, which would counteract racism and misrepresentation, and begin to reconstitute the public sphere as a pluralist cultural space based on dialogue and social negotiation between different voices, values and interests. This would also contribute to the revival of local participatory politics.

The need for such a strategy has intensified as traditional organizations of political socialization such as trade unions and political parties have declined in influence, so more groups are left disenfranchised. This problem has been enormously exacerbated by the demise of universal service provision and the restructuring of the local political system to rely more heavily on ad hoc coalitions of public and private interests (Borja, 1996; Jacquier, 1995: 37; Mayer, 1992) which has made collective self-organization of the weak more imperative. The unequal distribution of organizational resources is directly impeding the democratic participation of a growing sector of society – those without voice, representation or exit. In a media-dominated politics and economy of symbolic production, just as cultural capital converts into political capital, lack of cultural capital converts into political exclusion.

In order to address the problems of social polarization and political exclusion, cities have actively to solicit the self-organization of ethnic minorities and other disadvantaged social groups and their access to the policy-making process, so they can demonstrate the relevance of their ideas, aspirations and skills to the city's overall development. The city has a vital role in creating an inter-cultural space, through establishing venues for cultural exchange, public forums for cultural debate and policy making, and by fostering inter-cultural practice in the city, not least in the city government. In Berlin, such a policy has been pursued by the Berlin Senate Commission for Foreign Affairs through campaigns and inter-cultural festivals such as STREET '94 aimed at immigrant youths under the slogan 'To stay is my right' with street art, music and films and workshops on graffiti and rap (Soysal, 1996); through a local public radio station, Radio Multikulti, run mainly by non-German DJs, which broadcasts world music and debate in sixteen languages, on constructing Berlin as a multi-cultural and global city; through the Werkstatt der Kulturen (Workshop of Cultures) which has a concert hall, auditorium, laboratories and studios, run jointly by representatives of German and migrant organizations for young people who engage in joint production projects (Vertovec, 1995).

An embedding strategy, which capitalizes on the unique features of the city and the talents of its people, to prevent the haemorrhaging of skills and talent away from the city, has to guard against the danger of reinforcing a closed mentality to the wider world and 'ethnic' assertiveness of the purity or superiority of native 'insiders' against newcomers. Thus, it has to embrace external influences, ideas and outsiders and enable their creative integration in the public life of the city.

City governments have been more responsive than national governments to the cultural needs and aspirations of grassroots groups and more sensitive to multi-culturalism. They need now to promote cosmopolitanism as a positive virtue, as testimony to their openness to the world and to new influences. Festivals have already provided fertile ground for this kind of celebration of diversity and inno-vativeness, but all branches of urban life from architecture and the design of housing to forms of shopping and recreation could benefit from such an infusion.

The development of trans-European networks of co-operation between local authorities, such as Eurocities, which counteract destructive rivalry in the European urban system, can help to build new international relationships at local level – from which a genuinely democratic and inclusive 'Europe of the cities' could emerge. This will be based on multi-layered and overlapping sovereignties and a multi-faceted concept of culture, not confined to the high culture narratives of national grandeur. The example of the Biennale of Young Artists from Mediterranean Countries indicates how one such international network of cities can further inter-cultural literacy. It is based on an art festival-cum-trade fair, covering the performing and visual arts, craft and high-tech industrial forms, including live music, mime, photography, computer graphics and cartoons, rotating between cities including Bologna, Barcelona, Marseilles, Tunis and Turin on an annual basis. The inclusion of Mahgreb, Balkan and Middle Eastern cities in the network adds a further dimension bridging the gap between Europe and North Africa, retrieving the Mediterranean basin as a centre of cultural fusion (Bloomfield, 1993).

Interventions by the European Commission could also build on the achieve-ments of existing initiatives such as the European Film Distribution Office

(EFDO) which provides financial support for the distribution of low-budget films produced in EU countries to European cinemas. The EFDO model could be applied to the creation of mechanisms for supporting networks of independent cultural producers from ethnic and racial minority communities based in different European cities – for example Turkish publishing, or Afro-Caribbean music industries. These networks could make an important contribution to a culturally pluralist European civil society.

In order to move towards this new notion of citizenship, however, a more integrated approach to urban cultural policy making is needed. This would rest on a very broad anthropological definition of 'culture' as 'a way of life'. Such a strategy would audit and deploy all the cultural resources of the city, from its physical layout and design, its architectural and industrial heritage, local craft traditions, skill pools, arts, to the public spaces, educational and cultural institutions, tourist attractions and images of the city which the interaction of myths, conventional wisdom, cultural and media representations produce. It would cut across the divides between the voluntary, public and private sectors, different institutional concerns and different professional disciplines. It would involve the development of more consultative and open approaches to policy making and the provision of more broadly based forms of training for policy makers. Such an approach – defined by Mercer and Bianchini as 'cultural planning' (Mercer, 1991) – could provide an imaginative and integrative basis for future urban regeneration strategies. Such a strategy would have to balance and integrate the economic, physical, cultural, symbolic, social and political dimensions of the city. It would also harness the different types of creativity – artistic, political, organizational, economic – present in civil society to strategic development objectives. City authorities will have to let go of their prescriptive power and prejudice in promoting some forms of cultural production over others and recognize that creativity is a critical force in society which generates debate and alternative solutions to problems.

To establish a more explicit and intellectually grounded legitimation for cultural citizenship in the city, we need to retrieve the radical idea of the city as a *project* for the widening of cultural horizons and enhancing the capacity to redesign everyday life and the public sphere. This view was expressed by Nicolini, the Cultural Assessor for Rome City Council 1976–85, when he defined the city as 'a system of life which develops desires'. More recently, Jordi Borja, International Officer for Barcelona City Council, has reiterated this view: 'The city must be perceived as a cultural project. The city is a series of collective projects. There is no social integration without participation in collective projects' (Borja, 1995: 412).

Cultural policies will only be able to revitalize citizenship if they contribute to the revitalization of local politics itself through opening up the local media and city planning to popular participation. Furthermore, such an approach could no longer demonize the hedonism of young people, but would recognize the erosion of a Weberian conception of the self based on the work ethic, and positively embrace the wish to reconcile work and pleasure in an integral self. Likewise, it would welcome efforts to reconcile urban life and the protection of nature through environmental action. In so doing, it would seek to reconnect the cultural innovativeness and critical energy of young people and social movements to the local political sphere.

References

Althusser, L. (1971) 'Ideology and Ideological State Apparatuses' in *Lenin and Philosophy and Other Essays*. London: NLB.

Bacon, R. and Eltis, W. (1976) *Britain's Economic Problem: Too Few Producers*. London: Macmillan.

Bader, V.-M. (1996) 'The Institutional and Cultural Conditions of Postnational Citizenship'. Paper at Conference on Social and Political Citizenship in a World of Migration, European University Institute, Florence, February.

Baumann, G. (1997) 'Dominant and Demotic Discourses of Culture. Their Relevance to Multi-Ethnic Alliances' in P. Werbner and T. Madood (eds), *Debating Cultural Hybridity*. London/New Jersey: Zed Books.

Bennett, O. (1995) 'Cultural Policy in the United Kingdom: Collapsing Rationales and the End of Tradition', *European Journal of Cultural Policy*, I (2).

Bianchini, F. (1989) 'Cultural Policy and Urban Social Movements: the Response of the "New Left" in Rome (1976–1985) and London (1981–1986)' in Peter Bramham (ed.), *Leisure and Urban Processes. Critical Studies of Leisure Policy in West European Cities*. London: Routledge.

Bianchini, F. and Bloomfield, J. (1996) 'Urban Cultural Policies and the Development of Citizenship: Reflections on the West European Experience', *Culture and Policy*, VII (1): 85–114.

Bianchini, F. and Landry, C. (1994) *Indicators of a Creative City. A Methodology for Assessing Urban Viability and Vitality, Creative City Working Papers, No. 3*. Bournes Green: Comedia.

Bianchini, F. and Landry, C. (1995) 'The Contribution of Urban Cultural Policies to Human Development, Unpublished Background Paper 4'. The European Taskforce on Cultural Development (Council of Europe).

Bianchini, F. and Schwengel, H. (1991) 'Re-imagining the City' in J. Corner and S. Harvey (eds), *Enterprise and Heritage. Crosscurrents of National Culture in the 1980s*. London: Routledge.

Blair, T. (1995) *New Britain: My Vision of a Young Country*. London: Fourth Estate.

Bloomfield, J. (1993) 'Bologna: Laboratory of Cultural Enterprise' in F. Bianchini and M. Parkinson (eds), *Cultural Policy and Urban Regeneration: The West European Experience*. Manchester: Manchester University Press.

Bodo, C. (1988) 'La spesa culturale degli enti locali: un 'analisi quantitativa' in M. Salvati and L. Zannino (eds), *La cultura degli enti locali (1975–1985)*. Milano: Franco Angeli.

Borja, J. (1995) 'Transformations in Public Policy and Urban Social Management: Roundtable' in C. Jacquier (ed.), *Urban Territories and Social Cohesion in Europe: What Public Action?*, ACTS Seminar Proceedings, May, Paris.

Borja, J. (1996) 'European Citizenship: Introductory Aspects of Contribution by the Cities and Local Authorities to the Definition, Protection and Development of European Citizenship', Eurocities report: Barclenona Council.

Bourdieu, P. (1977) *Outline of a Theory of Practice*. Cambridge: Cambridge University Press.

Bourdieu, P. (1984) *Distinction: A Social Critique of the Judgement of Taste*. London: Routledge & Kegan Paul.

Bourdieu, P. (1992) *Language and the Symbolic*. Cambridge: Polity Press.

Boyle, R. and Hughes, G. (1991) 'The Politics of the Representation of "the real": Discourses from the Left on Glasgow's Role as European City of Culture, 1990', *Area*, 23.3: 217–228.

Brittan, S. (1975) 'The Economic Contradictions of Democracy', *British Journal of Political Studies*, 6.

Brubaker, W.R. (1992) *Citizenship and Nationhood in France and Germany*. Cambridge, MA: Harvard University Press.

Calhoun, C. (ed.) (1994) *Social Theory and the Politics of Identity*. Oxford: Blackwell.

Castells, M. (1994) 'European Cities, the Informational Society and the Global Economy', *New Left Review*, 204: 27.

Clarke, J., Hall, S., Jefferson, T. and Roberts, B. (1975) 'Subcultures, Cultures and Class' in S. Hall and T. Jefferson (eds), *Resistance through Rituals*. London: Hutchinson.

Clifford, C. (1993) 'Citizens' Chartism. The Citizen's Charter, Quality and the Civil Service', Policy Studies Association of the UK Annual Conference, University of Leicester, April.

Crouch, C. and Marquand, D. (1989) 'The New Centralism', special edition of *Political Quarterly*. Oxford: Blackwell.

Enzensberger, H.- M. (1974) *The Consciousness Industry*. New York: Seabury Press.

Feist, A. and Hutchison, R. (1990) *Cultural Trends in the Eighties*. London: Policy Studies Institute.

Fraser, N. (1995a) 'Recognition or Redistribution? A Critical Reading of Iris Young's Justice and the Politics of Difference', *Journal of Political Philosophy*, 3 (2), June.

Fraser, N. (1995b) 'From Redistribution to Recognition? Dilemmas of Justice in a "Post-Socialist" Age', *New Left Review*, 212, July/August.

Friedman, M. (1976) 'The Fragility of Freedom', *Encounter*, November.

Gaspard, F. and Khosrokhavar, F. (1995) *Le Foulard et la République*. Paris: La Découverte.

Gelder, K. and Thornton, S. (1997) *The Subcultures Reader*. London: Routledge.

Gellner, E. (1983) *Nations and Nationalism*. Oxford: Blackwell.

Gramsci, A. (1971) in Q. Hoare and G. Nowell Smith (eds), *Selections from The Prison Notebooks*. London: Lawrence & Wishart.

Habermas, J. (1986) *Autonomy and Solidarity*. London: Verso.

Habermas, J. (1994) 'Struggles for Recognition in the Democratic Constitutional State' in C. Taylor and A. Gutman (eds), *Multiculturalism. Examining the Politics of Recognition*. Princeton: Princeton University Press.

Hannerz, U. (1990) 'Cosmopolitans and Locals in World Culture' in M. Featherstone (ed.), *Global Culture. Nationalism, Globalisation and Modernity*. London: Sage.

Hannerz, U. (1996) 'Seven Arguments for Diversity' in *Transnational Connections*. London: Routledge.

Hebdige, D. (1979) *Subculture: The Meaning of Style*. London: Methuen.

Hobsbawm, E. and Ranger, T. (1983) *The Invention of Tradition*. Cambridge: Cambridge University Press.

Hurd, D. (1988) 'Citizenship in Tory Democracy', *New Statesman*, 29 April 1988.

Ignatieff, M. (1990) The Milner Gray Lecture, London Chartered Society of Designers 12 December.

Irwin, J. (1970) 'Notes on the Status of the Concept Subculture' in D. Arnold (ed.), *Subcultures*. New York: Glendessary Press.

Jacquier, C. (1995) 'Transformations in Public Policy and Urban Social Management: Introductory Report: Towards New Initiatives in Urban Social Management' in C. Jacquier (ed.), *Urban Territories and Social Cohesion in Europe: What Public Action?*, ACTS Seminar Proceedings, May, Paris.

Jordan, G. and Weedon, C. (eds) (1995) *Cultural Politics: Class, Gender, Race and the Post-Modern World*. Oxford: Blackwell.

Kymlicka, W. (1989) *Liberalism, Culture and Community*. Oxford: Clarendon.

Kymlicka, W. (1995a) *Multiculturalism: A Liberal Theory of Minority Rights*. Oxford: Clarendon.

Kymlicka, W. (ed.) (1995b) *The Rights of Minority Cultures*. Oxford: Oxford University Press.

Lash, S. and Urry, J. (1994) *The Economy of Signs and Space*. London: Sage.

Marshall, T.H. and Bottomore, T. (1992) *Citizenship and Social Class*. London: Pluto.

Mayer, M. (1992) 'The Local Urban Political System' in M. Dunford and G. Kafkalas (eds), *Cities and Regions in the New Europe*. London: Belhaven Press.

McRobbie, A. (1989) 'Secondhand Dresses and the Role of the Rag Market' in A. McRobbie (ed.), *Zoot Suits and Second-Hand Dresses: An Anthology of Fashion and Music*. London: Macmillan.

Melucci, A. (1989) *Nomads of the Present*. London: Hutchinson Radius.

Mercer, C. (1991) 'Brisbane's Cultural Development Strategy: the Process, the Politics and the Products' in EIT The Cultural Planning Conference, Mornington, Victoria, Australia.

Moss Kantor, R. (1995) *World Class: Thriving Locally in a Global Economy*. New York: Simon & Schuster.

Nederveen Pieterse, J. (1994) 'Globalisation as Hybridisation', *International Sociology*, 9 (2): 161–84.

Nozick, R. (1974) *Anarchy, State and Utopia*. New York: Basic.

Offe, C. (1987) 'Challenging the Boundaries of Institutional Politics: Social Movements Since the 1960s' in C. Maier (ed.), *Changing Boundaries of the Political*. Cambridge: Cambridge University Press.

Pakulski, J. (1997) 'Cultural Citizenship', *Citizenship Studies*, 1 (1).

Park, R. (ed.) (1925) *The City*. London and Chicago: University of Chicago Press.

Preuss, U. (1995) 'Problems of a Concept of European Citizenship', *European Law Journal*, 1 (3), November.

Rawls, J. (1973) *A Theory of Justice*. Oxford: Oxford University Press.

Rigby, B. (1991) *Popular Culture in Modern France. A Study of Cultural Discourse*. London: Routledge.

Rogerson, R., Findlay, A. and Morris, A. (1987) 'The Geography of Quality of Life', *Geography Department Occasional Papers, no. 22*. University of Glasgow, November.

Rogerson, R. et al. (1989) 'Measuring Quality of Life: Some Methodological Issues and Problems', APRU Working Papers 2, University of Glasgow Quality of Life Group and Applied Population Research Unit, University of Glasgow.

Soysal, Y. (1996) 'Boundaries and Identity: Immigrants in Europe', EUI Working Papers, 96/3.

Taylor, C. (1994) *Multiculturalism. Examining the Politics of Recognition* (A. Guttman, ed.). Princeton: Princeton University Press.

TEST (1988) *Quality Streets: How Traditional Urban Centres Benefit from Traffic Calming*. London: TEST.

Thornton, S. (1995) *Club Cultures: Music, Media and Subcultural Capital*. Cambridge: Polity Press.

Touraine, A. (1981) *The Voice and the Eye*. Cambridge: Cambridge University Press.

Turner, B. (1993), 'Contemporary Problems in the Theory of Citizenship' in B. Turner (ed.), *Citizenship and Social Theory*. London: Sage.

Vertovec, S. (1995) 'Berlin Multikulti: Germany, "Foreigners" and "World-Openness"', *New Community*, 22 (3): 381–399.

Waldron, J. (1995) 'Minority Cultures and the Cosmopolitan Alternative' in W. Kymlicka (ed.), *The Rights of Minority Cultures*. Oxford: Oxford University Press.

Walzer, M. (1983) *Spheres of Justice*. Oxford: Blackwell.

Weber, E. (1977) *Peasants into Frenchmen: The Modernization of Rural France, 1870–1914*. London: Chatto & Windus.

Willetts, D. (1994) *Civic Conservatism*. London: Social Market Foundation.

8

THREE DISCOURSES OF CULTURAL POLICY

Jim McGuigan

It is curious that as the security and rights of social citizenship were weakened in the older industrialized and de-industrializing parts of the world, with the decline of the social welfare state, the issue of cultural citizenship rose up the agendas of public and academic debate. To some extent this reflects how issues that were once considered 'social' have come increasingly to be thought of as 'cultural'. Questions of identity and a sense of belonging appear to have superseded questions of material entitlement in much social and cultural theory as well as in cultural politics. While, in the USA, to take the most notable example, public spending on urban programmes and welfare was slashed (Davis, 1993a, 1993b), thereby exacerbating the problems of the black 'underclass', the meaning of African-American identity became hotly debated amongst black intellectuals (Dent, 1992) and infused the very language of the public sphere to the extent that Nelson Mandela was addressed by a witless young journalist on his visit to the States a few years ago as 'African-American'. The status of cultural citizen of the United States was thus casually bestowed upon the President of another state, albeit by a slip of the tongue.

The question of cultural citizenship is extremely diffuse and reflexive, signifying perhaps how we have come to think of politics and public identity very broadly as a matter of signs. Its range vastly exceeds what has usually been instituted as *cultural policy* and the ways in which such policy has addressed social subjects. Cultural policy itself, however, is an unstable concept. It has had an uneven and often detached relationship to *communications* and *media policy*. These latter nominations have largely been thought of in terms of political economy, signifying their industrial and economic importance and the role of the communications media in politics as narrowly conceived. In comparison, *cultural policy* is still, in spite of attempts to broaden its remit, quite closely associated with *arts policy*, the objects of which are the aesthetic, the affective, value and values. From a practical point of view, this is, to be sure, unsatisfactory: yet the emphases on symbolic representation and on the subjectivity of civic and national identity do meet up with the more diffuse idea of cultural citizenship.

Another feature of cultural policy – and, to a great extent, communications and media policy as well – is its close historical association with the nation-state. In a globalizing economy and culture and a world of political interrelatedness, the nation-state in general and its cultural policies in particular are frequently said to be redundant. So many premature obituaries have been written of the nation-state that one might be forgiven for believing, against the palpable evidence of experience, that it is indeed dead or at least in its death throws. Yet, the nation-state stubbornly persists as a major constitutive power of politics, economy and culture in the late-modern world: and, specifically, it is still the key focus for the defence and extension of social citizenship and for many claims that are made for cultural citizenship. To argue thus is not to deny the importance of international and local formations, for instance, the role of 'Europe' in defending the social rights of citizenship in Britain during the eighteen years of Conservative government that ended in 1997, or, the several forms of cultural identity that transcend the national habitat and create localized enclaves within and sometimes against the territorial command of the nation-state. And, in any case, the nation-state is not the same as the nation. A crucial feature of state cultural policies in places like Malaysia – and one might also add Britain – is the object of reconciling different ethnicities and national identities with one another.

In this chapter, my concern is not, however, so much with unpacking the relations between the nation and the state, the local and the global, as with how the state's cultural policies have been constructed and deconstructed, assuming that the nation-state was and continues to be important for the conditions of both social and cultural citizenship. My examples are mainly though not exclusively drawn from Britain. There are two reasons for this: first, that I live there; and, second, that what has happened in Britain can be taken as a particular case study of how cultural policy is connected to citizenship historically. My principal concern in this account is to trace the rise of market reasoning within the state cultural sector during the recent period of neo-liberal hegemony and to explore the theoretical grounds for alternative and radical democratic policies. The approach is to consider the discursive framing of cultural policy and to outline the role of discourse ethics in reframing the cultural rights of citizenship.

I want to distinguish between three very general discursive formations of cultural policy in admittedly an over-simplification but one with a specific purpose. These formations are not confined solely to 'culture' and cultural policy. The three discourses of cultural policy – *state, market* and *civil* – all have a number of variants and are by no means internally unified. Yet, they all, however, function in some sense to define 'the real world' of culture and to position agents and subjects, producers, consumers and mediators within the discursive space of the cultural field.

To digress for a moment on the question of discourse: in a commentary on Foucault's inaugural lecture at the College de France, 'The Order of Discourse', Robert Young (1981: 48) once remarked that the 'effect' of 'discursive practices' is 'to make it virtually impossible to think outside of them'; which is not dissimilar to the Wittgensteinian dictum that language sets the limits to our world. To say that it is impossible to think outside of a discourse, in Young's explication of Foucault, is to say something more than this, however: it points to the operations of power in the regulation of discourse, procedures of exclusion, reason and truth, internal policing and conditions of application.

The prevailing ideological feature of particular discourses, according to Pecheux (1982: 115), is secured interdiscursively by the dominant ideological discourse of the social formation. Also, 'interdiscourse' suggests that no discourse is ever completely closed off from other discourses or without internally disruptive elements. From these considerations, I would like to make two broad observations. First, discourses of cultural policy do not exist in splendid isolation from the leading discourses of the day. Secondly, although discourses are indeed porous and there is interaction between them, one cannot help but notice how some discourses 'make it virtually impossible to think outside of them'.

It is interesting, at a time when 'the dominant ideology thesis' fell out of favour in social and cultural theory, that there should have been in strengthened existence such an outstanding candidate for designation as the dominant ideology: I mean, the all-encompassing discourse of market reason on a global scale. I shall eventually return to this point about the spread and pervasiveness of market reasoning across many practices after outlining selectively how the modern state has operated discursively in cultural policy, which is a necessary preliminary to examining the marketization of everything.

State Discourse

Modern cultural developments have been closely linked to the state, going well beyond earlier forms of monarchical and aristocratic patronage and building upon, for instance, the public museum and library legislation of the nineteenth century which became associated in Britain with Matthew Arnold's view of the state as society's 'better self'. The grander idea that the modern nation-state could command the whole of society, regulate the economy and cultivate appropriate selves, was extremely widespread until quite recently. This was never just a socialist or communist imaginary. It was generally accepted within the framework of advanced capitalism as a means of containing capitalism's recurrent crises by the middle decades of the twentieth century. Fordism and Keynesian economics called forth and legitimated the interventionist state.

That cultural policy might function to re-engineer the soul became a commonplace assumption of both totalitarian and, indeed also, although to a much lesser extent, social-democratic thought and practice. Nazism, for instance, promoted the Aryan ideal, especially in its bodily form, and attacked 'degenerate art'. There is, in addition, the key instance of Soviet communism in which culture came to be seen as a device for social engineering. According to the notorious Soviet Writers' Congress of 1934, the purpose of cultural policy was to create 'socialist man', both representationally and in lived reality (Gorky et al., 1977). That was a crucial moment of ideological closure around 'socialist realism' in the Soviet Union, reacting to the controversies and clash of diverse aesthetic tendencies and avant-garde practices during the 1920s. Vladimir Mayakovsky of Lef (the Left Front of Art), who was vilified as a 'petit-bourgeois individualist and anarchist' in the late 1920s, had already committed suicide in 1930. His reinstatement as an icon of 'socialist man' in 1935 was especially ironic (Shklovsky, 1974).

The operations of official cultural policy and artistic practice in the Soviet bloc were a good deal more complex and internally contradictory, however, than the image of a dictatorial and robotic culture for which it was known in 'the West'. The Hungarian writer, Miklos Haraszti's (1989) *The Velvet Prison – Artists Under State Socialism* shows, in a fascinating account, how 'dissidence' had actually become by the 1980s a normative aspect of the system amongst officially approved and rewarded cultural workers themselves. Anne White (1990) gives a different yet equally compelling account of the actual effects of communist cultural policy in her study, *De-Stalinization and the House of Culture*. White was interested in the fate of 'cultural enlightenment' as a strategy of socialist socialization after Stalin in the Soviet Union, Hungary and Poland. The houses of culture, arts centres, were established in order to inculcate humanistic and egalitarian ideals and to foster belief in human perfectability under socialism. However, by the time White was researching the practical outcomes during the period of glasnost in the late 1980s, she found that liberalization had occurred alongside political disillusion in general and with such cultural policy in particular amongst not only the people but also communist leaders. She says:

> Social changes – notably widespread disillusionment with, and rejection of, Stalinism and Stalinist cultural institutions, the spread of television and individual flat ownership, higher education levels, the emergence of organized dissent and the greater exposure of ordinary citizens to Western culture – had led to a situation by the 1980s in which the leading role of the party in determining how leisure time was spent was becoming seriously eroded. (White, 1990: 4)

In a much less detached tone, Ernest Gellner made the sour yet incisive observation that:

> Far from creating a new social man, one freed from egotistic greed, commodity fetishism and competitiveness, which had been the Marxist hope, the system created isolated, amoral, cynical individualists-without-opportunity, skilled at double-talk and trimming within the system, but incapable of effective enterprise. (1996: 5)

Great and no doubt mistaken expectations were also vested in state cultural policy under social democracy and even within the terms of liberal democracy throughout Western Europe. In Britain, there is the phenomenon of the intermediary body, organizations of the state but not supposed to be directly under the sway of the current government (Williams, 1979), organizations such as the BBC, the Arts Council and English Heritage. These bodies were modelled historically on the University Grants Committee, established in 1919. That the BBC should function in a similarly 'impartial' manner, secured by the greater authority of the state over the market as well as, in theory, protected from the present whims of government, was an aim of political liberalism in the 1920s, although actually brought into being by Baldwin's Conservative administration. John Reith, then, had his way in fashioning the BBC as the key institution of a liberal national culture, the guardian of a certain kind of communicational or cultural citizenship, and a bulwark against extremes of Left and Right. That card-carrying Liberals played leading roles in founding the welfare state in general and 'the welfare state model' of cultural policy in particular is itself significant historically: British social democracy to a degree, in effect, realized a Liberal programme. The central figures were Beveridge, in the case of social welfare, and Keynes, both as the economic guru of social democracy and architect of the Arts Council of Great Britain as an agency for enhancing national prestige. It was this thread which became so knotted in the 1960s and 1970s.

The key terms to consider with regard to the forms, contradictions and tensions of social-democratic cultural policy in Britain are 'extension' and, more latterly, 'access'. The discourse was not, however, just that of political liberalism: it was enunciated and fought over within the terms of social democracy itself. In his 1929 lectures on *Equality*, R.H. Tawney had set the agenda for appropriating 'culture' from the sole possession of a privileged elite and extending it to the masses. It is worth quoting Raymond Williams at length on the problems inherent in this Tawneyan agenda:

> The case for extension (the entirely appropriate word) is strong; the dangers of limitation are real and present. But to think of the problem as one of 'opening museums' or of putting the specimens in the market-place is to capitulate to a very meagre idea of culture. Tawney's position is both normal and humane. But there is an unresolved contradiction, which phrases about broadening and enriching merely blur, between the recognition that a culture must grow and the hope that 'existing standards of excellence' may be preserved intact. It is a contradiction which, among others, the defenders of inequality will be quick to exploit. The question that has to be faced, if we may put it for a moment in one of Tawney's analogies, is whether the known gold will be more widely spread, or whether, in fact, there will be a change of currency. If the social and economic changes which Tawney recommends are in fact effected, it is the latter, the change of currency, which can reasonably be expected. (Williams, 1971: 222–223)

The 1964 to 1970 Labour governments sought to realize the Tawneyan agenda by increasing the Arts Council's annual grant-in-aid threefold as part of a general programme for raising public access to the arts and culture. This was also the period of comprehensivization in secondary education and a comparatively well-funded, by present standards, expansion of higher education. Such policies were enacted in the name of 'access' to opportunities and pleasures that were previously denied to most people. But, as Williams had already noted back in the 1950s, in his discussion of Tawney, what was supposed to be disseminated more widely was bound to change with the dissemination. Trouble arose around the meaning of 'access'. Was it confined to creating the conditions for more people down the social hierarchy and in the regions to consume established art forms? Or, did it mean popular control over the means of cultural production, redefining what counts as 'culture' and participation for groups hitherto excluded by the established structures of public patronage? – facilitating ethnic minority arts, proletarian theatre, feminist film-making, and so on.

Much of the trouble centred upon alternative theatre and community arts. By the 1970s, the Arts Council was supporting both the National Theatre in its then newly palatial premises on the South Bank of the Thames and a range of practices throughout the country variously called 'community', 'fringe' and 'political' theatre. Although there was considerable variation within the field of alternative theatre, few were aiming to widen audiences for the theatrical culture of the National but many were trying to challenge what it represented aesthetically and socially, for instance, in the work of John McGrath (1981) and the 7.84 Theatre Company. Although in retrospect such oppositional practices are often seen to characterize the cultural action of that period, it should be remembered just how marginal they really were. In 1978, thirty travelling theatre companies received just less than £1 million between them in Arts Council grants while the National and the Royal Shakespeare Company shared more than £4 million (Itzin, 1980). The Arts Council was also spending about a million on community arts a year. That same year, Su Braden provoked a bitter counter-attack against community arts when she denounced the Arts Council's support for 'bourgeois' culture in her book, *Artists and People* (see, for example, Hoggart, 1979). In fact, by this time, grants to explicitly leftist theatre groups were already being cut off and community arts were soon to be devolved to the regional arts associations.

Although it was eventually argued from within the community arts movement (Kelly, 1984) that community arts should never have become so dependent upon state subsidy, it is now quite striking how typically the cultural campaigning of the '68 Generation was couched within the terms of the social-democratic discourse of access, a discourse which assumed that the state was the principal actor in the cultural field, contrary to the manifest powers of capital and commodified culture. To a considerable extent, then, the oppositional movements were about taking such discourse seriously by redirecting resources and control to 'the people'. This was also, in effect, part of an erosion of the social-democratic project from inside and which contributed ironically to its vulnerability to the populist assault coming from the New Right.

Market Discourse

The Senior Finance Officer at the Arts Council of Great Britain, Anthony Field, said in 1982:

> It is difficult to persuade people in control of funds that the most difficult time is that involving a real expansion of activity consequent upon a growth of funds. In the period from 1970 to 1980 the Arts Council experienced such a growth and gave priority to the growth of drama groups…The great achievement of the Arts Council subsidies is that they have made the best theatre available so widely…[I]n the last resort, the Arts Council has to hang on to the very best – the rest will survive (or not!) without public subsidy – the dregs of theatre, the mediocre, the work that is up-and-coming or on the way out. What needs subsidy is the forum in which the very best can develop and there are indications that it will have taken the Arts Council a decade to come to terms with how best to utilize new monies. (Field, 1983: 89, 95)

This is the voice of an accountant and, subsequently, an educator of arts administrators at the City University in London. It was not yet the authentic voice of the British New Right in cultural policy since it was still primarily in dispute over cultural value according to the elitist/populist divide, the struggle between 'the best' and 'the dregs' that were said to have flourished under social democracy. But, what Field is saying here already hints at the increasingly powerful language of money and efficiency whereby all value would be reduced to exchange value, the discourse of the market in cultural policy as in everything else.

Soon afterwards, in a position paper for the 1983 GLC (Greater London Council), conference on cultural policy, Nicholas Garnham said:

> [W]hile this tradition [of public cultural policy] has been rejecting the market, most people's cultural needs and aspirations are being, for better or worse, supplied by the market as goods and services. If one turns one's back on an analysis of that dominant cultural process, one cannot understand the culture of our time or the challenges and opportunities which that dominant culture offers to public policy makers. (reprinted in Garnham, 1990: 155)

When Garnham wrote this, the Labour GLC was, in fact, already doomed by Margaret Thatcher's 1983 General Election pledge to abolish it and thus rid the capital city of socialist government. This concentrated minds wonderfully at the GLC, which in its remaining years initiated an influential if only modestly realized policy of investment in 'the cultural industries'. It also showed how public sector culture could be popular fun with its festivals and how exclusion could be countered, for instance, in its encouragement of black film-making and positive discrimination in training.

Of course, Garnham was merely pointing to the glaring fact that state-subsidized and sponsored culture is not the means of cultural provision that captures the attention of most people most of the time, as Mulgan and Worpole (1986) also later insisted in their important book, *Saturday Night or Sunday Morning?*, which signalled a new economic realism and managerialism on the Left of cultural policy debate in Britain. Public cultural policy was indeed small beer, and remains so, when compared with the economic power of cultural business and the popular appeal of commodified culture. However, here I want to make two general and qualifying points, the second more fully than the first. The first is this: to have permitted, for example, Rupert Murdoch to buy up a big chunk of the British press and have allowed News Corp to seize command over satellite broadcasting in Britain were policies, in effect (see Curran and Seaton, 1991, and Chippindale and Franks, 1991). Decisions were taken by government. Such events in the history of what Bernard Miege (1989) has called 'the capitalization of cultural production' are not just 'trends that cannot be bucked'. They are trends that were actively promoted in Britain and elsewhere from the 1970s onwards. And, as now is so acutely evident in Britain – and also, for instance, in Australia and the USA – it does not necessarily seem to matter a great deal what is the apparent political hue of the party in government when dealing with international operators in global and national media markets like Murdoch. Whether there is an ineluctable combination of economic and technological determinism at work here or a pervasive abrogation of public responsibility by national governments is open to debate.

We are plunged, then, into a discourse where it is indeed 'virtually impossible to think outside of'. It is difficult to overestimate how pervasive it became throughout politics and practice. GLC-inspired policies of public cultural investment, for instance, to achieve economic regeneration and urban renewal, were pursued enthusiastically by a number of Labour-controlled local governments through the 1980s and into the 1990s with variable results. The point is not only to evaluate the practical outcomes of such policies in their specific contexts but, rather, to note how the language of cultural policy changed in relation to these and other practices. Simon Frith (1991: 136) posed the question, 'How have local Labour parties come to deploy terms like "market niche" and "corporate image" in their cultural arguments?' Evidently, and putting it very summarily, because of the reality-generating power of market reasoning and the new managerialism that was functioning ubiquitously across the institutions of British society and, for that matter, the world at large.

Perhaps this is 'reality' and, no doubt, we do have to be 'realistic'. We can at least appreciate, however, that it has been constructed, which is an elementary enough observation for social and cultural analysis. This is not only about the actual 'privatization' and 'de-regulation' of communicational and cultural resources. Major cultural businesses do indeed operate on an awesomely global scale and which, in many respects, transcends the powers of any nation-state, with the exception of the USA. Yet, the rhetorics of 'globalization' and of 'rolling back the state' should not be taken too literally at face value. In Britain, the state was not only rolled back with the official aim of returning its powers to 'the people'; it was also rolled forward and centralized (Gamble, 1994). That is why it is necessary to remark upon the colonization of the public sector by market reasoning and to identify some illustrative examples of the discourse in play.

First, there is William Rees-Mogg's at-one-time famous and dubious syllogism on the economic utility of 'investing' in the arts, delivered in his 1985 lecture, 'The Political Economy of Art' at IBM's British headquarters on the South Bank in London. It went like this: in 1984–85, the £100 million of 'taxpayer's money' spent by the Arts Council resulted in £250 million of turnover, creating 25,000 jobs. This produced £75 million of revenue for the Exchequer that was made up of the national insurance and income tax paid by arts workers and VAT on box-office receipts. £50 million was saved in unemployment benefits. For an outlay of £100 million, then, £125 million was returned to the public coffers, a very healthy profit. The quality of Rees-Mogg's reasoning is not primarily what is at stake: it is the discourse of such reasoning itself which is of interest. The justification for public expenditure on the arts is given as making money and, moreover, 'the taxpayer', so beloved of Conservative party discourse, is simultaneously redefined as a shareholder in Yookay PLC.

That same year (1985), the Arts Council issued its *A Great British Success Story*, subtitled 'An Invitation to the Nation to Invest in the Arts'. Again, the significance of this report was not so much its substantive content as the rhetorical form. *A Great British Success Story* presented the case for continuing public expenditure on the arts in the format of a glossy and colourfully illustrated company prospectus, addressing an ideal investor who is seeking a good return on share capital. This was enunciated in the same discursive space as the selling-off of public utilities by the Thatcher governments and the much-vaunted 'spread' of share-ownership during the 1980s. It is hard to recall and appreciate just how novel and controversial it was, in the 1980s, for the state to deploy the techniques of business promotion with such brashness because we have grown so accustomed to the normalization of that discourse in the public sector since then.

The other ideal subject of such discourse, in addition to that of shareholder, is that of His or Her Majesty The Customer, the mythical sovereign consumer who must be obeyed. So, for example, there has been an increasing use of marketing techniques in the arts, which are never simply about giving the customer what he or she is said to want but, rather, a means of increasing sales through a careful profiling of audiences and putting in the effort where it counts. Subscription marketing schemes (Diggle, 1984), for instance, are now ubiquitous, targeted upon increasing attendance by 'attenders' and encouraging 'intenders' to actually attend; and, not wasting time, effort and money on attracting 'non-attenders', as social-democratic cultural policy was supposed to do. A good deal of time and effort is probably wasted, however, on attracting business sponsorship to the arts in Britain, rather differently perhaps from, say, the USA. Business sponsorship in the British case is usually a small fractional supplement to public subsidy and box-office takings. Although that fraction may be seen as vital to survival for many arts organizations, other effects also come into operation. There is a strong case for arguing that the actual effects of business sponsorship have been more ideological than material, most notably by exerting an influence over programme planning and by giving the impression that an arts event has been subsidized solely by the business corporation that has, in fact, only contributed marginally to its production. In addition to functioning as an ostentatious leisure perk for managers and cheap promotional advertising, there is the further problem of rapid turnover in business sponsorship for the arts. However, much public subsidy today has been tagged to the willingness and capacity of arts organizations to attract private funding and to having a properly worked-out business plan.

In his 1993 McTaggart Lecture at the Edinburgh Television Festival, the late Dennis Potter, who in his day was Britain's leading television dramatist, attacked the 'new managerialism' at the BBC. He entitled the lecture, 'Occupying Powers'. This sense of the public sector being occupied by alien power had become intense and widespread by the beginning of the 1990s. Potter virtually spat out the following words at Marmaduke Hussey, then chair of the BBC governors, and his director general, John Birt: 'You pretend to be the commercial business that you cannot be.' Such 'pretence' was not confined to the public sector of arts and broadcasting. It is there in education, health and in the offices of national and local government. This is 'the new public management', described by Andrew Gamble (1994: 135) as 'a set of ideas for managing all institutions in the public sector and involving devices such as internal markets, contracting out, tendering and financial incentives'. All of this is now very familiar in the everyday life of British society and has been most controversial in the National Health Service. With regard to the NHS, John Clarke and Janet Newman (1993: 428) have identified '*managerialization*' as an ideological discourse 'which aims to make management the driving force of a successful society'.

The ur-text for the managerialization of the public sector is the American book, *Reinventing Government*, by David Osborne and Ted Gaebler, which British as well as American politicians, not only on the Right, took to quoting approvingly. It is said to have been hugely influential at the higher echelons of both the Democratic and Labour Parties (Painter, 1994). Osborne and Gaebler are disciples of the renowned management gurus, Peter Drucker and Tom Peters. They claim, however, that their managerial principles are inferred primarily from the practical experiments of US city governments in response to the 'tax revolts' of the late 1970s and, more generally, derive from the structural transformations that were brought about by the transition to a 'postindustrial' society. Under tight budgetary constraints and faced with radically changed economic circumstances, governments have had to become much more 'enterprising' than they were during what Osborne and Gaebler call the 'bureaucratic-industrial' era. Their book is typical of the rhetoric of management texts. It presents a set of simple and supposedly irrefutable propositions that are driven home through didactic repetition and to each of which a chapter is devoted. Osborne and Gaebler's 'ten principles' are as follows:

> Most entrepreneurial governments promote *competition* between service providers. They *empower* citizens by pushing control out of the bureaucracy, into the community. They measure the performance of their agencies, focusing not on inputs but on *outcomes*. They define their clients as *customers* and offer them choice – between schools, between training programs, between housing options. They *prevent* problems before they emerge, rather than simply offering services afterwards. They put their energies into *earning* money, not simply spending it. They *decentralize* authority, embracing participatory management. They prefer *market* mechanisms. And they focus not simply on, providing public services, but on *catalysing* all sectors – public, private, and voluntary – into action to solve their community's problems. (Osborne and Gaebler, 1992: 199–20; original emphasis)

Although Osborne and Gaebler denied they were asking for government to be 'run like a business', it is difficult to see quite how they could justify such a denial. Their ideas were clearly formed by the practical discourses of the most dynamic business corporations in the USA: theirs is a capitalist utopia in which the techniques of upbeat and 'postmodern' capitalism hold sway. The affinities with Conservative government in Britain during the recent period were plainly evident. The election of the New Labour government in Britain in 1997, however, did not result in a sudden change of affinity. The suits with their management bibles did not go away, whether at the level of elected government or anywhere else throughout the public or private sectors of British governance.

Civil Discourse

Nicholas Garnham (1995: 376) has remarked, 'the question of the Public Sphere now occupies a central position on the media studies agenda. In the face of the demonstrable crisis in the forms and practices of democracy in Western capitalist polities, and of attempts to reconstruct forms of democratic politics in the ex-socialist countries, it has taken over the central role previously occupied by the dominant ideology or hegemony.' So, the best critical hope, according to Garnham, is the reconstitution of what was a progressive bourgeois and extremely contradictory discursive formation dating from the eighteenth and early nineteenth centuries. It would seem, for example, a long way from the anarchistic delight in the liberating powers of 'virtual community' on the Net (Rheingold, 1995). And, yet, when *Wired* put Tom Paine on the cover of its first British edition, the connection was there to be seen. That the British version of *Wired* failed because its American agenda was only thinly veiled does not alter the general point about this virtualization of radical democracy, the way in which political hopes thus engendered have been so much associated with the magical powers of computer networking.

There is a perennial issue of debate concerning Habermas' (1962/89) original account of the rise and fall of the bourgeois public sphere and its latterday manifestations: is the public sphere actual or ideal? (see Calhoun, 1992). For Habermas, I believe, it is both: the public sphere has demonstrably existed in the past, although undermined by manipulative communications in the present, yet still serving as a beleagured actuality, and may yet function as a normative guide and refreshment of democratic practice in the future. Something similar can be said of Habermas' much more abstract theoretical treatment of the recursive conditions for satisfactory communication, which he has described as 'undistorted communication' (1970) or 'the ideal speech situation' (1979). For Habermas (1990), the validity claims that are made and subjected routinely to criticism in everyday discursive interaction demonstrate the human capacity for mutual understanding. This also connects up with Habermas' (1987) distinction between 'lifeworld' and 'system'. Communicative action to achieve mutual understanding is an ordinary feature of everyday life and which exceeds mere instrumentality. In contrast, the systemic imperatives of the state and capital operate according to an instrumental rationality in strategic pursuit of predefined goals, not a communicative rationale for debating and agreeing goals. The central problem of contemporary societies, then, according to Habermas' theory of communicative action, is 'the colonization of the lifeworld' by instrumental reason and the resistance that is waged with the communicative resources of everyday life.

Habermas' reasoning is directly relevant to discussion of cultural policy and, if nothing else, indicates why many who are interested specifically in 'culture' prefer not to talk of cultural policy. To talk of cultural policy is to run the risk of potentially instrumentalizing culture, of reducing it to something other than what it is. The discourses of state and market, in effect, instrumentalize culture, to make it, for example, a means of simply embellishing the nation-state (Williams, 1984), or, as I have suggested, by reducing all value to exchange value through the marketization of everything in a globalizing cultural economy. The notion of a civil society, closely associated with the historical phenomenon of the bourgeois public sphere, has been a means of checking the powers of the state whilst simultaneously creating the conditions for market relations to develop, which is very much how civil society was imagined in Eastern Europe in the late 1980s and early 1990s. The paradoxical problem is, however, that the liberalizing force of rational–critical debate, which is what the public sphere is about, has contributed historically to a liberalization of the economy that eventually threatens civil society itself as the space between the state and the market: and, in our present historical conjuncture, it is again 'the market' which is the main encroachment upon the lifeworld of civil society.

To speak of 'the public sphere', 'civil society' and 'the lifeworld' is to speak of formations less immediately tangible than the powers of the nation-state or the capitalist market. Yet these remain concepts which though not necessarily named as such, nevertheless, animate alternative and oppositional practices. For instance, Nancy Fraser (1992) has spoken of 'the subaltern counterpublic' of American feminism with its communicative networks and its cultural and political impact on the system. Paul Gilroy (1993) has spoken of the diasporic public sphere of 'the Black Atlantic'. Douglas Kellner (1995) has urged critical intellectuals to use modern media and information technologies in the struggle to revivify the public sphere under late-modern conditions. Generally, I would suggest, social and cultural critique is dependent upon some notion of a public sphere or civil discourse as a critical measure of democratic blockage and as a practical check on systemic abuse of democracy.

In his latest major work, *Between Facts and Norms*, Habermas has returned to the theme of the public sphere in the context of a discussion of law (see Carleheden and Gabriel, 1996). There he says:

> The public sphere is a social phenomenon just as elementary as action, actor, association, or collectivity…The public sphere cannot be conceived of as an institution and certainly not as an organization. It is not even a framework of norms…The public sphere can best be described as a network for communicating information and points of view (i.e. opinions expressing affirmative or negative attitudes); the streams of communication are, in process, filtered in such a way that they coalesce into bundles of topically specified *public* opinions. (Habermas, 1996: 360)

Placing less stress now on the colonization thesis, though not discarding it, Habermas emphasizes the 'sluice gate' role of the public sphere between life-world concerns and systems of governmental administration and business. Talking of 'the great issues of the last decades', including the arms race, the risks of nuclear energy and scientific applications such as genetic engineering, damage to the environment, famine and global economic inequality, feminism, increased migration and multi-culturalism, Habermas (1996: 381) remarks, '[h]ardly any of these were *initially* brought up by exponents of the state apparatus, large organizations, or functional systems'. The key players have been critical intellectuals, social movements and new subcultures.

It is sobering to consider, however, in conclusion, just how many specifically cultural movements, movements that are concerned directly with symbolic process in its own right and not only as a mediation of emergent political issues, have been animated by conservative resistance to post-traditional morality. These too are participants in the public sphere. They do not typically fulfil the criteria of reasonable argumentation required by Habermas' discourse ethics: their validity claims are usually asserted in a manner which they believe is uncriticizable. When it comes, for instance, to questions concerning children's use of media, their conviction that children's attitudes and behaviour are effectively harmed by viewing representations of violence usually ignores or rejects out of hand the more complex arguments about meaning and affect that are made by libertarian and anti-censorship intellectuals, who on the other hand wind up, however, often in practice and perhaps unwittingly, simply defending the capitalist conflation of free speech and the free market (see, for instance, Barker and Petley, 1997). As I have argued elsewhere (McGuigan, 1996), the libertarian defence is flawed by a refusal to pay attention to reasonable and widespread parental anxieties about children's consumption of media products, which are thus left to be exploited by conservative moralists; and, furthermore, such libertarianism is unable to contribute much to critical public debate about the role of media corporations in the moral education of children.

That is just one example of how critical and oppositional forces tend to exclude themselves from effective participation in the democratic process. Other examples, and more generally, might include the embrace of marginality predicated upon an assumption that the centre or mainstream of social and cultural life are utterly and hopelessly benighted. Some kinds of identity politics, with their particularism and anarchism, frequently constitute a retreat from effective political engagement and, often in practice, a certain acquiescence with dominant powers.

The systemic forces of state and capital are no guardians of a public sphere, though they do need its feedback mechanisms to prevent system ossification. In that sense, the formal 'democracy' of the capitalist West has indeed been much superior to the spurious 'democracy' of the failed communist East. However, systemic forces cannot be relied upon to maintain a properly functioning public sphere; only citizens feeling and acting vigilantly in their own and others' interests can do that effectively. Social and cultural movements of one kind or another, and not always 'progressive', unfortunately, contesting conventional wisdoms and demanding greater equitability against the enormous odds that are stacked in favour of the state and capital, are the actual and potential means of sustaining and developing the rights of citizens, cultural and otherwise. The value, then, of an active civil discourse – and, when necessary, civil disobedience – is not only a matter of utopian optimism but a vital safeguard of what little democracy we have in a world dominated by instrumental rationality whether of the nation-state or common-market variety.

Note

An earlier version of this chapter was presented as a paper at the University of Sussex's 'Teaching Culture and the Cultures of Teaching' conference in March 1996. I thank the participants in my session and, in particular, Georgios Daramas and Richard Johnson for their comments on what I had to say then. I also thank the editor of this book Nick Stevenson for pointing out that my fascination with Habermas' discourse ethics should not cause me to forget Williams' stress on political struggle.

References

Arts Council (1985) *A Great British Success Story – An Invitation to the Nation to Invest in the Arts.* London: ACGB.

Barker, M. and Petley, J. (eds) (1997) *Ill Effects – The Media/Violence Debate.* London/New York: Routledge.

Braden, S. (1978) *Artists and People.* London: Routledge.

Calhoun, C. (ed.) (1992) *Habermas and the Public Sphere.* Massachusetts Institute of Technology.

Carleheden, M. and Gabriel, R. (1996) 'An Interview with Jurgen Habermas', *Theory, Culture & Society,* 13 (3).

Chippindale, P. and Franks, S. (1991) *Dished – The Rise and Fall of British Satellite Broadcasting.* London: Simon & Schuster.

Clarke, J. and Newman, J. (1993) 'The Right to Manage – A Second Managerial Revolution?', *Cultural Studies,* 7 (3).

Curran, J. and Seaton, J. (1991) *Power Without Responsibility – The Press and Broadcasting in Britain.* London: Routledge.

Davis, M. (1993a) 'Who Killed LA? A Political Autopsy', *New Left Review,* 197.

Davis, M. (1993b) 'Who Killed Los Angeles? Part Two – The Verdict is Given', *New Left Review,* 199.

Dent, G. (ed.) (1992) *Black Popular Culture.* Seattle: Bay Press.

Diggle, K. (1984) *Guide to Arts Marketing.* London: Rheingold.

Field, A. (1983) 'Experiment and Public Accountability', in J. Shanahan (ed.), *Economic Support for the Arts.* Association for Cultural Economics/University of Akron.

Fraser, N. (1992) 'Rethinking the Public Sphere – A Contribution to the Critique of Actually Existing Democracy', in C. Calhoun (ed.), *Habermas and the Public Sphere.* Massachusetts Institute of Technology.

Frith, S. (1991) 'The Culture of the Cultural Industries', *Cultural Studies from Birmingham* 1, University of Birmingham.

Gamble, A. (1994) *The Free Economy and the Strong State – The Politics of Thatcherism.* London: Macmillan.

Garnham, N. (1990) *Capitalism and Communication – Global Culture and the Economics of Information.* London: Sage.

Garnham, N. (1995) 'The Media and Narratives of the Intellectual', *Media, Culture & Society,* 17 (3).

Gellner, E. (1996) *Conditions of Liberty – Civil Society and Its Rivals.* London: Penguin.

Gilroy, P. (1993) *The Black Atlantic.* London: Verso.

Gorky, M., Radek, K., Bukharin, N., Zhdanov, A. et al. (1977) *Soviet Writers' Congress 1934 – The Debate on Socialist Realism and Modernism.* London: Lawrence & Wishart.

Habermas, J. (1962/89) *The Structural Transformation of the Public Sphere.* Cambridge: Polity.

Habermas, J. (1970) 'Toward a Theory of Communicative Competence', in H. Dreitzel (ed.), *Recent Sociology No. 2 – Patterns of Communicative Behaviour.* New York: Macmillan.

Habermas, J. (1979) *Communication and the Evolution of Society.* London: Heinemann.

Habermas, J. (1987) *The Theory of Communicative Action, Volume Two – The Critique of Functionalist Reason.* Cambridge: Polity.

Habermas, J. (1990) *Moral Consciousness and Communicative Action.* Cambridge: Polity.

Habermas, J. (1996) *Between Facts and Norms.* Cambridge: Polity.

Haraszti, M. (1989) *The Velvet Prison – Artists Under State Socialism.* London: Penguin.

Hoggart, R. (1979) 'How Should We Pay for the Arts?', *New Society,* 2 August.

Itzin, C. (1980) *Stages in the Revolution – Political Theatre in Britain Since 1968.* London: Methuen.

Kellner, D. (1995) 'Intellectuals and New Technologies', *Media Culture & Society,* 17 (3).

Kelly, O. (1984) *Community, Art and the State – Storming the Citadels.* London: Comedia.

McGrath, J. (1981) *A Good Night Out – Popular Theatre, Audience, Class and Form.* London: Methuen.

McGuigan, J. (1996) *Culture and the Public Sphere.* London: Routledge.

Miege, B. (1989) *The Capitalization of Cultural Production.* New York: International General.

Mulgan, G. and Worpole, K. (1986) *Saturday Night or Sunday Morning? – From Arts to Industry, New Forms of Cultural Policy.* London: Comedia.

Osborne, D. and Gaebler, T. (1992) *Reinventing Government – How the Entrepreneurial Spirit is Transforming the Public Sector.* Reading, MA: Addison-Wesley.

Painter, C. (1994) 'Public Service Reform – Reinventing or Abandoning Government?', *Political Quarterly,* 26 (3).

Pecheux, M. (1982) *Language, Semantics and Ideology.* London: Macmillan.

Rees-Mogg, W. (1985) 'The Political Economy of Art', Lecture, IBM. London: ACGB.

Rheingold, H. (1995) *The Virtual Community – Surfing the Net.* London: Minerva.

Shklovsky, V. (1974) *Mayakovsky and His Circle.* London: Pluto.

White, A. (1990) *De-Stalinization and the House of Culture – Declining State Control Over Leisure in the USSR, Poland and Hungary 1953–89.* London: Routledge.

Williams, R. (1971) *Culture and Society.* London: Penguin.

Williams, R. (1979) 'The Arts Council', *Political Quarterly,* 50 (2).

Williams, R. (1984) 'State Culture and Beyond', in L. Apignanesi (ed.), *Culture and the State.* London: Institute of Contemporary Arts.

Young, R. (ed.) (1981) *Untying the Text.* London: Routledge.

9

FEMINISM AND CITIZENSHIP

Anna Yeatman

I think the time will come when men and women will wonder that they ever found it necessary to form a league to gain for women the right to choose those who make the laws she must obey; when it will be recognized everywhere that woman, man's inferior in some respects, his superior in others, is absolutely his equal in her right to govern herself; when it will be thought absurd that drunkards, fools and reprobates should make the laws they live to break, while only women, classed with children and idiots, should be silent.

> (From a speech by the Australian suffragist Marybanke Wolstenholme in 1891, and published verbatim in *The Daily Telegraph*, cited by Roberts, 1996: 27–28)

It was not an uncommon rhetorical resort for white suffragists of the nineteenth and early twentieth centuries in such societies as Britain, the United States and Australia to point out what they saw as an obvious and stark anomaly. Namely, that men either of backgrounds marked by Western racist discourse as oriental or uncivilized (as black and aboriginal 'races' were seen to be), or who were white but uneducated, drunkards or generally uncouth, might have the vote and become citizens before white, educated and temperate women did. The suffragist argument turned on the proposition that these women were more capable of governing themselves than uncivilized men and uncivilized races. In their insistence on this, suffragists reinforced the idea that citizenship was a matter of self-government. It linked self-governing individuals to the government of a self-governing political community.

Contemporary feminism is historically positioned in ways which require it to have a more complex and ambivalent relationship to what we may see as the classical-modern project of citizenship: self-government both for individuals as citizens and for the national citizen community. Where nation building is still salient as an historic project, as it is for instance in both the contemporary republican debate in Australia and the post-apartheid South African state, when it is oriented to this project feminism operates in terms of the metaphors of self-government. In these contexts, feminism pursues a politics of inclusion. Thus, for example, in the Australian case feminist groups are seeking to be included in whatever constitutional convention on making Australia a republic for the new millennium may still eventuate. This type of feminism is exemplified in these remarks of the then highly respected leader of the minority party Australian Democrats, Cheryl Kernot (1996: 84–85):

Feminists have a vital role to play in ensuring that constitutional change focuses on substantive reforms to achieve equality between women and men – and that sort of change is certainly not going to become a key plank of the republican movement unless women take action to force it onto the republican agenda…

The future meaning of citizenship must also form a central focus of the republic debate. We cannot develop a truly comprehensive pro-republic position without canvassing the issue of what it means to be an Australian – and that is a discussion which is highly relevant to Australian women.

At the same time, the conception of citizenship in terms of self-government has become problematized in a number of respects. The politics of difference which is tied to issues of recognition and reparation in relation to indigenous peoples within the white settler nations of Canada, New Zealand and Australia is central to this problematization. How is it possible to determine 'what it means to be an Australian' when both these 'peoples' are to be accommodated within the one national jurisdiction?[1] It is for this reason that the meaning of the term 'New Zealander' has thinned in the face of contemporary reference to Pakeha (white settler New Zealanders) and Maori (indigenous New Zealanders), and only gets revived in rugby matches between New Zealand and Australia (or South Africa etc.).

Contemporary feminism has also contributed to the problematization of citizenship defined in terms of an independent self-governing national community. Along with movements such as the disability movement, contemporary feminism questions whether citizen standing should be confounded with a conception of self-government in terms of independence (see for example Kiss, 1997; Narayan, 1997), and at what price for individuals who are so positioned that they cannot be independent, that is function without depending on the assistance of others. Contemporary feminism is exploring different conceptions of political personhood (Fraser, 1996; Kiss, 1997; Narayan, 1997). I call this a post-patrimonial conception of personhood for reasons I shall explain. Finally, post-colonial currents within feminism are questioning the equation of citizenship with nationality and the implications which follow from this for the increasing number of individuals in national jurisdictions who are non-citizen residents or illegal aliens (Narayan, 1997; see also Ang, 1996).

These currents in contemporary feminism depart from the kind of feminism which has been shaped by the modern democratic project of citizenship as (individual and national) self-government. Like other contributors to a post-national conception of human rights and citizenship, these currents operate in another paradigm altogether. A paradigm that does not equate citizen standing with a capacity for self-government but extends human rights to all who are communicative beings where communication is understood to involve more than clearly articulated speech. A paradigm also that refigures citizen standing in terms of human rights which are claimable within jurisdictions that are not coterminous with nation-states. These jurisdictions may be trans-national or, in the case of dialogic co-existence and negotiated settlement between settler and indigenous stakeholders within a nation, sub-national. Participation in these jurisdictions is not tied to 'membership' of a national citizen community. In this way it is a post-national type of democratic participation.

In what follows, I discuss first the feminism which is oriented to inclusion within and completion of an independent national citizen community. I select examples of first wave feminism in the Anglo-American democracies because it comes into being in relation to the classical nation-building projects of the nineteenth century. As I have indicated, echoes of this type of feminism persist and will do so as long as democratic nation building has any salience. I argue that the kind of democratic citizenship which is implicated in metaphors of nation building as a project of self-government is patrimonial in character. In the second section, I discuss post-patrimonial and post-colonial currents of contemporary feminism as they bear on a new paradigm of democratic citizenship.

Feminism is a creature of these historical trajectories of democratic citizenship. There is no single story to tell about its relationship to citizenship, only many stories which bring out the internal and changing complexity of feminism in relation to the historical dynamics of democratic citizenship.

Feminism and the Self-governing National Citizen Community

The dominant or hegemonic conception of citizenship is tied to a construction of what it means to be self-governing either as an individual or as a political community. This conception has its roots in the Aristotelian account of politics. In that account, the individual is self-governing only because he is an independent head of a household and is thus placed in a position of domestic government over others; the self-governing political community or *polis* is the political association of such self-governing or 'free' individuals. I call this a patrimonial conception of democratic citizenship because citizenship is associated with a condition of propertied independence which is expressed as a relationship both of self-government and government of those who are one's dependants. The democratic component of this conception refers to the political association which is consensually brought into being and sustained by individual independent householders (or citizens). This is a *patrimonial* conception of citizenship because the political personhood on which it depends is ethically modelled after the household authority of a master over his dependants (Weber, 1968: 1010–1013). The ethos of the patrimonial *oikos* underwrites the authority of the imperial and colonizing projects of modern Western nations in relation to peoples who these nations regard as uncivilized and incapable of self-government. It also informs the authority of the twentieth-century welfare state which is exercised over all those who are deemed deserving of 'protection'.

Within the discourse of patrimonial democratic citizenship, then, individuals get access to citizenship only if they can demonstrate that they are self-governing; and a nation is constituted only when independent statehood is achieved of a kind that licenses this political community to assume patrimonial-imperial authority over subject peoples in non-nations. What distinguishes modern patrimonial democratic discourse from the Aristotelian one is the former's attachment to the doctrine of natural right in its early modern Christian versions. On this doctrine all human beings are born equal as God's creatures, and they are the species upon whom God has endowed the capacity to reason. Independence or self-government in this frame of reference is associated with a mature, educated and thus independent capacity to reason which is not the same thing as household headship. There is then a tension which arises within modern democratic citizenship between its patrimonial and natural right components, a tension that might be termed one between the patriarchal and natural right versions of patrimonialism. It is this tension which calls modern feminism into being in the seventeenth century as is exemplified in Mary Astell's question (cited by Mitchell, 1976: 387) of John Locke's political reasoning in his *Two Treatises of Government*: 'If all Men are born free, how is it that all Women are born slaves? As they must be if the being subject to the inconstant, uncertain, unknown, arbitrary Will of Men [as heads of households], be the perfect condition of Slavery?'

Feminism develops as a political movement on behalf of women's accession to citizenship which exploits the tension between the patriarchal and patrimonial-natural right conceptions of modern-patrimonial citizenship. In order to bring women into citizenship, feminism has to elaborate on the assumptions of natural right in such a way that women can claim an independent capacity to reason and thus be self-governing rather than be the dependants of patriarchal household heads. In order to argue this, feminism has to work within the paradigm of citizenship conceived as self-government. This commits feminism to a feminine version of patrimonial independence, one where educated women are fit to be self-governing citizens who can extend their feminine rule of patronage and protection to the weak and needy, those who lack the capacity for self-government. This type of feminism thus makes its own distinctive contribution to the hierarchical humanist discourse of the duty of 'protection' which those who are self-governing subjects owe to those who are not.

It may seem odd to call feminist conceptions of individual independence patrimonial. They are patrimonial because they sustain the conception of property or propriety which is at the root of patrimonialism: namely the idea that an individual is his/her own person because he/she owns his/her will, person and all that is necessary by way of things to secure this propriety of self-hood. It is this independence or property in the self which constitutes a capacity for political independence that arises from an individual's ability to rationally govern both himself and those who fall under his protection. These are individuals who are not subject to the authority of any other except by their consent, and they are free to withdraw this consent if once they give it. Property in this sense of a right to be one's own person and freedom are co-determining ideas in this construction of the political personality.[2] Property in this conception refers to an exclusive right of ownership (in one's will, person, things) which cannot be shared with others if the individual is to be independent. The propertied individual in this way owns his/her will, embodied person, and material things. It is obvious that individuals who do not have the capacity to move, think, or will independently cannot be propertied, free citizens and that they must fall under the 'protection' of those who are.

Patrimonial feminism, then, takes the humanist egalitarianism of natural right only so far, and perhaps as far as the natural right type of egalitarianism can go.

Arguably, natural right even in its most egalitarian Protestant versions tacitly presupposes patrimonial right: the individual can be 'naturally' free only because he or she is endowed with patrimonial resources of independence. Individuals have to naturally become independent in the sense of cultivating their divinely endowed capacity to reason. In this framework, there can be no reference to a conception of government which positively constitutes in all regardless of their degree of 'independence' individualized capacities for participation in social life. This would be a post-patrimonial conception of the bases of individualized personhood (see Yeatman, 1997a).

As an historical project, feminism, then, comes into being within a 'patrimonial' conception of democratic participation in terms of self-government. For this reason, this type of feminism is not a champion of the rights of those who cannot effectively claim to be self-governing: for example, children and all adults who for reasons of cognitive and/or moral impairment are not accorded the right to be self-governing. First-wave feminists in arguing that women, civilized women at least, were capable of self-government had to contest the masculinist-patrimonial models of self-government that prevailed at this time. On these models, self-government was possible only if an individual possessed the kind of propertied independence that permitted him to be head of a household. By the second half of the nineteenth century, it was increasingly accepted that property of this kind could be property in one's own capacity to labour, not just property in land and capital (see Hall, 1994; Scott, 1996: Ch. 3; Stanley, 1988). Accordingly, working-class men were able to claim inclusion within a universal male suffrage and the status of independence that followed upon a patrimonial household headship. For the wives of propertied men to be also included within the franchise and to be granted citizenship, patriarchal forms of patrimonial independence had to give ground to individualized conceptions of patrimonial independence. Self-government was no longer tied to patrimonial household headship but to the political and social adulthood of individuals educated to use their reason and who are constituted as the owners of their wills and capacities. Property as the basis of a capacity for political independence and self-government is sustained in this shift. Political personality is still identified with the capacity to be one's own person in a way that firmly rules out of citizenship those who for some reason cannot aspire to or attain this condition.

The masculinism of nineteenth century working men's movements, as well as that of the post-bellum movement on behalf of the ex-slave freedmen, continued to emphasize a patriarchal construction of patrimonial independence. Patrimonial independence positions male household heads in a relationship of dominion to their wives, children and household servants. The household head possesses a 'property right in his family' (Stanley, 1988: 480; also Scott, 1996: 63–64).

In order to claim for women accession to the individualized capacity for self-government, and thus qualification for citizenship, nineteenth century suffragists had to offer an alternative conception of political personhood. They rejected the domestic despotism which they saw as inherent in conceptions of the franchise which maintained men's independence as householders in governance over women as their dependants. As Stanley (1988: 480–481) puts it in relation to the

American republican discourse of Reconstruction which extended individualized contractual standing to freedmen: 'To conceive the wife as a contracting individual was to subvert the animating principles of republicanism, which defined the free-man, the citizen, as a household proprietor whose rights embraced dominion over his wife, including title to her person, labor, and wages.'

Nineteenth century feminists had to refuse patriarchal models of independence and self-government, but they did not, and given the terms of political discourse of the time, could not, refuse the association of citizenship with an individualized capacity for self-government. Such a capacity cannot be stripped of its patrimonial associations even when it is made over to the cause of women in process of eman-cipating themselves from patrimonial domination. Self-government makes sense only as it is contrasted with an incapacity to govern oneself. Correlatively, those who are constituted as self-governing subjects are simultaneously positioned as subjects who being free and independent in this way are capable of governing those who are not. A feminist deployment of the classical democratic rhetoric of self-government maintains patrimonialism but gives it a distinctive feminine and maternalistic cast. In this way, emancipated women come to share in the patri-monial authority of self-government both as individuals and as members of self-governing political communities.

The patrimonial-natural right cast of first wave feminism explains the complex interweaving of the discourses of egalitarianism and imperial racism in move-ment rhetoric. It explains also the rancour of such feminist-suffragists when 'their' men give preference to the enfranchisement of men of class or race back-grounds that are seen as making them less educated and civilized, and thus less equipped for self-government and the government of others, than themselves. Grimshaw (1996: 77–78) offers a particularly good Australian example of such rancour with reference to Vida Goldstein, a prominent Victorian suffragist, who in 1900 began editing *The Australian Woman's Sphere*:

> On the cover page of the October edition of the journal, Goldstein spelt out pictorially one of the arguments on which suffragists based their case, in a cartoon entitled 'Voters and Voteless'. Depicted at the centre is a young woman, neatly attired in academic gown and mortar, reading a book; behind her are shelves filled with further scholarly volumes. She stands, apparently, as the model of modern elevated womanhood, edu-cated, knowledgable and serious. She is also 'voteless', defined as undeserving of the boon of citizenship. The female graduate is surrounded by a series of crude caricatures of men who are, by contrast, citizens, and hence exercise the vote. Six men are white: an effete dandy; a hopeless drunk; an uncouth, aggressive lout; a prize fighter; an igno-rant, fatuous politician; and a wife-beater, his boot captured in the act of kicking the prostrate form of his fragile wife. The remaining two of these male figures are not white. One is an Aborigine, dishevelled, bare-chested, shoeless, a boomerang in one hand, a bottle of alcohol in the other. 'I Have a Vote' runs the simple but telling caption. The second is Chinese, portrayed as overweight and smoking a long pipe, his facial features exaggerated: 'So Havve Ah Chew Fat Plenty Savee Vote'.

On the other hand, the egalitarian assumptions of natural right positioned first wave feminism as an ally of the nineteenth century abolitionist movement which sought to end the system of slavery in the United States and European colonies such as the West Indies. As long as their male citizen allies supported the enfranchisement of women and slaves, nineteenth century feminists were willing to sustain an egalitarian discourse of natural right. When their male citizen allies broke with this egalitarianism in favour of a patriarchal conception of patrimonial right, thus favouring working class and black men over women, nineteenth century feminists could not help but bring out the distinctive racism of patrimonial democracy in their insistence that the kind of women they represented were better equipped for self-government than many men.

In the Australian case, by the time of federation in 1901 suffrage feminism was generally committed to the cause of a 'white' Australia, a virtually consensual cause shared with their white settler counterparts, and advocated for by the young Australian labour movement (see Grimshaw, 1996).[3] On the other hand, in New Zealand, suffrage feminism was oriented with an egalitarian conception of political rights for both Pakeha and Maori. These two white settler colonies saw Maori as people who possessed the key traits of civilization in a way that Australian Aborigines did not.[4] Because the citizens of the newly established Australian Commonwealth still wanted to entice New Zealand to join it at a time when both Maori men and women could vote alongside their Pakeha counterparts (Grimshaw, 1996: 84–86), the Australian Commonwealth Franchise Act extended to adult women the right to vote and stand for the federal parliament, but excluded all Aboriginal natives of Australia, Asia, Africa and the Pacific, with the exception of Maori (Grimshaw, 1996: 78). Thus, it was how the historical terms of their case for an equal title to membership of the national citizen community were set that determined whether and in what ways egalitarianism prevailed over patrimonial racism in nineteenth century feminism, or the reverse. The history of the relationship of the women's suffrage movement to abolitionism both before and after the Civil War in the United States is instructive of this complexity in feminism's relationship to the democratic patrimonial discourse of self-government.

Prior to the Civil War, feminism and abolitionism were partners in a shared cause of enfranchisement for both slaves and women. The rhetoric was one of common and equal humanity. The analogy between the condition of slaves and wives as both dependants of patrimonial masters was often made. Stanley (1988: 478) comments: 'Employing the imagery of slavery, woman's rights advocates assailed the anomalies of marriage in a society that discountenanced bondage and dependence and paid homage to the equal rights of sovereign individuals.' After the Civil War, during Reconstruction, the male leaders of abolitionism pursued the cause of the freedmen and dropped their support for female suffrage (see Du Bois, 1978: Chs 2 and 3). The leaders of the women's suffrage movement attempted to maintain the pre-bellum abolitionist association between the enfranchisement of women and that of slaves with Susan Anthony in 1866 calling the movement for women's rights a movement for *human* rights. However, the historical alliance between these two causes broke down with the introduction into Congress of the fourteenth Amendment to the Constitution in 1865, the principal thrust of which was to establish the supremacy of national citizenship over state provisions with regard to the civil and political rights of ex-slaves, of freed*men*. Ellen Du Bois as she tells this history comments:

From the very beginning of Reconstruction, abolitionist leaders indicated that woman suffrage would not be part of their efforts. They believed that the demand for women's enfranchisement was a burden they could not carry if they were going to overcome the enormous opposition to black suffrage. (Du Bois, 1978: 59)

Two decades of women's rights agitation had destroyed the centuries-old assumption that political rights applied only to men. Accordingly, the Republican authors of the Fourteenth Amendment...had to decide between enfranchising women or specifying male citizens as the basis of representation. They chose the latter, writing the word 'male' into the amendment and introducing an explicit sexual distinction into the Constitution for the first time. (Du Bois, 1978: 60)

By 1868, after the definitive abandonment of the women's suffrage cause by the abolitionists and Republican Party in the Kansas referenda in 1867, Anthony had resorted to what nowadays would be called a separatist conception of the feminist movement, namely an attachment to the women's rights movement as an autonomous political movement.[5] This positioned her in the race politics of the United States at that time as a potential ally of white supremacists within the Democratic Party (discussed by Du Bois, 1978: Ch. 3) and permitted her co-leader of the women's rights movement, Elizabeth Cady Stanton, to say:

It becomes a serious question whether we had better stand aside and see 'Sambo' walk into the kingdom first...'This is the negro's hour'. Are we sure that he, once entrenched in all his inalienable rights, may not be an added power to hold us at bay...it is better to be the slave of an educated white man, than of a degraded ignorant black one...(cited by Hall, 1994: 25)

It was also obvious to these nineteenth century feminists that children, idiots, lunatics and prisoners should not be enfranchised. Individuals who fell into these categories were not capable of self-government, that was demonstrably clear, and most certainly could not be put in a position of the government of others. By positioning themselves alongside adult, civilized men as capable of governing themselves and others, these feminists maintained the identification of citizenship with a modified form of patrimonial independence. If independence is the *sine qua non* of individualized political personhood, this is a discourse which will require distinctions to be made between those who are capable and those who are incapable of such independence.

When democratic participation is confounded with a cluster of values that bring together terms such as independence, autonomy and self-determination, there are stringent tests of the kind of personhood that is admitted into democratic participation, tests that a great many human beings cannot pass. Equality in this context refers to the equality of self-governing, independent persons or, at least, to the equality of those who can reasonably aspire to be independent. In the context of patrimonial democratic discourse, the historical project of feminism has been to claim for (white, educated) women this status of self-government. This attachment to citizenship conceived as a propertied independence and capacity for self-government has also characterized the class-based and anti-colonial movements that have their roots in nineteenth century rhetorics of emancipation: the union movements and post-colonial movements for independent statehood, for example.

Feminism and Post-patrimonial/Post-national Citizenship

While the paradigm of citizenship conceived as self-government still has considerable salience, it is being displaced by a number of developments which it cannot accommodate. The first of these concerns the extension of human rights to individuals who are not capable of governing themselves. Children are an obvious case in point but such individuals also include older people with dementia and many people with intellectual and/or psychiatric disabilities. The second involves the displacement and decentering of a state-centric national policy by various kinds of strategic alliance and negotiated interaction between different kinds of stakeholder, both governmental and non-governmental. For example, the national-centrist dynamics of the Australian state in the 1990s are not as significant as they were in the 1970s and for most of the 1980s in the face of the enterprise of provincial level (state) governments in developing strategic links with other national governments in the region (e.g. the growing relationship between the Northern Territory and Indonesia). Moreover, the idea that there can be a sub-national, regional negotiated settlement across key stakeholders in relation to indigenous Australians' native title to use of the land is already practically exemplified in the Cape York Heads of Agreement in North Queensland, even if it has lacked in (both national and provincial) governmental recognition and does not get off the ground. Such an agreement is indicative of a stakeholder politics that is not containable within the established governmental process of a bounded unitary decisionism. Finally, the reciprocal enmeshing of commercial markets and the new information technologies at this time has opened up networks of interaction and participation which cannot be subsumed within or mapped onto the jurisdictional boundaries of governments and intergovernmental entities.

All of these developments suggest possibilities of participation which cannot be grasped by the democratic-patrimonial model of citizenship as membership of an independent, self-governing citizen community. Contemporary feminism is responding to these developments in ways which are suggestive of a post-patrimonial and post-national conception of citizenship.

First, feminist scholars are reconceptualizing political personhood so that it refers to rights of participation which can be exercised by anyone who is able to participate in what Seyla Benhabib calls in a revisionist reworking of Habermas' communicative ethics, an ideal communication community. As Benhabib makes clear, respect for the equality and autonomy of individuals even when they are dependent on the assistance of others in order to move, eat, think, etc., can be tendered or not tendered. For a parent to respect the equality and autonomy of an infant, for example, is to invite the infant to participate in the communicative interaction which this relationship constitutes.[6] An individual's lack of independence, in other words, does not have to invite an ethic of paternalistic or maternalistic protection; instead, it can invite an ethic of universal moral respect and egalitarian reciprocity, to use Benhabib's (1992: 31) terminology. This is why there has been such a bitter struggle in the service areas of accommodation for people with disabilities and people who are frail and aged to get service providers to move beyond an ethic of patrimonial care where independent care-givers provide services in ways that position those who need them as people who cannot look after themselves. Policy is now moving in the direction of providing services in ways which respect and respond to the individualized personhood of those who need them.

Feminist political and legal theorists as well as feminist policy practitioners have offered theoretical models and practical protocols for what citizenship as a reciprocal and intersubjective ethic of respect for individualized personhood may mean. Narayan (1997: 53–54) argues that the central concept needed to ground the rights of citizenship is 'social dignity':

> If rights are understood as instruments for *preserving basic social dignity for all individuals*, we can avoid a bifurcated theory of rights that sees 'negative rights' as grounded in 'human capacities for self-government' and 'positive rights' as *separately grounded* in a vision of 'human needs'…Human dignity is at risk when humans are left without protection for important vulnerabilites. Human dignity is at risk when humans are rendered vulnerable to intrusions on their capacities for self-government and autonomy, and to a lack of *adequate means* for the satisfaction of basic needs. Rights can then be seen as social means to *minimize such vulnerabilities*, as attempts to ensure a minimum amount of *social dignity* to all members of society…. (Narayan, 1997: 53–54, emphases in the original)

Here Narayan recontextualizes the meaning of self-government away from its moorings within a patrimonial model in the direction of a universalistic conception of individualized personhood. This shift depends upon the construction of a post-patrimonial individualized subject, one who has an integrity that needs to be respected but whose boundaries as a self do not preclude dependency on others nor sustained interconnectedness with others (on this conception of the rights of a post-patrimonial self, see Kiss, 1997; and Yeatman, n.d.).

A conception of citizenship in terms of individualized personhood is exemplified in recent statute law and policies. As I have argued elsewhere (Yeatman, 1997b: 154) the significance of anti-discrimination, affirmative action and equal employment types of legislation is 'the statutory constitution of women as right-bearing subjects, where these rights are attached neither to property nor to protection but to personhood'. Legislation of this kind creates the space for a discourse of what it means to be constituted as a person, how this constitution works, in what ways and in what contexts. Instead of it being assumed that there are always already natural persons – the discourse of 'natural rights' – the implication of this type of legislation is that persons have to be positively constituted through the agency of the state in ways that are not prejudicial to some for reasons of their sex, or any other assumed aspect of identity (for development of this point see Yeatman, 1997a, and Yeatman, n.d.).

Legislation of this kind is universalistic in a way that was not true of earlier statutes enfranchising certain categories of political subject. As we have seen the statutes which extended suffrage were conceived in ways which sustained a hierarchical humanism, one where those who had the capacity for self-government had an undemocratic authority over those who did not. The universalism of patrimonial self-government is one which harbours racism of a particular kind as well as stigma for all subjects who cannot attain the condition of independent self-hood.

Exemplary of policy which materializes an anti-discriminatory ethos of respect for individualized personhood is the Australian federal government report on residents' rights in nursing homes and hostels offered by the feminist lawyer, Chris Ronalds (1989). It is no accident that Chris Ronalds also was one of the architects of Commonwealth Government Affirmative Action legislation (see Ronalds, 1990). Ronalds recommends the following principles for policy regarding the rights of nursing home residents:

- the principle of individuality in a communal setting:
- 'The right to be treated as an individual with dignity and respect goes to the very heart of the relationship between the resident and the facility in which they live. It should govern every aspect of that relationship, including the basis of tenancy, the routines within the facility and the way in which staff carry out their duties' (Ronalds, 1989: 2).
- the principle of provision of information as a 'basic component of [resident] decision making' (Ronalds, 1989: 3).
- the principle of consultation and participation 'It is recognized that the capacity of residents to be consulted and to participate will vary according to a number of factors such as their intellectual capacities, their experience in decision making and their interest and willingness to be involved. However, such varying capacities cannot be seen as reducing the necessity or desirability of involving residents in decisions' (Ronalds, 1989: 5).
- the principle of advocacy: 'The fundamental difficulty which emerges in relation to this issue is that difficulty in personally exercising rights should not mean that those rights no longer apply. Rather it means that some effective method of assisting the person to exercise their rights must be found. In practical terms, the notion of an advocate or advocacy service is seen as one mechanism designed to meet this need' (Ronalds, 1989: 5–6).
- the principle of accountability: 'accountability of service providers not just to government funders but also to their consumers, that is the residents' (Ronalds, 1989: 7).
- the principle of redress: without such an effective mechanism of redress, which can be exercised without fear of reprisal, 'the concept of rights can be of no practical value' (Ronalds, 1989: 8).

Citizenship reconfigured as respect for individualized personhood can be extended to respect for group rights as long as those who belong to the group in question elect to belong to it, that is, this groupness is itself congruent with respect for individualized personhood. This is a conception of citizenship that recasts how we think of democratic government. The purpose of democratic government on this account is not that of realizing the independence of a national citizen community. Rather, it is one of producing whatever jurisdictional materiality is required in order to secure respect for individualized personhood. That the integrity of this kind of governmental jurisdiction can be shared across established governments is shown in cases where trans-national instruments of law and policy (e.g. the various United Nations conventions) are accorded standing and legality within national and sub-national governmental jurisdictions. Cross-governmental juris-dictional integrity of this kind dilutes and thins the type of national government we have been used to. This is why the struggle of nostalgic defenders of the patrimo-nial imagined community of the nation-state against the resituation of govern-ments within a post-patrimonial trans-national ethos of respect for individualized personhood is so passionately and bitterly made. For example, in the Australian case, the conservative parties which constitute the Coalition government in power at the federal level since 1996 are seeking to release the Australian federal and state legislative jurisdictions from being bound by rights-oriented covenants of the United Nations.

The contemporary 'politics of difference' is suggestive of a likely reconfigura-tion of jurisdictions so that they constitute an assemblage of governance rather than clearly bounded governments which, when they interact, come into the sphere of international law and treaties. In order to make effective multi-cultural responses to the politics of immigration, on the one hand, and the politics of recognition of the claims of indigenous peoples, on the other, jurisdictional governance will have to make policy in accordance with non-discriminatory and trans-national standards of citizenship. Such policy both as process and outcome will have to have an inbuilt tolerance for explicitly stated unresolved and ongoing issues as well as to facilitate trans-national regional approaches to the movement of people and capital investment. Such approaches will have to include also shared policy responses to taxation and public service provision. In this context, the salience of being a citizen of one nationality or another is likely to be displaced in relation to a growing trans-national regional sense of identity and membership.

Contemporary post-colonial feminist theorists who are working with ideas of diasporic, non-hegemonic and fractured identities can be seen as portending such developments. These theorists refuse any closure that comes with notions of a singular, bounded and propertied identity of the patrimonial kind. This passage from Ien Ang's critique of how hegemonic 'national' feminism responds to the challenges of the politics of difference is instructive:

> I want to stress the *difficulties* of 'dealing with difference'...To focus on *resolving* differences between women as the ultimate aim of 'dealing with difference' would mean their containment in an inclusive, encompassing structure which itself remains uninterrogated...In such a case, difference is 'dealt with' by absorbing it into an already existing feminist community without challenging the naturalised legitimacy and status of that community *as* a community. By dealing with difference in this way, feminism resembles the multicultural nation – the nation that, faced with cultural differences within its borders, simultaneously recognises and controls those differences amongst its population by containing them in a grid of pluralist diversity.... (Ang, 1996: 59–60, emphases in the original)

A post-patrimonial and post-national democratic citizenship is the emergent paradigm. While the fierceness of contestation over this development may suggest its emergence is more embryonic than real, in fact, the new paradigm is more established than most realize. Contemporary feminism does not have the privilege of a special relationship to this new paradigm any more than it did in relation to the old patrimonial-national one. In each case, contemporary feminism, from the standpoint of the positioning of women in the citizenship politics in question, offers theoretical insight and practical interventions alongside those offered by other movements championing a post-patrimonial ethic of difference and respect for individualized personhood.

Notes

1 The term 'co-existence' is used in the Australian High Court's majority judgement on the Wik case: the two indigenous groups (the Wik and the Thayorre) 'contended, successfully, that...pastoral leases were particular kinds of proprietary interests created by the relevant statutes, leaving room for the co-existence of rights of other persons such as native title holders' (Hiley, 1997: 3). As one of the dissenting judges saw, this introduces a new principle of property which implies against all the tradition of patrimonial liberalism and republicanism that something can have more than one owner, the corollary of which is that, in order to be a person, a subject does not have to have a clearly bounded property in his/her will, person, things of a kind that excludes others. The patrimonial conception of self-hood is elaborated later in this chapter.

2 J.G.A. Pocock appropriately insists that the significance of 'property' in seventeenth century political debate is its work on behalf of the constitution of political personality. Pocock (1985: 56) comments: '...it does no harm to recall that the word is spelt in seventeenth-century printing both as property and as propriety...The point is that property was a juridical term before it was an economic one; it meant that which was properly one's own, that to which one properly had a claim, and words such as proprium and proprietas were applied as much as to the right as to the thing, and to many things as well as the means of sustenance or production.' For further discussion of this see Richard Tuck's *Natural Right Theories* (1979).

3 Grimshaw (1996: 84) points out that there were within the new Australian federal House of Representatives some members who defended Aboriginal rights, but it 'contained too many who opposed non-white immigration, and were willing to link Aborigines to the same exclusion'.

4 Grimshaw (1996: 85) argues: 'Explanations for the different positions of the two indigenous peoples are complex, grounded in cultural, demographic and historical differences. There was really never a serious doubt as to whether Maori women would be granted the vote alongside pakeha women when the measure was under debate in the late 1880s and early 1890s [it was granted in 1893]. Many Maori women owned land, had conducted cases before the Maori Land Court, and had shared equal access to free primary education with European girls since the 1870s. White suffragists noted that whereas all Maori men could vote, not a single white woman could, however well-educated, but this allusion was rare, and muted in tone.'

5 Equal rights organizers had begun the Kansas campaign by trying to forge a joint voting bloc in favor of suffrage for blacks and women, but Republicans had sabotaged their efforts...Blacks and women did not begin the campaign as enemies of each other's enfranchisement. To the degree they ended it that way, they were victims of the Republicans' policy of dividing them. Yet the swiftness and energy with which Stanton and Anthony turned from their own abolitionist traditions to [the Democrat] Train's racism remains remarkable. At this point, their racism was opportunist and superficial, an artifact of their anti-Republicanism and their alienation from abolitionists. However, it drew on and strengthened a much deeper strain within their feminism, a tendency to envision women's emancipation in exclusively white terms. They learned from Train how to transform white women's racism into a kind of sex pride, a technique to which they were later to turn in building the woman suffrage movement. (Du Bois, 1978: 95–96)

6 If communication is not understood narrowly and exclusively as language but if body gestures, behavior, facial expressions, mimics and sounds are also viewed as non-linguistic but linguistically articulable modes of communication, then the 'ideal communication community' extends well

beyond the adult person capable of full speech and accountable action. Every parent of a young infant knows that the act of communication with a being not yet capable of speech and action is the art of being able to understand and anticipate those body signals, cries and gestures as expressing the needs and desires of another human and to act such as to satisfy them. Every communication with an infant counterfactually presupposes that infant is a being who must be treated as if she had fully developed wants and intentions. I would say that the same is true of our relation to the disabled and the mentally ill. In mothering, nursing, caring and in education we are always counterfactually presupposing the equality and autonomy of the being whose needs we are satisfying or whose body and mind we are caring for, curing or training. When this counterfactual presupposition of equality, certainly not an equality of ability but one of claims, fails then we have poor pedagogies just as we have stifling, over-protective or punitive care, mothering or nursing. (Benhabib, 1992: 58–59)

References

Ang, I. (1996) 'I'm a feminist but…"Other" women and postnational feminism', in B. Caine and R. Pringle (eds), *Transitions: New Australian Feminisms*. St Leonards: Allen & Unwin, pp. 57–74.

Benhabib, S. (1992) *Situating the Self: Gender, Community and Postmodernism in Contemporary Ethics*. New York: Routledge.

Du Bois, E. (1978) *Feminism and Suffrage: the Emergence of an Independent Women's Movement in America 1848–1869*. Ithaca and London: Cornell University Press.

Fraser, N. (1996) 'Gender Equity and the Welfare State: a Postindustrial Thought Experiment', in S. Benhabib (ed.), *Democracy and Difference: Contesting the Boundaries of the Political*. Princeton, NJ: Princeton University Press, pp. 218–243.

Grimshaw, P. (1996) 'A White Woman's Suffrage', in H. Irving (ed.), *A Woman's Constitution*. Sydney: Hale & Iremonger, pp. 77–98.

Hall, C. (1994) 'Rethinking Imperial Histories: the Reform Act of 1867', *New Left Review*, 208: 3–29.

Hiley, G. (1997) 'Introduction', to G. Hiley (ed.), *The Wik Case: Issues and Implications*. Sydney: Butterworths, pp. 1–6.

Kernot, C. (1996) 'Breaking up the Boys' Club: Making the Republic Relevant to Australian Women', in J. Hoorn and D. Goodman (eds), *Vox Republicae: Feminism and the Republic*. Victoria: La Trobe University Press, pp. 81–87.

Kiss, E. (1997) 'Alchemy or Fool's Gold: Assessing Feminist Doubts about Rights', in M.L. Shanley and U. Narayan (eds), *Reconstructing Political Citizenship: Feminist Perspectives*. Cambridge: Polity Press, pp. 1–25.

Mitchell, J. (1976) 'Women and Equality', in J. Mitchell and A. Oakley (eds), *The Rights and Wrongs of Women*. Middlesex and New York: Penguin Books, pp. 379–400.

Narayan, U. (1997) 'Towards a Feminist Vision of Citizenship: Rethinking the Implications of Dignity, Political Participation and Nationality', in M.L. Shanley and U. Narayan (eds), *Reconstructing Political Citizenship: Feminist Perspectives*. Cambridge: Polity Press, pp. 48–68.

Pocock, J.G.A. (1985) *Virtue, Commerce and History*. Cambridge: Cambridge University Press.

Roberts, J. (1996) 'Maybanke Anderson: the Domestic and the Public', in H. Irving (ed.), *A Woman's Constitution*. Sydney: Hale & Iremonger, pp. 21–42.

Ronalds, C. (1989) *Residents' Rights in Nursing Homes and Hostels: Final Report*. Canberra: Australian Government Printing Service.

Ronalds, C. (1990) 'Government Action Against Employment Discrimination', in S. Watson (ed.), *Playing the State: Australian Feminist Interventions*. Sydney: Allen & Unwin, pp. 105–121.

Scott, J.W. (1996) *Only Paradoxes To Offer*. Cambridge, MA and London: Harvard University Press.

Stanley, A.D. (1988) 'Conjugal Bonds and Wage Labor: Rights of Contract in the Age of Emancipation', *The Journal of American History*, 75 (2): 471–501.

Tuck, R. (1979) *Natural Right Theories: Their Origin and Development*. Cambridge: Cambridge University Press.

Weber, M. (1968) *Economy and Society*. New York: Bedminster Press.

Yeatman, A. (1997a) 'Contract, Status and Personhood', in G. Davis, B. Sullivan and A. Yeatman (eds), *The New Contractualism*. South Melbourne: Macmillan Education Australia.

Yeatman, A. (1997b) 'Feminism and Power', in M.L. Shanley and U. Narayan (eds), *Reconstructing Political Citizenship: Feminist Perspectives*. Cambridge: Polity Press.

Yeatman, A. (n.d.) 'Relational Individualism,' unpublished manuscript.

10

EXTENDING CITIZENSHIP: CULTURAL CITIZENSHIP AND SEXUALITY

Diane Richardson

In recent years various writers have critiqued both historical and contemporary accounts of citizenship for failing to acknowledge the gendered nature of citizenship. Feminist analyses in particular have examined the relationship between concepts of citizenship and gender, pointing out how, despite claims to universality, a particular version of the normal citizen/subject is encoded in dominant discourses of citizenship (Lister, 1990, 1996; Phillips, 1991; Walby, 1994; Williams, 1998). Just as women were excluded from the classic concept of citizenship, so too in contemporary accounts the paradigmatic citizen is male (Wilton, 1995). This has, in turn, prompted discussion about how gender can be integrated into citizenship. Much of this debate is focused around the question of whether acknowledgement of the gendered nature of citizenship strengthens the notion of universalism through such incorporation, or whether we need a differentiated notion of citizenship (see Lister, 1997 for a discussion).

Despite growing interest in and recognition of how ideas of citizenship are gendered, as well as racialized, discussion of sexuality and its connection to citizenship remains largely absent from contemporary studies of citizenship, including much feminist work. Although social movements concerned with sexual politics have fought for specific rights, such as the right to a self-determined sexuality which was one of the early demands of the women's liberation movement, such claims have not been theorized in broader debates about citizenship until relatively recently.

There are two main observable trends in the inclusion of sexuality in work on citizenship: the question of the relationship of sexuality to citizenship and the development of a notion of sexual citizenship. Surveying the literature, it seems that a distinction can also be made between two common forms of usage of the term sexual citizenship.[1] First, it may be used to refer specifically to the sexual rights granted or denied to various social groups (Bell, 1995; Evans, 1993). That is, the question that is addressed is 'How are we entitled to express ourselves sexually?' In this sense we may conceptualize sexual citizenship as a collection of rights. For example, within feminist discourses sexual rights have primarily been seen in terms of the right to sexual self-determination and freedom from coercive and abusive relationships. By this logic it could be argued that the term sexual citizen would not extend to those who are not considered to be capable of sexual self-determination i.e. are not sexual subjects. For example, laws governing age of consent define the age that children are considered to be sexually self-determining and can be legitimately regarded as sexual citizens with the right to engage in various sexual practices.

Lesbian and gay movements have emphasized the extension of specific sexual rights, including an equal age of consent, as well as more broadly the right to freely choose consenting adult sexual partners and the right to be lesbian, bisexual or gay. Some writers (Binnie, 1995; Evans, 1993, 1995) also include in their discussion of sexual citizenship the right to consume 'sexual commodities', which can be defined as services and goods related to sexual practices and identities. Such 'commodities' might include sex education, gay and lesbian magazines, contraceptives, abortion services, prostitution and pornography.

Although it is useful in providing a grounded basis for discussion, sexual citizenship defined in terms of sexual rights is problematic in a number of respects. There are, for instance, competing claims for what are defined as sexual rights and lack of rights, in part reflecting the fact that there is no singular agreed definition of sexual citizenship. In his book *Sexual Citizenship*, for example, David Evans (1993) provides examples of what he delineates as different forms of sexual citizenship, including the experience of male homosexuals, bisexuals, transvestites, transsexuals and children. While this is useful in developing an understanding of what might be termed sexual rights, Evans does not offer an explicit, clear and succinct definition of the term sexual citizenship. There are also problems arising from the interpretation of sexual rights (Richardson, 2000). Debates within feminism, sometimes characterized as the 'sex wars' (Jackson and Scott, 1996), are illustrative of this. For example, one of the objections to feminist critiques of S/M practices and butch/femme put forward by Jeffreys (1990, 1994) and others, is that they contravene the feminist assertion of a woman's right to a self-defined sexuality. Such debates and disagreements touch on another problematic aspect of sexual citizenship, the extent to which we can usefully talk about rights if sexuality is an important mechanism of patriarchal control (see Jackson and Scott, 1996; Richardson, 1997; Walby, 1990). For example, the right to freely choose one's sexual partner raises important questions relating to consent and power, especially in heterosexual relations (Holland et al., 1996).

In addition to competing claims over what are defined as sexual rights, and how these are interpreted, there is also the question of obligation. Traditionally citizenship has been conceptualized as a set of rights and obligations. How does this model translate when we consider the relationship between sexuality and citizenship? What are our sexual obligations if we are granted sexual rights? To put it a slightly different way, what issues, attitudes or actions in relation to sexuality are considered to be important for good citizenship?

In one sense, it could be said that sexual obligations are already part and parcel of many forms of citizenship. For example, in the case of social rights the questioning of the welfare rights of lone mothers who have children outside of marriage reflects the way in which access to and eligibility for benefits is often linked to normative assumptions about sexuality (Carabine, 1996). Indeed, many citizenship rights are grounded in sexual coupledom, marriage in particular, rather than rights granted to us as individuals (Delphy, 1996). Similarly, Anna-Marie Smith (1995) makes the point that, in relation to homosexuality, the 'good homosexual citizen' is constructed as occupying the private sphere. In return for certain rights the obligation of the homosexual citizen is to keep themselves to themselves, out of public view.

The focus on obligations is particularly important in the area of sexuality because the assertion of rights does not guarantee protection from the harmful effects of various forms of sexual practices. For example, the right to consume pornography in private, with certain restrictions on content, is critiqued by many feminists in terms of the potentially harmful effects it may have, both at a direct level, in terms of incitement to violence, and at an indirect level, in terms of inculcating misogynist attitudes and beliefs (Itzin, 1993).

In addition to considering sexual citizenship in terms of access to a set of rights to sexual expression and consumption, we can conceptualize sexual citizenship in a much broader sense in terms of access to rights more generally. That is, how are various forms of citizenship status, and access to social, civil, political and other rights, dependent upon a person's sexuality? More specifically, what is the impact of being of a different sexuality to the prescribed heterosexual norm? At both international and national levels, political campaigns and struggles have highlighted how heterosexuals have access to certain rights that others do not. For example, in Britain campaigning groups like Stonewall have drawn attention to, amongst other things, the denial of same-sex relationships the same social rights of welfare as heterosexual couples; affecting pension rights, taxation and inheritance rights.

A further distinction can be drawn between analyses of sexual citizenship which place greater emphasis on the discussion on rights per se and struggles for rights acquisition, and those which are concerned with the wider theoretical implications of access to or exclusion from certain rights on the grounds of sexuality. For example, does a consideration of the sexualized nature of citizenship demand a re-evaluation of models of citizenship and if so, in what ways? Related to this, it might be argued that the recognition of legal and social rights for lesbians and gay men, for example, may broaden the interpretation of rights as well as citizenship. Jeffrey Weeks (1995), for instance, suggests that 'an argument for sexual rights is inevitably concerned with expanding or, perhaps better, stretching to the limits, the scope of the rights discourse. By arguing for a more extended definition of rights, we are actually changing the definition of what can be regarded as a right' (Weeks, 1995: 119). Conversely, the exclusion of lesbians and gay men from certain rights draws attention to the socially constructed nature of citizenship, highlighting both the heterosexual colonization of the public sphere and the normative construction of the citizen as heterosexual (Phelan, 1995; Richardson, 1996, 1998).

This broader concern with sexuality and citizenship, rather than a narrower focus on sexual citizenship, includes the work of Giddens (1992) on the democratization of intimate relationships, which he takes to include sexual relations. Giddens argues that the 'transformation of intimacy', in which women have played the major part, holds out the possibilities of a radical transformation of the personal sphere, which will have consequences for wider social and political citizenship. Conversely, Giddens also claims that democratization in the public domain shapes democratic practice in personal relationships, what one might call 'intimate citizenship'. Thus, for example, women's social and legal status as citizens has been significant in their right to freedom from coercive and abusive relationships both within and outside of marriage. Giddens himself uses the term 'pure relationship', defined as 'a relationship of sexual and emotional equality' (Giddens, 1992: 2), to refer to the democratic restructuring of intimacy.

We can infer from Giddens' analysis that sexuality and citizenship, as it has traditionally been defined in terms of rights and obligations in the public sphere, are seen as linked through a dynamic process whereby citizenship status has implications for how sexual relations are ordered and vice versa. Thus, Giddens remarks 'the advancement of self-autonomy in the context of pure relationships is rich with implications for democratic practice in the larger community' (Giddens, 1992: 195). Within a different framework of understanding to that espoused by Giddens, the idea that there is a dynamic relationship between democratic norms and sexuality can also be found in the earlier work of writers like Marcuse (1970) and Reich (1962). According to their interpretation, modern civilization depends upon a high level of sexual repression; liberating erotic potential is a prerequisite to a more civilized, egalitarian society.

Plummer's (1995) discussion of citizenship is also concerned with intimacy rather than sexuality specifically, although much of the spheres he mentions cut across the terrain of sexual relationships. He proposes that a 'fourth notion of citizenship' be added to those based on the traditional Marshallian model of civic, political and social rights (Marshall, 1950) – the idea of intimate citizenship. Plummer offers a very loose definition of what he means by intimate citizenship, using the term to suggest 'a cluster of emerging concerns over the rights to choose what we do with our bodies, our feelings, our identities, our relationships, our genders, our eroticisms and our representations' (Plummer, 1995: 17).

Clearly, like cultural citizenship, what we mean by sexual/intimate citizenship is still in the process of being defined. Part of the difficulty resides in the use of the word 'sexual' which is employed in various and often vague ways, and may refer to identities, activities, desires and/or specific relationships. The term intimacy is equally ill-defined, and further problems arise when, as I have attempted to do above, we try to link discussions of sexual citizenship with those concerning intimacy and intimate citizenship. Although in contemporary Western societies sexuality and notions of intimacy are closely linked, sexual relations need not be experienced as intimate just as intimate relations need not be sexual.

Acknowledging these difficulties of definition, I want to examine the relationship between sexuality and cultural citizenship. The main focus of writers who have been concerned with cultural citizenship are education and mass communication (Stevenson, 1996). Although there are important debates concerning the kinds of sexual citizenship that are promoted (and denied) through the regulation of education, particularly in the light of Section 28 of the Local Government

Act prohibiting the 'promotion' of homosexuality in maintained schools (see Stacey, 1991), this is not the focus of the remainder of this chapter. Rather, I will attempt to explore issues of cultural citizenship through a consideration of the following: the contribution of lesbians and gay men to cultural production; cultural practices/sites through which the lives of lesbians and gay men are represented or excluded; and, finally, lesbians and gay men as consumers of cultural products/ spaces.

Sexuality and Cultural Exclusion

Elsewhere (see Richardson, 1996, 1998) I have outlined how citizenship, conceptualized both as a set of civil, political and social rights and as common membership of a shared community, is closely associated with the institutionalization of heterosexuality. Here I want to focus on how understandings of citizenship as *cultural citizenship* can also highlight the sexualized, as well as gendered, nature of social inclusion and exclusion and access to 'rights and entitlements'. In order to explore the relationship between sexuality and cultural citizenship, I intend to examine the representation and participation of lesbians and gay men in various cultural sites. In art, film, music, theatre, literature, dance and advertising, there is a long history of controversy over how sexual relations can be depicted, including heterosexual relations. Such controversies reveal the intersection of sexualities and culture, and the 'boundaries' of regulation of cultural consumption and production of sexualities in any given period.

Visibility is a key issue in the social exclusion of lesbians and gay men and the development of possible strategies of resistance. Other communities have been culturally deprived of visibility in the dominant culture and have raised objections to the way images have stereotyped, for example, women, disabled groups and black communities. (Clearly, these 'groups' are overlapping and inclusive of lesbians and gay men.) However, because lesbians and gay men are not identifiable in the way that, say, racially defined or gendered individuals usually are, it is easier to ignore their presence in society. Equally, this makes it easier for lesbians and gay men to choose to avoid certain forms of discrimination and prejudice through 'passing' as heterosexual, thereby reaffirming their social invisibility. The lack of visibility of lesbians and gay men in social and cultural life can also be explained in terms of the public/private structuring of social relations. Sexuality is commonly understood to belong to the 'private' sphere, but more especially lesbian and gay relationships. For lesbians and gay men the private has been institutionalized as the boundary of sexual citizenship and social tolerance. For example, in the case of male homosexuality the 1967 Sexual Offences Act decriminalized sexual relations between consenting adult males over the age of 21 under certain specific conditions, in particular it stipulated that such relationships should be carried out in private (Moran, 1996).[2] Indeed, in terms of the sociology of rights lesbian and gay rights claims have been primarily viewed in this way, as private individual rights rather than as human rights. Thus, for example the right to recognition of lesbian and gay life-styles and identities as a legitimate and equal part of social and cultural life is commonly understood as seeking 'a better deal' for sexual minority groups, rather than an extension of the right of freedom to choose one's sexual partner to all human beings.

The public/private division is, then, fundamental to a liberal model of lesbian and gay citizenship, which has predominated since the 1960s, based on a politics of tolerance and assimilation. Lesbians and gay men are granted the right to be tolerated as long as they remain in the private sphere and do not seek public recognition. The 'I don't mind what they do in their own homes as long as I don't have to see or hear about it' argument. This relative exclusion from the public does not only pertain to 'homosexual persons', but also to 'homosexuality' as a topic of discussion, affecting claims to civil, social, political as well as cultural citizenship.[3] Indeed if, as Pakulski (1997) points out, claims to rights are negotiated through public fora, then the negotiation of citizenship rights will be seriously restricted if one is disallowed from those fora, either formally or informally, through fear of stigmatization or recrimination if one identifies publicly as a lesbian or gay man. The ability to be 'out' and publicly visible is therefore crucial to the ability to claim rights.

As Turner (in this volume) points out, citizenship is also closely associated with ideas about moral behaviour; what is and is not considered fit and proper conduct. The continued belief among certain individuals and social groups that engaging in lesbian or gay relationships is immoral, if not criminal behaviour, is clearly relevant here. Unlike many other 'problematic' people and images, it can be argued that 'homosexuality' has no legitimate place in mainstream media on the grounds not merely that it is a private matter, but also that public manifestations may cause offence. It was certainly the case that until relatively recently lesbians and gay men were regarded as not 'fit and proper' people to appear on television. For example, when an item about the novelist Angus Wilson was proposed by a producer for the BBC in the late 1950s the editor of the programme, Huw Wheldon, ruled that 'we can't have someone who is overtly queer on the programme' (Ferris, 1993: 159).

Historically, lesbian and gay communities have been systematically denied and ignored in popular culture. In mainstream cinema, lesbian and gay themes were rarely articulated. For example, in a comprehensive survey of images of lesbians and gays in films, Vito Russo (1981) found only a handful of examples. Similarly, the history of broadcasting reveals that there has been relatively little lesbian and gay coverage on radio and TV. It was the mid-1950s before 'homosexuality' was first mentioned on British TV; thirty years later coverage remained minimal (Sanderson, 1995). For example, one study which monitored one week's output of the broadcasting media found that the proportion of lesbian/gay characters and issues on television was extremely low; only 4.5 per cent of the week's total output included any such references. The denial of media space affected lesbians more than gay men. The study found that the representation of lesbians during the monitoring period totalled just one minute and thirty-five seconds (Lesbian and Gay Broadcasting Project, 1986).

Lesbians and gay men have also been culturally deprived of visibility in advertising (Clark, 1993), popular music (Stein, 1993), theatre (Freeman, 1997), literature and the visual arts (Smyth, 1996). Similarly, where are the representations of lesbian and gay lives in museum exhibitions, public monuments, or heritage parks?[4] In thinking about cultural citizenship, it is therefore important to address the history of invisibility that positions the lesbian and the gay subject in relation to cultural practices. Generally, when lesbians and gay men have appeared in popular and consumer culture their sexuality is rarely named, although this does not preclude lesbian and gay readings (Dyer, 1990). Where lesbian and gay characters, images or relationships are occasionally made explicit, it is usually in highly unidimensional and often negative representations. Thus, for example, the classic lesbian stereotypes are the image of the mannish 'butch' woman, such as Beryl Reid in the title role of the film *The Killing of Sister George* (Robert Aldrich, 1968), the predatory lesbian, as exemplified by Coral Brown in the same production and the neurotic, often closeted lesbian. Encoded in this way, we are encouraged in particular readings of lesbianism as, primarily, social deviance and sexual titillation or threat. However, in so far as the meaning of a text is derived from the interaction of the text with its audience, it is important to recognize the possibility that audiences, especially lesbian and gay audiences, may read against the text and derive alternative meanings to those which stereotype and denigrate lesbian and gay relationships (Griffin, 1993).

Lesbian and gay characters are further marginalized by the fact that there is a long tradition in granting a certain visibility, a cultural space, only on the grounds that such characters did not have a permanent or successful existence; thereby affirming normative sexual and social roles for women and men. Typically, fictional representations of lesbians have achieved this erasure through one or more of three main narratives: the character becomes heterosexual, dies or dis-appears, often without explanation (Cottingham, 1996). A good example of the heterosexual resolution is the classic lesbian novel *The Well of Loneliness* by Radclyffe Hall, first published in 1928 and subsequently prosecuted and banned until the late 1940s, which provoked the first major public debate about lesbianism in Britain and the United States (Wilton, 1995). A novel about the love between two women, it is Stephen, masculine in name and nature, who is left by the femi-nine Mary at the end of the story when she opts for heterosexual married life rather than a lesbian 'existence'. The sub-theme within this form of representa-tion is unrequited love, that of the 'real' lesbian whose sexuality is denied fulfilment. This relates to the second of the three main narratives, where the lesbian character dies. The character Martha played by Shirley MacLaine in the film adaptation of Lillian Hellman's play *The Children's Hour* (William Wyler, 1962) offers a good example of how suicide is often presented as a resolution of unre-quited lesbian desire. A more contemporary example which illustrates the 'death' narrative, is the case of the British television series *Brookside*, where the lesbian character Beth Jordache dies in prison following her conviction for the killing of her father who had raped her.

The reproduction of negative images and meanings associated with lesbians and gay men has also been a staple aspect of the popular press. Although, by the mid-1980s, lesbian and gay events and opinions were being covered in the British press, 'serious representation was scattered and infrequent' (Sanderson, 1995: 2). Coverage, especially in the tabloids, has primarily been hostile rather than sympathetic and is often used as a means of titillation through, for example, sexual scandal and expose stories.

Going Mainstream

Resistance to exclusion from popular culture and negative media coverage, in addition to other issues of citizenship conflict in particular focused on civil rights, has been an important focus of political activity. Feminist and gay movements from the 1970s onwards have been concerned with issues of representation, albeit with considerable debate and disagreement not only over how to interpret particular images and texts, but also what strategies should be employed in response (Marshment, 1993). Out of such political movements has emerged, over the past twenty five years in Britain, but more especially in the US, a plethora of cultural efforts including feature films, videos, documentaries, theatre productions, popular music and the publication of books and magazines, aided by the setting up of feminist and gay presses.

The distinction that is made between such activities, although undoubtedly significant, and the recent appearance of lesbian and gays in various cultural sites, is that whereas previously the focus was subcultural it is now becoming increasingly mainstream. Since the 1990s, lesbian and/or gay characters have appeared in popular television series in the UK, such as *Brookside*, *Eastenders* and *Emmerdale*, and even in the long running BBC radio series *The Archers*. In addition, Channel 4 launched the 'gay series' *Queer As Folk*, which focused on 'gay life' in Manchester.[5] A similar pattern has emerged in the US with series such as *Roseanne* and *Friends* including minor lesbian or gay characters and, perhaps more significantly, *Ellen* offering the first out major lead role. A few mainstream feature films have been made which have lesbian or gay characters or associated themes, including *Philadelphia*, *Basic Instinct*, *My Private Idaho*, *The Birdcage*, *Heavenly Creatures, Bound, In and Out* and *American Beauty*. In addition, independent films with lesbian and gay storylines have found some funding and distribution such as *My Beautiful Laundrette, Go Fish, Show Me Love* and *Beautiful Thing*. Similarly in music, fashion, artwork and publishing it would seem that we are witnessing a gradual increase in the participation and representation of lesbians and gay men in contemporary culture. There are, for example, contemporary museum exhibitions which occasionally include artwork by and about lesbians and gay men. For example, in 1997 the lesbian painter Sadie Lee had a show at the National Portrait Gallery in London. At the same time, there is a new visibility of especially lesbian imagery in popular music which extends beyond the alternative subcultural 'women's music' networks into the mainstream, including performers such as k.d. lang, Melissa Etheridge, Michelle Shocked and The Indigo Girls (Stein, 1993).

One could regard the inclusion of lesbian and gay images and narratives in dominant culture as constituting an important form of social recognition and access to cultural citizenship. Alternatively, the greater visibility of lesbians and gay men in mainstream social and cultural life can be seen as less an acknowledgement of cultural rights than a process of commodification and assimilation into dominant culture.[6] Thus, for instance, various writers have argued that even as lesbians are accorded more mainstream visibility, the images and narratives currently being produced generally treat lesbianism ambivalently, which serves to diffuse and contain the challenge to dominant definitions of gender and sexuality (Cottingham, 1996; Torres, 1993). For example, mainstream media texts tend to employ representational strategies that refer to lesbians in individualistic terms; they are different but also similar to other women and can therefore be incorporated. In this normalizing process, the specificity of lesbian desire and practice is de-emphasized (Torres, 1993). Lesbians are represented as heterosexuals with alternative private lives.

Despite certain 'sociological shifts', then, it would seem that cultural space is still primarily constructed as heterosexual territory. The basic narrative of contemporary entertainment is premised on heterosexuality as the normative form of social organization, which structures and organizes the ways in which lesbian and gay themes, if they appear, are represented and are likely to be interpreted by audiences (Richardson, 1996). Even when the story takes place on another planet or galaxy with radically different life forms and forms of social organization, dominant (apparently trans-galactic) meanings of sexuality and gender tend to be reproduced (see Cottingham, 1996). Indeed, responses to greater lesbian and gay visibility within media institutions reveal the extent to which it is implicitly assumed that cultural space is normatively constituted as heterosexual. Thus, for example, from the letters page of the British newspaper *The Guardian* there have been complaints about its coverage of lesbian and gay issues e.g. 'Why are homosexual/lesbian issues occupying so many column inches in your newspaper when these people form a minute subculture?' (*The Guardian*, 29 July 1995).

This example serves to highlight how normative assumptions about sexuality are important in media reception as well as production. The 'audience', the imagined community of readers, listeners and viewers are normatively constructed as heterosexual. Such assumptions have not only influenced audience research, but have helped to reinforce the exclusion of certain sections of society in mainstream cultural production. The situation is compounded by the fact that lesbians and gay men have become more visible in mainstream culture at a time when deconstructive approaches to political/social/sexual identities are fashionable. Emphasizing the fragmentation and fluidity of identity, new forms of sexual politics such as 'queer' have emerged in the 1990s which seek to displace the categories lesbian and gay *and* heterosexual (Warner, 1993). Paradoxically, the radical critique of sexual categories queer offers can be interpreted as enabling visibility of the 'lesbian' or 'gay' subject on the grounds that it undermines the construction of the 'lesbian' or 'gay' as a distinct category of being. In other words, one of the factors that makes it possible for lesbians to be granted cultural space is a cultural discourse which rejects the notion of a separate and authentic lesbian subject and divests lesbianism of its current political meaning(s).

Consumer Cultures

Another argument for the greater cultural presence and visibility of lesbians and gay men reasons that it has less to do with the growing acceptance of lesbian and gay rights, than with the political economy of media institutions and the identification of new consumer markets. Indeed, it is when we come to define citizenship as *consumerism* (Evans, 1993; Richardson, 1998) that 'non heterosexuals' seem to be most acceptable as citizens, as consumers with identities and life styles which are expressed through purchasing goods, communities and services. This has often been referred to as the power of the 'pink pound', although this commercialization has been predominantly Western and male (Woods, 1995). In the last few years, however, there have been signs of a new commercialism associated with lesbians as consumers, for example witness the appearance of lesbian 'life styles' magazines such as *Diva*, in the UK, and *Girlfriend* and *Curve*[7] in the United States, which contain features on and advertisements for fashion items, cosmetics, books, videos, holidays and sexualized commodities.

Speaking of lesbian and gay visibility in advertising, Danae Clark points out that in the past advertisers have been afraid to openly appeal to a lesbian and gay market on the assumption that if a product becomes associated with 'homosexuality' it will be avoided by heterosexual consumers perceived as the main market. Recently, however, advertisers have begun to recognize the purchasing power of lesbians and especially gay men, striving to create a 'dual marketing strategy' which will open up consumer culture to lesbians and gay men in a way that does not negatively affect the heterosexual market. This 'dual marketing strategy' has been referred to as 'gay window advertising', a good example of which is the Calvin Klein jean and perfume advertisements. Typically, such advertising texts avoid explicit reference to heterosexuality and contain elements which can be read as signifiers of sexual ambiguity or difference. In this way, Clark argues, we are witnessing an appropriation of lesbian and gay subcultural style which is incorporated into commodified representations and offered back to the lesbian and gay consumer in a form which, although it can still be 'claimed and coded' as lesbian (or gay), 'consciously disavows any explicit connection to lesbianism for fear of offending or losing potential customers' (Clark, 1993: 196). Thus, whilst in one sense the connection that has traditionally been made between heterosexuality and consumerism is challenged, in seeking to assure a lesbian and gay market, consumer culture continues to rely on heterosexual norms and institutions which contribute to the invisibility of lesbians and gay men.

Despite this, some have identified this commodification of lesbian and gay sexuality – the creation of lesbian and gay 'life style culture' – and the development of consumer power as important for formal civil, political and social rights. As Evans, for example, remarks:

> Sexual minorities have progressively become distinct, formal, though not necessarily formally clear, participants within the citizenship of developed capitalism, whilst simultaneously becoming, not surprisingly for of course the two are closely connected, legitimate consumers of sexual and sexualized commodities marketed specifically for their use and enjoyment. (Evans, 1993: 2)

As I have implied above, others take the different view that a politics oriented around consumption is unlikely to foster a more inclusive sexual citizenship (Woods, 1995). It is argued that, as with other forms of citizenship, the dominant model is one of access to the right to consume within the boundaries of heterosexual tolerance. This is well illustrated by the fact that one of the largest sponsors of the 1997 Gay Pride festival in London, United Airlines, does not extend partnership benefits to its lesbian and gay employees. However United clearly recognize lesbian and gay consumer citizenship. In a full-page advertisement in the festival programme the company states: 'We would be proud to fly you to Pride festivals around the world. It's the kind of things we do for you every day at United, rising to meet your needs, rising above your expectations.' Commenting on this, Peter Tatchell of the direct action campaigning group OutRage! stated: 'United Airlines seems only interested in the Pride festival as a marketing opportunity. It wants gay customers but doesn't seem to give a damn about gay human rights' (*Time Out*, 2–9 July 1997).

In addition to being structured by access to time and money, consumer citizenship is also limited by the boundaries set on the cultural and spatial contexts where lesbian and gay 'life styles' can be consumed. The development and marketing of areas of Soho and Manchester as gay commercial districts, for instance, whilst significant in terms of increasing the public visibility of lesbians and gay men, is 'queer space' (Binnie, 1995) whose contested boundaries are defined through heterosexual constructions of public space (Bell, 1995).

If the charge of assimilationist politics has been made in relation to the development of the new lesbian and gay commercialism and consumer culture, then so too can it be said of other forms of lesbian and gay politics. Indeed, the view that lesbians and gay men are legitimate citizens who have been wrongly excluded from various forms of citizenship can also be seen in this way, in so far as it leads to the seeking of rights through recognition and reform by the State, which will allow for inclusion within the present order. This form of lesbian and gay politics has become increasingly dominant in relation to citizenship claims. In Britain, the Stonewall lobby group is an example of this approach. Formed in 1989, Stonewall is an all party parliamentary working group on lesbian and gay rights which lobbies for legal reforms such as lowering the age of male homosexual consent to sixteen and legal recognition of same sex couples.

By contrast, more radical gay, lesbian/feminist and queer politics have been critical of what have been labelled assimilationist and commercially oriented values. (Hence, the slogan: 'We're here, we're queer and we're *not* going shopping.') Despite certain differences, what these movements largely share is a politics which questions the 'normality' of the citizen and, rather than seeing inclusion as achievable through the extension of common rights, seeks the deconstruction of heterosexism. It is around these politics that issues of cultural citizenship, in particular media representation, have been largely addressed in recent years.

Conclusions

In this chapter I have focused specifically on the question of lesbian and gay rights in relation to certain aspects of cultural citizenship, in order to highlight how the construction of the legitimate citizen is related to the institutionalization of heteronormative forms of social and cultural life. This is evidenced in the limits to full citizenship experienced by lesbians and gay men; albeit in varying ways in so far as this is also a racialized and gendered process. In developing notions of cultural citizenship, and for that matter sexual citizenship, it is important to recognize such debates and the questions they provoke. For instance, how might sexuality be integrated into models of cultural citizenship? Or, is it less a question of integration than a radical rethink of approaches to understanding citizenship that is required?

Inevitably, there are many other important questions which deserve attention that I have not had the space to deal with here. For example, how are appeals to cultural traditions and cultural heritage sometimes employed to deny access to citizenship to lesbians and gay men (see Richardson, 1996, 1998)? Related to this, what kinds of sexual citizenship are promoted in national cultures? Equally, to what extent have lesbian and gay claims to citizenship been based on appeals to a specific cultural and historical heritage. That is, how far has ethnicity, where lesbians and gay men are perceived as an ethnic minority group (Altman, 1982; Epstein, 1992), been the dominant paradigm in arguing for access to rights? Finally, what are the implications of changes in mass communication, in particular electronic media, for sexual citizenship? These are some of the issues which will need to be addressed in the development of future analyses of the relationship between sexuality and cultural citizenship.

Notes

1 It should be pointed out that in making a distinction between a narrow and a broad meaning of the term sexual citizenship I do not wish to suggest that these interpretations are exclusionary. Indeed, they are often used by writers concurrently.

2 This was replaced, in 1994, with an 'age of consent' of 18. It was further decreased, in 1998, to 16 years of age as part of the Crime and Disorder Act. However, this decision was subsequently overturned by the House of Lords and at the time of writing the legal age of consent for sexual practices between two men remains at 18.

3 Interestingly the campaign by the City of Amsterdam to attract international gay tourism to Amsterdam, including an idea for a museum charting the historical development of the city's lesbian and gay cultures, was withdrawn seemingly on the basis of public concern over how Amsterdam would be represented abroad, but also perhaps reflecting concern over public spending. The responsibility for marketing the city as 'the gay capital of Europe' has been transferred from public bodies to gay businesses themselves (see Binnie, 1995).

4 A notable exception is the Homomonument in Amsterdam, at Westermarkt on the Keizergracht, which consists of three pink granite triangles forming a larger triangle commemorating lesbian and gay victims of homophobia.

5 Alongside this there have been specially commissioned series made by and for lesbians and gay men such as the Channel 4 series *Out on Tuesday* and, on the BBC, *Gay TV* and *Dyke TV*.

6 In the case of lesbians this has often been referred to as 'lesbian chic' (Cottingham, 1996).

7 The original title was *Deneuve* but after a legal action brought by the French actress Catherine Deneuve the magazine changed its name to *Curve*.

References

Altman, D. (1982) *The Homosexualisation of America*. Boston: Beacon Press.

Bell, D. (1995) 'Perverse Dynamics, Sexual Citizenship and The Transformation of Intimacy', in David Bell and Gill Valentine (eds), *Mapping Desire. Geographies of Sexualities*. London: Routledge.

Binnie, J. (1995) 'Trading Places: Consumption, Sexuality and the Production of Queer Space', in David Bell and Gill Valentine (eds), *Mapping Desire. Geographies of Sexualities*. London: Routledge.

Carabine, J. (1996) 'Heterosexuality and Social Policy', in Diane Richardson (ed.), *Theorising Heterosexuality: Telling it Straight*. Buckingham: Open University Press.

Clark, D. (1993) 'Commodity Lesbianism', in Henry Abelove, Michele Aina Barale and David M. Halperin (eds), *The Lesbian and Gay Studies Reader*. London: Routledge.

Cottingham, L. (1996) *Lesbians Are So Chic...That We Are Not Really Lesbians At All*. London: Cassell.

Delphy, C. (1996) 'The Private as a Deprivation of Rights For Women and Children', paper given at the International Conference on Violence, Abuse and Women's Citizenship, Brighton, 10–15 November.

Dyer, R. (1990) *Now You See It. Studies on Lesbian and Gay Film*. London: Routledge.

Epstein, S. (1992) 'Gay Politics, Ethnic Identity: The Limits of Social Constructionism', in E. Stein (ed.), *Forms of Desire*. New York: Routledge.

Evans, D. (1993) *Sexual Citizenship. The Material Construction of Sexualities*. London: Routledge.

Evans, D. (1995) '(Homo)sexual Citizenship: A Queer Kind of Justice', in Angelia R. Wilson (ed.), *A Simple Matter of Justice? Theorizing Lesbian and Gay Politics*. London: Cassell.

Ferris, P. (1993) *Sex And The British. A Twentieth Century History*. London: Michael Joseph.

Freeman, S. (1997) *Putting Your Daughters on the Stage: Lesbian Theatre from the 1970s to the Present*. London: Cassell.

Giddens, A. (1992) *The Transformation of Intimacy: Sexuality, Love and Eroticism in Modern Societies*. Cambridge: Polity Press.

Griffin, G. (ed.) (1993) *Outwrite: Lesbianism and Popular Culture*. London: Pluto Press.

Hall, R. (1928) *The Well of Loneliness* (reprinted in 1982). London: Virago.

Holland, J., Ramazanoglu, C. and Thomson, R. (1996) 'In the Same Boat? The Gendered (in) Experience of First Heterosex', in Diane Richardson (ed.), *Theorising Heterosexuality: Telling it Straight*. Buckingham: Open University Press.

Itzin, C. (ed.) (1993) *Pornography: Women, Violence and Civil Liberties*. Oxford University Press.

Jackson, S. and Scott, S. (eds) (1996) *Feminism and Sexuality: A Reader*. Edinburgh: Edinburgh University Press.

Jeffreys, S. (1990) *Anticlimax: A Feminist Perspective on the Sexual Revolution*. London: The Women's Press.

Jeffreys, S. (1994) *The Lesbian Heresy: A Feminist Perspective on the Lesbian Sexual Revolution*. London: The Women's Press.

Lesbian and Gay Broadcasting Project (1986) *Are We Being Served?* London.

Lister, R. (1990) 'Women, Economic Dependency and Citizenship', *Journal of Social Policy*, 19 (4): 445–468.

Lister, R. (1996) 'Citizenship Engendered', in D. Taylor (ed.), *Critical Social Policy. A Reader*. London: Sage.

Lister, R. (1997) *Citizenship: Feminist Perspectives*. London: Macmillan.

Marcuse, H. (1970) *Eros and Civilisation*. London: Allen Lane.

Marshall, T.H. (1950) *Citizenship and Social Class*. Cambridge: Cambridge University Press.

Marshment, M. (1993) 'The Picture is Political: Representation of Women in Contemporary Popular Culture', in Diane Richardson and Victoria Robinson (eds), *Introducing Women's Studies: Feminist Theory and Practice*. London: Macmillan.

Moran, L. (1996) *The Homosexual(ity) of Law*. London: Routledge.

Pakulski, J. (1997) 'Cultural Citizenship', *Citizenship Studies*, 1 (1): 73–86.

Phelan, S. (1995) 'The Space of Justice: Lesbians and Democratic Politics', in Angelia R. Wilson (ed.), *A Simple Matter of Justice? Theorizing Lesbian and Gay Politics*. London: Cassell.

Phillips, A. (1991) 'Citizenship and Feminist Theory', in Geoff Andrews (ed.), *Citizenship*. London: Lawrence and Wishart.

Plummer, K. (1995) *Telling Sexual Stories: Power, Change and Social Worlds*. London: Routledge.

Reich, W. (1962) *The Sexual Revolution*. New York: Farrar, Straus and Giroux.

Richardson, D. (1996) 'Heterosexuality and Social Theory', in Diane Richardson (ed.), *Theorising Heterosexuality*. Buckingham: Open University Press.

Richardson, D. (1997) 'Sexuality and Feminism', in Victoria Robinson and Diane Richardson (eds), *Introducing Women's Studies: Feminist Theory and Practice*, 2nd edn. Basingstoke: Macmillan.

Richardson, D. (1998) 'Sexuality and Citizenship', *Sociology*, 32 (1): 83–100.

Richardson, D. (2000) 'Constructing Sexual Citizenship: Theorizing Sexual Rights', *Critical Social Policy*, 20 (1): 105–135.

Russo, V. (1981) *The Celluloid Closet: Homosexuality in the Movies*. New York: Harper & Row.

Sanderson, T. (1995) *Mediawatch: The Treatment of Male and Female Homosexuality in the British Media*. London: Cassell.

Smith, A.M. (1995) *New Right Discourse on Race and Sexuality: Britain, 1968–90*. Cambridge: Cambridge University Press.

Smyth, C. (1996) *Damn Fine Art: By New Lesbian Artists*. London: Cassell.

Stacey, J. (1991) 'Promoting Normality: Section 28 and the Regulation of Sexuality', in Sarah Franklin, Celia Lury and Jackie Stacey (eds), *Off Centre: Feminism and Cultural Studies*. London: Unwin Hyman.

Stein, A. (1993) 'Androgyny Goes Pop: But Is It Lesbian Music?', in Arlene Stein (ed.), *Sisters, Sexperts, Queers: Beyond The Lesbian Nation*. New York: Plume.

Stevenson, N. (1996) 'Globalization, National Cultures and Cultural Citizenship', *The Sociological Quarterly*, 38 (1): 902–926.

Torres, S. (1993) 'Prime Time Lesbianism', in Henry Abelove, Michele Aina Barale and David M. Halperin (eds), *The Lesbian and Gay Studies Reader*. London: Routledge.

Walby, S. (1990) *Theorising Patriarchy*. Oxford: Blackwell.

Walby, S. (1994) 'Is Citizenship Gendered?', *Sociology*, 28 (2): 379–395.

Warner, M. (ed.) (1993) *Fear of a Queer Planet: Queer Politics and Social Theory*. Minneapolis: University of Minnesota Press.

Weeks, J. (1995) *Invented Moralities: Sexual Values In An Age Of Uncertainty*. Oxford: Polity Press.

Williams, F. (1989) *Social Policy: A Critical Introduction*. Cambridge: Polity Press.

Wilton, T. (1995) *Lesbian Studies*. London: Routledge.

Woods, C. (1995) *State of the Queer Nation: A Critique of Gay and Lesbian Politics in 1990s Britain*. London: Cassell.

11

DISABILITY AND CULTURAL CITIZENSHIP: EXCLUSION, 'INTEGRATION' AND RESISTANCE

Deborah Marks

This chapter argues that extensions of the concept of citizenship to include the right to 'endignified representation' offers a crucial tenet in ensuring full cultural citizenship rights for those people currently constituted as disabled. I begin by identifying the lack of civil and social rights held by disabled people, but go on to argue that the notion of endignified representation is intrinsically intertwined with civil and social rights. I explore the way in which an 'ablist' built environment might apparently relate purely to disabled people's civil rights, but in practice cannot be separated from aesthetic and psychological categories. In the last part of the chapter, I identify some aspects of disabled people's resistances which work both to gain civil rights and disrupt disabling images.

Extending the Concept of Citizenship Rights

It is helpful to begin by defining what we mean by citizenship. Citizenship confers a set of rights 'both claimed by and bestowed upon all members of a political community...citizenship rights are universalistic but restricted to "insiders" in society' (Pakulski, 1996: 73–74). Alongside these rights, citizens have responsibilities or duties to the political community to which they belong (see Turner and Crossley, this volume). Whilst in principle everyone is a de jure citizen, in practice the concept has always excluded certain sections of the population, such as slaves and women in Ancient Greece.

T.H. Marshall (1950) attempted to extend the apparent universality of citizenship rights so that they were practically attainable by working-class people. He traces the development of modern citizenship from the eighteenth century, which established civil rights, through the nineteenth century, which extended democracy to secure political rights, and finally the twentieth century which saw the establishment of social rights, aimed at preventing serious disadvantage and enabling people to make use of political and civil rights. Many commentators, particularly from a feminist perspective, have challenged Marshall's 'conditions' of citizenship (for example, the right to work), for failing to address the range of positions and experiences of different social groups (Young, 1989). Further, the development of social rights has, according to Pakulski, been hindered by the 'crisis in welfarism, the "shrinkage of the state", and globalization'. This has served to 'redirect the claims for rights towards a new domain of cultural rights that involve the right to unhindered and legitimate representation and propagation of identities and lifestyles through information systems' (Pakulski, 1996: 74).

For the purpose of this chapter, Pakulski's outline of what constitutes cultural citizenship is the most helpful.

> The claims for cultural citizenship involve not only tolerance of diverse identities but also – and increasingly – claims to endignifying representation, normative accommodation and active cultivation of these identities and their symbolic correlates. (Pakulski, 1996: 77)

Such an extension of our concept of citizenship is particularly helpful in attempting to understand the position of disabled people.

This chapter focuses on ways disabled people are currently denied recognition or respect in ablist culture. However, the call for 'endignifying representation' and 'active cultivation of disabled people's identities' can only be made within a social and civil rights context. Disabled people are denied not just full cultural citizenship, but also the formal rights and responsibilities which form the socio-political context for cultural association. Representation cannot be separated from structural issues.

Civil Rights

Disabled people still lack basic political rights, both in the narrow sense, since environmental barriers may prevent some disabled people from using their vote (Oliver and Zarb, 1989) and more significantly, because their 'interests' continue to be represented predominantly by non-disabled people (Oliver, 1996). In terms of civil rights the UK has no written constitution. However there are a number of legal protections which are extended to women and racialized minorities, but not to disabled people. The UK Disability Discrimination Act (1995) is much weaker than earlier anti-discrimination statutes and was initially passed without a commission to secure enforcement. Whilst this has changed under the current British Labour Government it will be some time before legal changes bring about a significant reduction in disabling barriers and prejudice against disabled people. The Act as it currently stands, is full of loopholes and justifications which condone continued discrimination against disabled people (Barnes, 1994; Doyle, 1995), such as the broad defence for employers of 'justifiable discrimination' which locates the problem within the disabled individual rather than environmental barriers. No such caveat exists in anti-racist or anti-sexist legislation. The experiences of people identified as having a mental illness or learning difficulty indicate some of the extreme restrictions placed on freedom of movement and control of bodies (Ryan and Thomas, 1987; Shakespeare et al., 1996). Both these groups are more likely to be subject to invasive surgery, neuroleptic drugs and physical constraints, as well as barriers which prevent some of the most basic autonomous choices, such as over sexual partners and diet. People with physical impairments have few recourses to the social apartheid produced by environmental barriers and discrimination. These exclusions have marked consequences for cultural membership.

Social Rights and Responsibilities

Disabled people are socially constructed as dependent, primarily because the social and built environment is designed for non-disabled people. Disabled people are then encouraged to 'integrate' into this ablist world. In order to assist entrance into 'the mainstream' disabled people are offered a range of special benefits and services. Given that much of this provision can only be accessed through complex professional gatekeeping (for example, the Disability Living Allowance form requires medical validation), disabled people are often positioned as compliant and grateful 'clients' rather than active consumers with rights and duties (Davis, 1994).[1]

Walmsley (1994) points out that disabled people are 'conceived of as net takers'. Yet when we subject this conception to critical examination we rapidly discover that disabled people's social responsibilities are just not acknowledged. Walmsley quotes evidence from Atkinson and Williams (1990), Potts and Fido (1990), Barron (1989) and Etherington et al. (1988) to show the extent to which people with learning difficulties have informal roles as carers, volunteers and undertake low-paid jobs which are not easy to fill by non-disabled people. 'Like women, a lot of the work they do is invisible, taken for granted, and somehow does not count as work' (Walmsley, 1994: 264).

Disabled people's 'rights' are constituted as 'special' rights *without* responsibilities. (As such, the benefits have much in common with charity in the way that they produce dependency.) Cultural images of disabled people draw heavily on individual and medical constructions of disability as mental or bodily pathology. Disabled people continue to be seen as occupying a 'sick role' which 'excuses' them of full responsibilities and rights accorded to the cultural citizen (Parsons and Fox, 1952). Whilst Western medicine has given up trying to 'cure' homosexuality (even the most conservative of bodies, the American Psychiatric Association Board of Trustees no longer sees 'ego-dystonic homosexuality' as a mental illness – see Wilson, 1993), disabled people are still seen as having their lives put on hold until a cure can be found.

Oliver shows how we might begin to deconstruct the medical model of disability, which locates the ultimate cause of disability in an impaired (malfunctioning or abnormal) body. For example, he reformulates the medically oriented question 'how difficult is it for you to get about your immediate neighbourhood on your own?' into the question, 'what are the environmental constraints which make it difficult for you to get about in your immediate neighbourhood?' (Oliver, 1990: 7–8). When we do this, we can see the extent to which different cultures (Bogdan, 1988; Groce, 1985) and technologies (Lynch, 1997) constitute certain differences (or what many refer to as 'impairments') as disabling.

In addition to examining technologies and access in relation to human differences, we need to examine some of the cultural and emotional investments which sustain disabling barriers. The starting point for this argument is to attempt to show that the opportunity for 'endignified' self-representation within the public sphere depends on the relationship between civil and social rights and cultural images of the citizen. The next section will examine idealized images and conceptions of personhood and the way these images relate to conceptions of the citizen.

Images of Citizenship and Disability

The Active, Fit and Autonomous Citizen

Whether our vision of the citizen comes from an image of the Athenian democrat attending his forum or from Rousseau's virtuous man, the term citizen conjures up an image of activity and physical prowess. The Greeks were particularly concerned with ideal depictions of man in their formulations of the citizen. Questions about how to perfect human existence have concerned thinkers and religious leaders since ancient times and remain a focus in contemporary Western culture with its emphasis on 'external activity, on outward visibility, on physical striving and action' (Dutton, 1995: 366).

Physical images of those in positions of authority serve in a democracy as an important model for citizenship. National rulers serve to represent the 'body' of the nation. As such, much energy is spent in ensuring an image of the political leader as physically strong. When Jimmy Carter collapsed during a run and Neil Kinnock slipped during an election campaign, these accidents were public relations setbacks. Where leaders have had some substantial physical impairment or illness, elaborate efforts are made to prevent it from becoming apparent to the population. Gallagher (1985) in his book *FDR's Splendid Deception* showed how President Roosevelt developed a carefully orchestrated strategy to disguise the extent of his paralysis. Indeed, many commentators and biographers talk about his polio as an 'illness' which struck him down during the prime of his life, but which he 'overcame'.

Once we have a positive image of a particular kind of person/citizen, we raise the question of exceptions. In ancient Greece, infants who were born with deformities were not merely denied citizenship, but life itself. In Sparta these policies were demanded by law (Tooley, 1983). Some versions of citizenship theory, particularly from a free market and conservative perspective, have elided the notion of the active independent citizen with Social Darwinian and utilitarian notions of personhood, which distinguish between the autonomous 'fit' citizens (see Williamson, 1997) and those humans who lack the mental capacities which would qualify them for citizenship. Utilitarian philosophers have devoted themselves to the task of establishing which individual human beings have, for example, a right to life. Philosophers such as Glover, Singer and Tooley all see the 'right' to life as depending on 'personhood' (Teichman, 1996). A person is someone who is capable of 'autonomous' and 'independent' action. Thus for utilitarian philosophers, a person with severe learning difficulties may be considered to lack the qualities defining 'personhood'. As such, they are seen as lacking the qualities required for the ideal and the fit citizen. It is noteworthy that ways of categorizing disabled people reflect their status as non-persons. Disabled people are constituted as 'racialized others', as in 'Siamese twins' and 'Mongols', as animals, as in the 'Elephant Man' and 'savages' (of both the innocent and dangerous varieties), and as vegetables such as 'persistive vegetative state'. Yet all these terms position disabled people outside the category of personhood which has such significant implications for citizenship rights.

The Engaged Citizen

Citizenship is defined by boundaries which demarcate inclusion and exclusion. The return to the concept of citizenship in contemporary social theory and politics seems in part to express frustration with the atomism of contemporary life. The notion of association provides a pivotal activity for the citizen of a clearly bounded community. As such, the question of who stands outside the boundaries of our community of citizens becomes a pressing one. The question of boundaries marking membership, or to use Sibley's (1996) term, 'geographys of exclusion' has become the key issue in citizenship debates.

Perhaps the most striking feature of contemporary images of the disabled person is that he or she is isolated and disengaged from the community (Nordon, 1994). Such an image is rooted in material reality, with the development of a range of 'special' residential (Humphries and Gordon, 1992) and educational (Tomlinson, 1982) institutions, segregated work schemes (Finkelstein, 1980), day centres (Barnes, 1994) and barriers excluding disabled people from public transportation and the built environment (Imrie, 1996). The isolation of disabled people has come to function as a central dramatic metaphor in the contemporary media, with disabled people functioning as objects of pity (Evans, 1988), objects of danger (*Without Walls*, 1996) and as exotic objects of 'anthropological' interest. Nordon identifies some of the key ways in which film-makers isolate disabled characters: 'framing, editing, sound, lighting, set design elements (e.g. fences, windows, staircase banisters) – [serve] to suggest a physical or symbolic separation of disabled characters from the rest of society' (1995: 6).

Evans (1988) identifies a series of photographic techniques to position the 'mentally handicapped' in charity advertising as Other. The complexity and range of experiences of impairment are rarely portrayed. Disability functions as an archetypal construction (see Darke, 1997) or metaphor (see Sontag, 1977). Disability stands outside community, offering a threat or rallying point through which citizenship is expressed.

In contrast to the image of the citizen as someone who is an active, autonomous, fit and relating person, disabled people are frequently constituted as being the isolated and dependent recipients of services rather than being productive and valued citizens (Morris, 1993). Given such constructions it is not surprising that disabled people are subject to a different version of the question, cited by Hall, as the most frequently asked of migrants: 'Why are you here?' and 'When are you going back home?' (Hall, 1990: 44). Disabled people are asked 'How did you get like that?' and 'Can you be cured?' Both questions interpolate an 'outsider', someone whose existence presents a problem to the fully fledged citizen. Before going on to examine some of the psychic investments which citizens have in the maintenance of the category of disability, it is important to show the extent to which sociology can be implicated in the exclusion of thinking about disability.

Sociology and the Marginalization of Disability

Whilst a masculinized (and also White) conceptualization of citizenship has been subject to critical social analysis disabled people's social position remains remarkably naturalized. Disability has, until recently, been marginal to mainstream sociological questions of difference and inequality. The study of disability tends to be treated as a specialized area open to empirical examination by practitioners in applied studies such as health care and social work. Work tends to focus on the question of the 'prevalence and character of chronic illness, and on patient compliance' (Barnes and Mercer, 1996: 3). As such, disability continues to be perceived as being *about* disabled people rather than as a relational concept which has ramifications for the social position and way in which everyone thinks, feels and acts. Whilst the last 10 years has seen a large body of critical and conceptual work, produced predominantly by disabled sociologists (Barnes, 1994; Finkelstein, 1980; Oliver, 1990; Shakespeare et al., 1996; Zola, 1982), this work has only recently come to occupy a place in mainstream sociological analysis. Davis (1995) points out that at academic conferences 'people don't come to sessions on disability'. Thus, despite the concepts of disability and ability playing a central role in contemporary understandings of normality, the body and intelligence – disability remains seriously under-theorized. It is likely that the omission of disability reflects contemporary cultures' unwillingness to think about disabled people as citizens within the Western cultural universe.

Psychic Investments in Segregating 'The Disabled'

Having suggested that disability represents a pervasive but segregated and repressed presence in Western culture, it is important to look at the investments which citizens have in maintaining the exclusion of disabled people. Why is cultural mindlessness about certain kinds of physical and mental 'differences' combined with an almost obsessional interest in disabled people as 'Other' – the object of pity, fear and revulsion? Having argued that disability is (to use the words of Walkerdine, 1990) a 'socially constructed fiction, lived as fact', I want to go on to look at the way in which it has become 'invested with fantasy'.

Western culture valorizes youth and constitutes the physical states associated with ageing (as with disability) as a return to the dependency of infancy. Moreover, the chances of re-entering this feared state are high. Statistically most people who live to the age of 75 will spend 13 years with some form of impairment or reduced functioning (Pope and Tarlov, 1995). Added to this is the pervasive fear of bodily vulnerability which is such a staple of movies. It is worth noting that a person's bodily or intellectual identity and status is far more open to change than their 'racialized' or gendered status. Despite the challenge which post-structural theory has presented to the notion of fixed identity (see for example, Butler, 1993), most of us live with the working assumption of a relatively stable racialized and gendered identity. Yet few of us have a similar existential security about the stability of our bodily and intellectual status.

One way in which able bodied people manage the (repressed) anxiety associated with earlier and later states is to avoid thinking about disability. To use the more engaging language of Sinason (1992), we go stupid in the face of certain kinds of impairments. As a consequence, we do not, as a culture, engage in mindful recognition of the likelihood of changes (currently constituted as impairments) in ourselves or in those we love. Rather than seeing 'impairment' as a mundane fact of life which may at times present a challenge, or even a crisis, we engage in a collective cultural refusal to recognize the commonality of 'impairment'. Instead, we constitute certain impaired people as 'Other', and their condition as tragic and unbearable (Oliver, 1990). If tragedy implies an unforeseen fall from a state of grace, or at least a privileged position, then surely non-disabled people are engaged in a rather grandiose denial of vulnerability and impairment? The energy and anger which is often directed towards those propounding a social account of disability indicates something of the threatening nature of the suggestion that pathology is not fixed in 'other' people.

I wish to suggest that disability is constituted on a split which involves projecting neediness and lack onto certain 'impaired' people. Disabled people are psychically necessary in order that non-disabled people may sustain the phantasy of invulnerability and ability. This is reflected in the clarion calls for prevention, cure and removal of 'damaged' people rather than looking at the social and cultural environment which constitutes certain differences as damaging. Impairment cannot be thought about or included within our cultural repertoire of possibilities, so must be removed from sight and from mind. Thus, the socially constituted split between able and disabled people is intensified.

Having speculated that the avoidance of mindful and mundane acceptance of certain differences which function as receptacles for unconscious fears, it is helpful to look at some of the mindless attempts to extend citizenship to include disabled people within the built environment.

The Built Environment

How does the language of architecture and design convey images of inclusion and exclusion? Design aesthetics reflect certain idealized assumptions about the inhabitants and users of the built environment. In different ways, designer 'ableism' is a central feature of classical, modern and postmodern architecture. The stairs, plinths and ornamentation characterizing classical architecture are concerned to exclude the powerless and demarcate zones of privilege. Modern architecture, by contrast, strives towards 'non-contextual pure design', based on 'universal laws' of human habitation. However, this approach assumes human bodies conform to a predictable 'able' type (Imrie, 1996). Le Corbusier commented that 'all men (sic) have the same organism the same functions...the same needs' (quoted in Imrie, 1996: 81). Finally, whilst postmodern architecture does, in theory, attempt to restore human proportions and reject the totalizing impulse of modernism, in practice 'the era of the so-called postmodern has been characterized by the decline of the public realm, the privatization of public spaces, the dismantling of welfare states, and the emergence of non elected local government, all of which seems anathema to forms of political emancipation for people with disabilities' (Imrie, 1996: 98). 'Ablist' design has a detrimental impact on everyone. Environments which fail to take account of people with sensory, mobility and learning 'impairments' tend to be environments which are complex and exhausting to navigate for everyone (Van Royan, 1997). Steps, badly co-ordinated navigational aids such as signs, heavy doors and narrow spaces often may present barriers for older people, those pushing strollers, people carrying a heavy load, people who are feeling tired and those unfamiliar with the environment. Given the difficulties which ableist design presents to everyone, it is surprising that the built environment continues to be thought of by many architects and designers as an abstraction which transcends socio-political context.

Many attempts to overcome the barriers to access for disabled people have been only partially successful. One commonly deployed 'solution' is to engineer a series of formulaic adaptations and introduce a system of 'special' access for 'the disabled'. Whilst such 'accommodations' may bring about some improvement in physical access, they are frequently designed, built and implemented in a thoughtless way, which require the user to engage in a series of complex negotiations to use facilities. A series of examples of mindless adaptation can be found if we address one key social setting.

Lavatories seem to offer a key signifier of the respect accorded to different people. Admittance to lavatories is governed by a set of rules regarding one's membership or use rights within a particular setting. Accessible lavatories may be locked, vandalized, used as a store cupboard, installed in such a way that they are difficult to use (for example, the soap dispenser may be placed too high). At my own place of work, an accessible toilet was installed without a mirror. The door was initially hinged so that it swung inwards. This meant that anyone going past would be able to see the wheelchair user back into the room fully before a series of complex manoeuvres would need to be undertaken in order to close the door. This made a particularly private activity, of slipping into the loo' a very public and visible activity. Such lack of privacy is common in facilities for people with learning difficulties, whose toilets are often designed for the convenience of care assistance than with the dignity of the user in mind. As Thomas has noted on his arrival for work at a hospital ward for the 'mentally handicapped', 'I was shown the shower-room and toilets – cold floors, high ceilings, glaring lights, a row of lavatories with no doors...' (1987: 32). In addition, disabled lavatories may be placed in the women's facilities. Frequently, there are non-gender specific baby changing facilities yet very few are accessible to wheelchairs. Thus, disabled people are positioned as people who are not accorded respect, sexual citizenship (see Shakespeare et al., 1996) or parental roles. Segregated facilities are symbolized with the hegemonic symbol of the wheelchair, such that disability is seen as the same as wheelchair use.

Thus, adaptations may provide a segregated special form of access which reinforces the position of disabled people as a group who, like the occasional foreign guest, 'we' must remember to think about and lay on extra facilities for. In addition to practical barriers, the lack of aesthetic sensibility in disability design also conveys the message that disabled people are a 'special' category rather than natural community members. Napolitano writes of elegant Victorian buildings, that they reflect and engender 'a sense of pride in citizenship, a sense of belonging to something larger than self and family' (1996: 34). When adaptations are made without consideration of the extent to which they are in tune with the environment, they reinforce associations of disability as something which cannot be harmoniously included into the 'able' world. Napolitano expresses this well:

> I wasn't at all happy with the idea that getting my share of what goes on in those buildings should inevitably produce an aesthetic blot on the cityscape. If my participation could only be made possible by some ugly contraption, what did that say about me? What would it do to my sense of pride in citizenship?. Being able to use the environment is about more than being able to 'get about'. At a deeper level it is about a sense of belonging. Until the environment supports mobility impaired people's participation with dignity and pride intact, this sense will continue to evade them. (1996: 34–35)

A more fundamental form of inclusion would involve a thorough-going adoption of the principles of universal design. Universal design is concerned to produce a 'flexible architecture' based on structures which are 'demountable, reasonable, multifunctional and changeable over time' (Weisman, 1992: 32). This would involve building which thought about difference at the outset or, when adapting a building, working in a way which is both thoughtful regarding the access requirements of a wide range of potential (rather than just current) users, and to aesthetics. 'Ramps could be constructed in the same stone as nineteenth century buildings and grab rails could be made of brass with elegant Victorian styling' (Napolitano, 1996: 34). Such a change would clearly need to be based on consultation with as wide as possible range of disabled people. This is not to say that environments can ever be made perfectly accessible to all people. As French (1994) has pointed out, many alterations in the environment cannot address all the needs of every single person since some people have conflicting needs. For example, some visually impaired people need bright lights whilst other visually impaired people need dim lights in order to see. However, recognition of the ways in which design aesthetics lack mindful consideration of certain oppressed groups is a central issue in disability campaigning.

Examining who the environment is built for and what messages architectural aesthetics convey shows the extent to which assumptions about citizenship are built into the environment. The exclusion of disabled people does not need to be expressed actively. It just appears as a natural fact of life, which is medicalized and located in impaired people's bodies. When disabled people are invited in to the 'able' environment, the split between ability and disability is left intact. The concept of 'integration' leaves the concept of a fantasized wholeness and normal educational ability intact. Hegarty et al., write,

> pupils with special needs do not need integration. What they need is education...there is the tendency to talk of the integration of the handicapped, implying that it is something done to or by the handicapped. Integration is their problem. (1981: 13–15)

What is needed is transformation of the built environment so that those who are currently disabled become citizens.

Earlier in this chapter I discussed images of the active citizen and his or her bounded community. These images relied on a visual aesthetic. For the final section of this chapter, I wish to discuss some particularly successful forms of resistance, on the part of disabled people. I identify the power of this resistance to disrupt the able/disable binary in the images of activity and engagement presented by a variety of disabled protesters.

Resistance to Cultural Exclusion: The Disabled People's Movement

If we examine some recent stories of disabled people's resistance, they are united by the powerful way they disrupt stereotypes of disabled people as passive and exclude impaired people for recognition and inclusion. They offer images of disabled people trespassing into a cultural terrain belonging to non-disabled citizens. Acts of civil disobedience use a variety of strategies, including humour, surprise and drama to challenge ablist assumptions that disabled people are lacking and need non-disabled support.

In the USA disabled people's acts of resistance, such as the ADAPT actions in the 1960s, have played an important role in challenging ablist structures and practices (Shapiro, 1994). One important watershed in disabled people's actions was the 1988 student protest at Gallaudet University, Washington DC. Gallaudet is a university for Deaf people[2] and the students were protesting against the appointment of a hearing president. Whilst there had been black presidents at Howard University and women presidents at Wesley College, Gallaudet had not, prior to 1988, had a Deaf president. When a hearing candidate was appointed to the post, student protests closed down the University. The protest was difficult to control using traditional police methods. The students hearing impairments led to particular difficulties in crowd control. Students pulled fire alarms and were able to ignore police megaphones with relative impunity. The protest presented a powerful visual image, of 'hundreds of outstretched arms signing "Deaf President Now" over and over, in a rhythmic choreography' (Shapiro, 1994). Gallaudet students were successful in securing the removal of the hearing president. Perhaps more important than the appointment of a Deaf University president, was the national image of activism and resistance.

Until the 1990s, many actions by disabled people went undocumented (see Campbell and Oliver, 1996). One was by residents of a Cheshire home for people with physical impairments, involving a trip to the pub in pyjamas, in protest against being made 'ready for bed' prior to a change in staff shifts at 6pm. More recent actions by DAN (Direct Action Network) have captured widespread public attention. The DAN symbol is of a wheelchair user breaking chains. DAN actions, which have succeeded in bringing sections of public transport in a number of UK cities to a halt, have brought to television screens images of disabled people in association, rather than in isolation, within public spaces, and engaged in independent activities.

Other examples of challenges to the cultural exclusion of disabled people include attempts to reconceptualize beauty and place disabled people within the orbit of classical beauty. In Alexander McQueen's recent feature in the style magazine *Dazed and Confused* physically disabled people model designer clothes in highly stylized poses, with the intention not of being 'controversial' but rather as a 'joyful celebration of difference' (1998: 68).

Having described what I identify as positive acts of resistance, it is important to add that the valorization of physical presence and active resistance cannot be a panacea in the struggle to obtain full civil rights for those impaired people who are currently disabled. Athletic or beautiful images of disabled people reinforce the association between physical activism and certain appearances with citizenship. The work of DAN might bring the minority of young and healthy disabled people into civil society but does not necessarily empower those disabled people who are older and chronically ill. Perhaps the confidence of the disabled people's movement, particularly in the USA with its emphasis on independent living plays into the ablist fantasy of the possibility of complete autonomy and independence. These caveats suggest what is needed is a range of forms of resistance. We must transform our image of citizenship so that all members of the community may occupy a range of social positions.

Ultimately, a disabling society will only be effectively transformed when all those who are currently constituted as 'impaired' people are accorded respect, recognition and the opportunity for full inclusion, rather than offered cures and 'special' provision. Returning to our concept of cultural citizenship, the disabled people's movement with its emphasis on self-representation and 'endignifying representation', might be characterized as a 'socio-cultural movement' (Pakulski, 1996). Disabled people share with others such as gay people, a core struggle to establish the right to be 'different'. It involves the 're-valu[ation of] stigmatised identities, to embrace openly and legitimately hitherto marginalised lifestyles and to propagate them without hindrance' (1996: 83). Such struggles play an important part in resisting the cultural exclusion of disabled people and transforming narrow assumptions about who is a member of a cultural community. Visible acts of performance and resistance represent an important challenge, but not perhaps a panacea to the problem of isolating and pathologizing disabled people.

Acknowledgement

Many of the examples and themes in this chapter are also discussed in my book *Disability: Controversial Debates and Psychosocial Perspectives*. London: Routledge.

Notes

1 The call for social responsibilities to accompany rights is a key issue for the disabled people's movement. Such responsibilities include the appeal for direct employment of personal assistants rather than having service delivery organized by a paternalistic state. Similarly disabled people have called for the removal of discrimination and barriers which prevent them from working and paying taxes.

2 When a capital is used in 'Deaf' the word refers to a community of sign language users, rather than to those people who have a hearing impairment.

References

Atkinson, D. and Williams, F. (1990) *Know Me As I Am: An Anthology of Poetry, Prose and Art From People with Learning Difficulties*. Sevenoaks: Hodder and Stoughton.

Barnes, C. (1994) *Disabled People in Britain and Discrimination: A Case for Anti-Discrimination Legislation*. London: Hurst & Company/BCODP.

Barnes, C. and Mercer, G. (1996) *Exploring the Divide*. Leeds: The Disability Press.

Barron, D. (1989) 'Locked Away: Life in an Institution', in A. Brechin and J. Walmsley (eds), *Making Connections*. Sevenoaks: Hodder and Stoughton.

Bogdan, R. (1988) *Freak Show: Presenting Human Oddities for Amusement and Profit*. London: The University of Chicago Press.

Butler, J. (1993) *Bodies That Matter: On the Discursive Limits of 'Sex'*. London: Routledge.

Campbell, J. and Oliver, M. (1996) *Disability Politics: Understanding Our Past, Changing Our Future*. London: Routledge.

Darke, P. (1997) 'From Polemical Theory to Defining Analysis', Book Three, Module One, MA Disability Studies Distance Learning Programme, published by Sheffield University.

Davis, K. (1994) 'The Crafting of Good Clients', in J. Swain, V. Finkelstein, S. French and M. Oliver (eds), *Disabling Barriers, Enabling Environments*. London: Sage.

Davis, L. (1995) *Enforcing Normalcy: Disability, Deafness and the Body*. London: Verso.

Doyle, B. (1995) *Disability, Discrimination and Equal Opportunities: A Comparative Study of the Employment Rights of Disabled Persons*. London: Mansell Publishing Ltd.

Dutton, K.R. (1995) *The Perfectible Body: The Western Ideal of Physical Beauty*. London: Cassell.

Etherington, A., Hall, K. and Whelan, M. (1988) 'What it's Like For Us', in D. Towell (ed.), *An Ordinary Life in Practice*. London: Kings Fund.

Evans, J. (1988) 'The Iron Cage', *Ten 8 Photographic Magazine*, 29.

Finkelstein, V. (1980) *Attitudes and Disabled People: Issues for Discussion*. New York: World Rehabilitation Fund.

French, S. (1994) 'Disability, Impairment or Something in Between', in J. Swain, V. Finkelstein, S. French and M. Oliver (eds), *Disabling Barriers – Enabling Environment*. London: The Open University and Sage.

Gallagher, H.G. (1985) *FDR's Splendid Deception*. New York: Dodd, Mead and Company.

Groce, N. (1985) *Everyone Here Spoke Sign Language: Heredity Deafness on Martha's Vineyard*. Harvard, MA: Harvard University Press.

Hall, S. (1990) 'Minimal Selves', in *M/F*, 22 Jan.

Hegarty, S., Pocklington, K. and Lucas, D. (1981) *Educating Pupils with Special Needs in Ordinary Schools*. Windsor: Nfer-Nelson.

Humphries, S. and Gordon, P. (1992) *Out of Sight: The Experiences of Disability 1900–1950*. Plymouth: C4/Northcote House.

Imrie, R. (1996) *Disability and the City: International Perspectives*. London: Paul Chapman Publishing.

Lynch, P. (1997) 'From Hard Blocks to Soft Braille – Reported Advances in Technology', MA Dissertation, Centre for Psychotherapeutic Studies, Sheffield University.

Marshall, T.H. (1950) *Citizenship and Social Class*. Cambridge: Cambridge University Press.

McQueen, A. (1998) 'Fashion Able?' in *Dazed and Confused* (46), September.

Morris, J. (1993) *Independent Lives: Community Care and Disabled People*. London: Macmillan Press.

Napolitano, S. (1996) 'Mobility Impairment', in G. Hales (ed.), *Beyond Disability: Towards an Enabling Society*. London: Sage, in association with The Open University Press.

Nordon, M. (1994) *Cinemas of Isolation: A History of Physical Disability in the Movies*. New Brunswick: Rutgers University Press.

Nordon, M. (1995) 'Politics, Movies and Physical Disability', *Kaleidoscope*, Winter/Spring, 30: 6–14.

Oliver, M. (1990) *The Politics of Disablement*. London: Macmillan.

Oliver, M. (1996) *Understanding Disability: From Theory to Practice*. London: Macmillan.

Oliver, M. and Zarb, G. (1989) 'The Politics of Disability', *Disability, Handicap and Society*, 4 (3): 224–239.

Pakulski, J. (1996) 'Cultural Citizenship', in *Citizenship Studies*, 1 (1): 73–86.

Parsons, T. and Fox, R. (1952) 'Illness, Therapy and the Modern American Family', *Journal of Social Issues*, 8: 31–44.

Pope, A.M. and Tarlov, A.R. (eds) (1995) *Disability in America: Toward a National Agenda for Prevention*. Washington DC: National Academy Press.

Potts, M. and Fido, R. (1990) *A Fit Person to be Removed*. Plymouth: Northcote Press.

Ryan, J. with Thomas, F. (1987) *The Politics of Mental Handicap*. London: Free Association Books.

Shakespeare, T., Gillespie-Sells, K. and Davies, D. (1996) *The Sexual Politics of Disability*. London: Cassell.

Shapiro, J. (1994). *No Pity: People with Disabilities Forging a New Civil Rights Movement*. New York: Times Books.

Sibley, D. (1996) *Geographies of Exclusion*. London: Routledge.

Sinason, V. (1992) *Mental Handicap and the Human Condition: New Approaches from the Tavistock*. London: Karnac Books.

Sontag, S. (1977) 'Illness as Metaphor', in *Illness as Metaphor and Aids and its Metaphors*. New York: Doubleday Anchor.

Teichman, J. (1996) *Social Ethics*. Oxford: Basil Blackwell.

Thomas, F. (1987) 'Everyday Life on the Ward', in J. Ryan with F. Thomas, *The Politics of Mental Handicap*. London: Free Association Books.

Tomlinson, S. (1982) *A Sociology of Special Education*. London: Routledge and Kegan Paul.

Tooley, M. (1983) *Abortion and Infanticide*. Oxford: Oxford University Press.

Van Royan, J. (1997) 'The Baby and the Bathwater', *The Squiggle Foundation Newsletter*, October. London: The Squiggle Foundation.

Walkerdine, V. (1990) *School Girl Fictions*. London: Verso.

Walmsley, J. (1994) '"Talking to Top People": Some Issues Relating to the Citizenship of People With Learning Difficulties', in J. Swain, V. Finkelstein, S. French and M. Oliver (eds), *Disabling Barriers – Enabling Environments*. London: Sage, in association with the Open University Press.

Weisman, L. (1992) *Discrimination By Design*. Illinois: University of Illinois Press.

Williamson, J. (1997) 'Survival of the Thinnest', *The Guardian* (Weekend Section), 22 March.

Wilson, M. (1993) 'DSM-III and the Transformation of American Psychiatry: a History', *American Journal of Psychiatry*, 150: 399–410.

Without Walls: Supercrips and Rejects (1996) Channel 4, 9 April, UK.

Young, I.M. (1989) 'Polity and Group Difference, A Critique of the Idea of Universal Citizenship', *Ethics*, 250–274.

Zola, I.K. (ed.) (1982) *Ordinary Lives: Voices of Disability and Disease*. Cambridge, Massachusetts: Applewood Books.

12

YOUTH MARGINALITY UNDER 'POSTMODERNISM'

Shane Blackman and Alan France

This chapter will focus on how the academic discourse on youth culture and citizenship has produced understandings of social and cultural processes relating to the status of young people in society. It will examine the way that academics, interested in youth issues within a British national context, have theorized both the notion of 'youth culture' and 'citizenship'. The discussion will explore how these concepts may be interconnected while also examining the extent to which they have been constructed in a theoretical discourse around either the notion of inclusion; linked to all young people, or exclusion; relating to only a small minority. In considering these issues we shall also discuss whether theoretical arguments give agency to young people or whether they are seen as passive. This chapter is concerned with agency which is expressed in terms of resistance to dominant cultural forms; a passive role would imply that young people are not resistant but dictated to, or in conformity with the dominant culture. However, using resistance as a means to gauge whether or not 'citizenship' and 'youth culture' has agency creates the effect of effacing the complex process whereby cultural forms which do express a challenge to the dominant culture are incorporated economically in ways that empty them of their resistant content and paradoxically make them support the dominant order.

The concept of marginality – and the celebration of difference – is relevant to this process. For some theorists working within a postmodernist approach, marginality is celebrated as an expression of resistance. But where postmodernism represents 'the cultural logic of late capitalism', difference is itself attractive to the market as a selling feature. On this basis youth cultures which express marginality can be taken up and exploited economically within a global market-place. This has the effect of translating an expression of difference into a mainstream commodity available for consumption. At the same time it is the decline of economic and social citizenship rights of the young that has placed them in a position of social exclusion within society. While much of this process has been the result of political ideology (Coles, 1995; France, 1996) its outcome aids the workings of capital accumulation by both excluding young people, and then exploiting the resistant cultural forms which arise from their marginality. Importantly, this process is neither automatic nor the only possible response, as shown by the development in Britain of cultural-political protest and DIY cultures during the 1990s (McKay, 1996, 1998). This is why a full understanding must be based upon the study of specific youth cultural forms within their own social context.

A Theoretical Critique of Youth Culture and Youth Subculture

Youth culture is historical and contemporary, it creates the opportunity for young people to forge roles and make identities. It enables degrees of differing partici- pation at different ages and at different periods in young people's lives. Youth culture is foreground and background for all young people's lives. It is both established by young people and made by others for young people (Rees, 1986). Within early teenage years it may be that youth culture is more fashion regulated, whilst for young adults there is a conscious decision to select from within the broad range of styles according to relevant social, cultural, ethnic and gender for- mation (see Blackman, 1995: 22–56).

The 1940s post-war period marks the origin and elaboration of the two terms 'youth culture' and 'youth subculture'. We argue that the articulation of the two concepts is an expression of the social divisions of inclusion and exclusion. At the same time, the concept of the 'teenager' was coined in 1945 by Eugene Gilbert, a 19-year-old student at Chicago University as a category of market research (Gilbert, 1957). Youth had emerged as a target for commodity produc- tion. Mark Abrams argues that there was 'a grand total of £900 millions a year to be spent by teenagers at their own discretion' (1959: 9). From the outset it can be asserted that youth culture is based upon consumerism and although participation is restricted according to economic resources, Abrams identifies the teenage con- sumer as an inclusive feature of youth culture. Through the idealism of consumer- promoted-identity young people were able to effectively discriminate and combine cultural artifacts to assert their generational difference from the parental culture.

Conceptually youth culture and youth subculture are derived from the func- tionalist paradigm of American sociological thought. The term youth culture was first employed by Talcott Parsons in his 1942 paper 'Age and sex in the social structure of the United States'. Parsons establishes the trend for youth to be seen as 'trouble' when he stated 'the orientation of the youth culture is more or less specifically irresponsible. One of its dominant features is "having a good time"' (1942: 92). Although Parsons assesses youth culture as representing values in conflict with the adult world, he also argues 'there is reason to believe that the youth culture has important positive functions in easing the transition from secu- rity of childhood in the family of orientation to that of the full adult in marriage and occupational status' (1942: 101). We would not wish to start a rather late functionalist revival, and we see the ideology within Parsonian analysis as flawed, but we would note that the value in Parsons' interpretation is that he identifies young people's activities in youth culture as inclusive.

The term subculture applied by A.K. Cohen (1955) had its theoretical origin in Robert Merton's elaboration of Durkheim's theory of anomie. Merton conceptu- alized deviance from the norm as an individual problem, whereas Cohen conceptualized deviance from the norm as a social group solution not an individual action. For Cohen subculture is inconsistently theorized as a deviant minority practice belonging to segments of the working class who experience 'structural strain' and 'status frustration'. On this basis the theoretical elaboration of the term subculture is applied to potentially all working class youths who refuse to adapt to the norm, for example the goals of success via institutional means such as school. These youths are then defined as not part of society and categorized as outsiders. Here subculture is inclusive and applied to a whole class culture, but is also used as an exclusive theoretical tool relating to a delinquent minority who are brushed with the dangerous attraction of marginality. Thus the theoretical origins of both youth culture and subculture belong in the school of deviance: the conceptual formulation identifies youth culture as 'generational trouble' and sub-culture as deviant.

Thus far it is possible broadly to state that the concept of youth culture is theorized as inclusive and subculture as exclusive; the two concepts were applied separately. During the 1960s criminologists David Downes, Stan Cohen and Laurie Taylor critically explored the theoretical link between deviance and sub-cultures, then in the 1970s Phil Cohen argues that 'it's important to make a dis-tinction between subculture and delinquency' (1972: 30). In an attempt to break the association of subculture with crime and pathology in an exclusive way, Cohen brought forth an inclusive argument that identified subcultures as belong-ing to the working class: he maintained that subcultures were 'produced by a dominated culture not a dominant culture' (1972: 30). Cohen's primary focus was on locale, he firmly identified subcultures as being at the heart of the working class community. He maintains that subcultures 'all correspond to the same parent culture and ... attempt to work out through a system of transformations, the basic problematic or contradiction which is inserted in the subculture by the parent culture' (1972: 23).

Cohen does not employ the term youth culture, because his assertion is that the specific youth styles are generated by the parent culture. On this basis he argues that subculture is an inclusive theoretical concept, whereby it is possible to explore these cultural forms as sites of resistance within a subordinate culture, the working class. In contrast, Willis (1977) does not apply the concept of subculture in *Learning to Labour* but refers to a 'counter culture' with its obviously greater political connotations. However, in an earlier study Willis explains his omission of the term subculture: 'The notion implies a relative positioning which seems to give an altogether misleading sense of absoluteness and dominance of the main culture' (1972, XLV–XLVI). He sees the concept of subculture as an exclusive category which is both 'mechanistic' and lacking rigour. In both cases each of the authors are advancing agency and inclusion for their theoretical propositions to understand youth. As Marcus states the rationale to their separate approaches is that 'Youths' culture is in fact positively meaningful and creative, that they are on to something rather than just being the alienated class both in conditions of work and spirit' (1986: 187).

The uniting of the concepts of youth culture and subculture was undertaken by the Centre for Contemporary Cultural Studies (CCCS) in their classic text

Resistance Through Rituals. However, it would be inaccurate to suggest that the aim of the CCCS was only unification. Clarke et al. state 'Our aim is to de-throne or de-construct the term, "Youth Culture", in favour of a more complex set of categories. We shall try, first, to replace the concept of "Youth Culture" with the more structural concept of "subculture". We then want to reconstruct "sub-cultures" in terms of their relations, first, to "parent" cultures, and, through that, to the dominant culture, or better, to the struggle between dominant and subordi-nate cultures' (1975: 16).

The CCCS analysis begins with the assumption that youth culture is tied to the market as a consumption-led means to exploit an affluent young working class and which may blunt consciousness. The differentiation between youth culture and subculture is undertaken on the basis that youth culture was 'most simply the crea-tion of a truly mass culture' (Clarke et al., 1975: 19). In this sense, youth culture is defined as an inclusive and passive form of consumer control, whereas subculture is manoeuvred into an active response to oppression under the dominant order. The youth subculture now takes on the mantle of the parental experience of class contradictions under capitalism. Clarke et al. state 'Subcultures are shown to address a common class problematic, yet attempt to resolve by means of an imaginary relation – i.e. ideologically – the real relations they cannot otherwise transcend' (1975: 33). On this basis subcultures are injected with agency and creativity through a cultural Marxist analysis, whilst youth culture is dismissed as an artificial and malleable imposition experienced by young people who are not part of the subculture.

The CCCS defines subculture in terms of a distinct social class expression, where gender and ethnic identity remained underdeveloped (Gilroy, 1987; Griffin, 1993). On this basis social class-defined subcultural styles are understood within a Gramscian framework as challenging the construction of hegemony through their relative autonomy. Young working class people are seen as being no different from their parents: in that 'working class culture has consistently "won space" from the dominant culture' (Clarke et al., 1975: 42). For the CCCS, the concept of subculture is inclusive because all working class youth are seen as having the potential to undertake differing forms of 'subcultural solutions', although of course these only solve in an imaginary way the structural 'prob-lematic of their class experience' (1975: 47). Within the CCCS it is initially Clarke and later Hebdige who advance the analysis of subculture onto the ana-lytical terrain of structuralism to establish the autonomy of the signifying prac-tices of subculture. The take-up of Levi-Strauss' concepts of bricolage and homology as a means to interpret subculture means the theory is able to generate an infinite number of meanings. Thus the concept of subculture is injected with literary theory to become a host which signifies refusal and displays resistance to powerlessness. The most advanced members of the subculture are those who are able to challenge the bourgeois order; they are seen to possess 'real' creative potential to win space (Amit-Talai and Wulff, 1995).

Without any substantive empirical ethnography on youth culture in the first three case studies of *Resistance Through Rituals*, the 'real' young working class who were part of such subcultures were made temporarily silent. Also those young people who were not identified as members of a subculture were seen as passive followers of commercial youth culture. The theoretical problem is that the 'rest', i.e. ordinary youth, were denied a place in the subculture. Empirically, the three major case studies in *Resistance Through Rituals* failed to talk to the bearers of subculture: youth were excluded from participation in the academic analysis. At the empirical level the CCCS concept of subculture was developed in isolation from youth. At the same time for Hebdige (1979) the theoretical movement towards structuralism led to what Harris calls 'a discursive genealogy of youth' (1992: 93). On this basis the concept of subculture becomes inclusive as a type of cultural response available to all young people regardless of class because subculture has lost its specific class origin and connotation. It is now possible to have an endless chain of structuralist interpretations of endless subcultures: here all youth can take part in variations of different subcultural gazes.

A number of studies to emerge from the Institute for Popular Culture at Manchester Metropolitan University assert that the tradition of youth studies established at the CCCS, either collected data or made interpretations which were determined by their ideological principles. Both Muggleton (1997) and also Lovatt and Purkis (1996: 258) argue that theorists at the CCCS 'are keen to use the research to support their own particular world view (in Willis' case Marxism) rather than letting the voices speak for themselves'. The Manchester Metropolitan University school of thought primarily represented by Steve Redhead (1990, 1993, 1997) argues that the CCCS approach to youth culture was elitist and presented a romanticized political interpretation. Such an approach according to Redhead 'has positioned conceptually youth culture and youth subculture in a relation of resistance to, or rebellion towards a dominant culture' (1990: 41). Redhead is critical of the CCCS theories because the young people in the subculture they described were the few who had not been incorporated into bourgeois society. *Resistance Through Rituals* (Hall and Jefferson, 1975) while remaining empirically weak on youth culture, did articulate the central importance of ethnography. The CCCS significantly retained E.P. Thompson's (1963, 1991) culturalist sensitivities which gave priority to conscious lived experience under contradiction or 'from below'. Rather than see the CCCS position as reductive it is perhaps more accurate to identify it as perhaps too 'romantic' an account of human agency. Willis argues in his conclusion to *Profane Culture* that 'At its best ethnography does something which theory and commentary cannot: it presents human experience without minimizing it, and without making it a passive reflex of social structure and social conditions' (1978: 170).

Unlike Redhead's critique of the CCCS, we consider that the 'real' illegalities and 'imagined' transgressions of youth cultures in fact ensure that some sense of marginality is retained and resistance shown. Redhead and colleagues are critical of the CCCS subculture theory, but their critique is neither substantially developed nor their 'new' theory fully explained. MacDonald critically notes the similarity between contemporary music composition and their application of cultural theory, in that they construct an account 'through sampling elements of Baudrillard's postmodernism' (1994: 100). Although Redhead (1990) is initially critical of Baudrillard's postmodernism, his account soon develops into a celebration whereby 'youth culture can be excavated by way of some of Baudrillard's signposts' (Redhead, 1993: 5). This approach deliberately assesses durable social structures, or the theorization of them, as impositions of determinism. Thus youth culture is 'free floatingly' theorized, in terms of a cultural implosion which recognizes the diversity and differences of individual experience 'without in any way applying some grand narrative' (1993: 5). Redhead and associates' theory of youth culture remains both implicit and essentially descriptive rather than analytical. One of their primary criticisms of the previous theory is that it is too 'old', although precisely what this means is not made clear.

Theoretically the result is that under this postmodernist analysis youth is denied a collective cultural response because this would represent a grand narrative. Their argument is that 1990s youth culture holds little real depth or authenticity. Thus there is no necessity to use critical theory because contemporary youth culture is merely a surface appearance. Their theorization derives from a selective combination of Baudrillard (1985) and Jameson (1991) which sees youth culture as flat and interchangeable, in contrast to the CCCS Marxist theory of youth culture with its focus on resistance. Unfortunately the new emphasis on fragmentation and individual identity seems to have left young people without agency or recognition of their imposed marginal status.

Furthermore, this analysis of contemporary youth culture is quite inaccurate when it asserts that youth culture is depthless. The 1990s has been a period of considerable youth cultural diversity as shown through the expansion of cross cultural identities in terms of youth style and popular music (Polhemus, 1994; Thornton, 1995). It is possible to identify the period from the late 1980s as one where youth culture became less divided, as differing groups such as goths, heavy metal, grunge, hip hop, indie, jungle, ravers, travellers, new age hippies and others were brought together. 1990s youth culture is not merely an age of superficial plunder, rather it has spawned a multiplicity of diverse and interconnecting youth cultures which mark festivals as a site of difference and unity: an inclusive collective action. In this sense Redhead's selected postmodernist theory may assert that youth culture is superficial and lacks critical reflection, but empirical reality supports the view that youth culture is more complex, diversified and meaningful than Redhead allows. As Collin identifies specifically in relation to ecstasy culture 'It has an open-access formula: rather than a defined ideology, it offers a series of possibilities that people can use to define their own identity, possibilities that can be adapted to each individual's background, social status and belief system. It is endlessly malleable, pragmatic to new meaning' (1997: 4). Throughout the 1990s popular youth culture has been in perpetual self-invention as a dynamic cultural force fragmenting but projecting a collective voice (Reynolds, 1998). Part of the radical element to contemporary dance culture has been its integral connection to other forms of DIY protest, including Free Festivals, Anti-Nuclear Groups, the Reclaim the Streets Movement and Anti-Road Groups, through specific dance collectives, such as Exodus. These forms of disparate protest were brought together via demonstration against the Criminal Justice Act. Currently, for government and media such non-traditional alternative life styles are understood to represent values which are in opposition to the mainstream. The loose coalition between the various DIY cultures, forms of protest, travellers and the dance scene gives the impression of an identifiable international youth subculture. The new British Labour government presents a more positive understanding of alternative cultures through its link with youth cultural icons; however, this has not prevented both government and media from negatively labelling such young adults as dangerous 'folk devils'.

Citizenship and the Exclusion of Rights for Young People

Here we will address the theorization of citizenship and challenge the dominance of the transitional approach, due to its under-emphasis on this aspect of young people's cultural and identity formation. We assert that recent theories of cultural consumption that fail to develop an understanding of the materialistic and structural constraints which shape young people's actions only serve to reinforce young people's marginality.

Since the mid-1980s the growth of modern citizenship is seen as being linked to the expansion of the modernity project. Contemporary citizenship was born out of the shift from 'traditional forms of living' to the 'modern' where anonymous, secular and egalitarian forms of social belonging dominated. In such conditions the social order is created around the notion of rationality (Turner, 1994). Recent debates in Britain on citizenship evolved after the Second World War. T.H. Marshall (1950) argued that increasing citizenship for all was a justifiable ideal for the newly established post-war welfare states. Built into Marshall's theory of citizenship were three main assumptions, all of which still have a major influence on the theorizing of citizenship. First, to be a full citizen you have to be an adult. Adulthood and citizenship are seen to be interconnected and interrelated. Secondly, citizenship is something that is bestowed on members of nation-states. Full citizenship is seen as being achieved when a person is seen as a legal member of a nation. Thirdly, 'being a member' brings with it certain forms of benefits. Not only does the state offer physical protection from outsiders but it also provides certain rights and benefits. In the early part of the post-war years this debate evolved around extending social rights to all, although young people's rights were never identified as being of central importance (France, 1996).

In relation to young people and citizenship the debate has been defined in terms of transition (Jones and Wallace, 1992). Being young is seen as being between 'childhood' and 'adulthood'. It is where either learning about adulthood takes place or where the 'rites of passage' are undertaken. The notion of 'transitional rights' has a tendency to ignore constraining factors which may be influential in shaping young people's movement into citizenship. Taylor (1989) argues that a rights-based society fails to recognize other sources of social power. Certain groups of young people, especially those who live in poor economic regions are clearly excluded and marginalized by the exercise of social power (Blackman, 1998; Brown, 1995). Not only is citizenship concerned with legal entitlement to a nation-state but it is also tied into a whole set of ideological practices associated with who holds power and who defines what it is to be a citizen. Citizenship rights are integral to young people as they enter the symbolic and political order of adult society although other forms of social power need to be recognized. For example, young people's entrance to civil society under a series of Conservative governments has resulted in contested entry: where both legislation and tabloid news media have been preoccupied with young people's transgression and oppression (Cohen, 1997; Holland, 1995).

The movement towards a long transition has been structurally based around principles of deferred citizenship, for example government policies such as the denial of an automatic right to Income Support in 1988 or the assumption of social security regulations which imposed age-related income. The stated aim of such policies is to encourage young people to stay within the parental home. This arrangement draws young people into closer relations of familial conflict and tension as they become more dependent, but also subject to parental control at a time when they should be more autonomous.

But theorizing of citizenship often ignores the exercise of political power and thus denies the real context of what it means to be young in late modernity. The focus on 'transitions as citizenship' suggests that there are a number of processes that young people need to either 'pass through' or 'gain' to aid their movement into adulthood. Within such an argument all activities are given equal weight, little attention is given to priorities. This therefore fails to recognize the centrality of an independent income, i.e. the wage and the role it plays, not only in aiding young people's movement into adulthood but also in giving them the resources to participate in their own social and cultural worlds. By locating the wage as 'one of many' it is given equal value to other aspects of transitions: activities such as leaving home, establishing intimate relationships and getting independent accommodation.

Levitas challenges the assumption that the only route to reverse social exclusion is through paid employment. We agree with her that employment is definitely a source of potential social integration because the wage allows for active consumption: without it transitions either grind to a halt or young people find themselves 'marginalized'. The primacy of paid work as she goes on to argue should not be taken as read because 'social integration may not result from labour market participation' (1996: 14). Under the ideological principles of citizenship young people may find that they have been socially included through access to paid work, but experience social exclusion through low wages and poor chances for mobility: thus young people are socially included and excluded at the same time. Whilst the New Labour government have made high profile policy presentations about challenging the social exclusion of young people through programmes such as New Deal little seems to have changed. Although New Deal aims to be 'inclusive' its chances of success are limited. First, New Deal focuses on tackling supply side difficulties and 'employability' not creating 'real' jobs. As Turok and Webster (1998) have argued such a position will not provide 'real' jobs where they are needed the most or improve the material base for the young unemployed. In fact it is more likely to increase their 'exclusion' as they find the only jobs available are in the low paid, service sector that offers little in terms of advancement. Secondly, recent evidence is suggesting that New Deal is not an 'inclusive' programme. Sections of unemployed youth are being 'excluded' at the point of entry. Others are 'excluding' themselves by developing 'strategies of resistance' (Hoogvelt and France, 1998) or by 'disappearing' at different stages of the programme (DfEE, 1998). Other developments, such as the removal of student grants, the continuation with age-related benefits and differentiation with adults for the minimum wage suggest the consolidation of young people's insecurity and the continuing tradition of viewing 'youth as trouble'. Where contradictory, involvement of young adults in different forms of protest and alternative cultures is not seen as acts of empowerment but identified as evidence to deny rights and increase dependency. Government and media identify this form of cultural citizenship as a direct challenge. As McKay argues 'The construction or reclamation of space for a group or a group event is a continual project, and indicates the extent to which DIY culture is active, does want to move by practical example rather than rhetoric' (1998: 26).

Where citizenship is theorized in transitional studies the focus tends to suggest 'passivity' where 'rights' and 'rites of passage' are handed down to young people. Wyn and White (1997) attempt to rethink the youth transition through asserting that such a separate stage does not exist. For them traditional notions of youth transition are a form of Western hegemony implying universalism where there is none. In Western nations youth is a distinct phase located in time and locked into specific spaces with social and cultural meanings: to be young has specific cultural significance. However, at the same time the theorization of transitions implicitly suggests rationality in terms of arrival and completion with respect to adult identity formation. Here youth is defined both legally and culturally in terms of the transition towards adulthood. This common-sense understanding of 'growing-up' fails to see the structural and institutionalized processes which systematically marginalize young people.

Cultural Citizenship and Postmodern Consumption

Under late modernity the new challenges for our understanding of citizenship are; the globalization of labour markets; nationalism and the changing nature of the state; and the rise of new right ideology (Roche, 1992). In terms of young people, much of this debate has been led by the political right around questions of young people's individual duty to their families and the state (France, 1996). Turner argues that the traditional method of theorizing citizenship ignores the importance of culture. He suggests that historically citizenship has been defined sociologically as 'a bundle of practices which are social, legal, and political' (1994: 159). With the massive growth of cultural artifacts and activities, citizenship is now being theorized in terms of the impact of economic participation in market relations through the purchase of, and participation in, culture. This leads Giroux to argue that under late capitalism the discourse of citizenship should be identified with 'a broader struggle for cultural democracy' (1992: 246).

Building on the analysis of youth culture in the first part of the chapter we argue that it is necessary to critically assess the relationship between cultural citizenship and forms of consumption by young people. Abu-Lughod sees the importance of locality where people actively 'select, incorporate and redeploy'

(1989: 8) global mainstream cultural media for their own ends. Much in the same way Willis argues 'against postmodernist pessimism' (1990: 26), seeing contemporary culture as a series of opportunities for young people's inclusion in youth cultural consumption and production. Willis talks of creative consumption: 'These processes involve the exercise of critical discriminating choices and uses which disrupt the taste categories and "ideal" modes of consumption promoted by the leisure industry and break up its superimposed definitions of musical meaning' (1990: 60). Willis in essence argues that young people's involvement in youth culture can be an act of 'symbolic creativity'. On this basis youth culture returns to an inclusive mode, where young people are able to participate and actively engage in youth culture which is locally organized and defined. Mitchell takes up Appadurai's notion of the 'repatriation of difference' to assert that globalized cultural forms, such as youth culture 'are given quite different meanings in different localities' (1996: 264) which offer creative possibilities for alternative meaning.

There is a connection here with Walter Benjamin's (1970) understanding that conscious meaning is produced at the moment of consumption. Under late capitalism youth culture becomes available to more young people making it a symbolic set of resources that can aid identity and critical awareness. In this sense Willis sees young people's participation in youth culture as necessary for critically advancing society and encouraging democratic debate. Willis puts priority on individuals' differing experiences of consumer culture although he tends towards an inflation of agency in terms of the personal meanings held by young people. Willis' theoretical aim is to make youth culture inclusive but also to identify individual consumerism with some form of critical distance. However, for Miles the analysis makes the 'mistake of exaggerating the extent to which young people can be symbolically creative within the parameters provided for them by consumer culture' (1995: 41).

In terms of cultural citizenship it would seem that for Willis (1990) young people are defined as creative through an individualistic interpretation of consumerism that allows for inclusion, where young purchasers discriminate on the basis of an informed consciousness. It is assumed that the critical distance for this informed consumption is provided by location within a subcultural context. However, individual consumerism and collective use of subcultural commodities do not necessarily contain radical possibilities. Connor asserts that 'it would be wrong to assume that its energies are necessarily in a liberalizing direction' (1989: 189).

However, it is under these material conditions that Willis (1990), quite rightly suggests, that even in adverse situations the young have both the ability and desire to be 'creative'. It is important to state that young people's cultural citizenship cannot be understood without a 'theory of materialism'. As Evans argues:

> Citizenship has become increasingly equated with consumer power under the 'New Right'. Unemployment cuts young people off not only from work, but also from exercising consumer power in their leisure time. Adults' monopolies on local politics and democratic structures may also make it difficult for young people to participate. (1995: 21–22)

Therefore, reliance upon the notion of consumer consumption or the 'force of the market' alone denies the importance of young people's need to have economic stability that is at a level which can aid them in participating in cultural practices. Such a focus on markets as providers of income or access to consumption goods will not provide the opportunities necessary for either creating stability or progressing into adult citizenship.

Globalization and Marginality: The Contradictions of Identity

Youth culture and music have moved beyond national borders, through an expansion and development of televisual communications resulting in Western youth culture being projected onto new audiences. Globalization is about the organization of production and exploitation of cultural and economic markets on a world scale. Youth cultures and popular music represent a major source of cultural commodities which can be exported around the planet for huge economic profit for capitalism. Globalization breaks the connection between local territory and culture. Youth becomes a marketable global commercial product via satellite systems which then create a type of electronic populism which has the appearance of being universally available. This has been shown through the growth of satellite TV channels, perhaps the most extensive being MTV. It is estimated that during the 1990s MTV will be broadcasting in over 40 countries and reaching over 204 million homes (Goodwin, 1993). Commercialism has also begun to dominate the contemporary dance scene. Rietveld states 'Clubland is being rationalized according to strategies worked out by lawyers, accountants and marketing specialists' (1998: 255). She notes the high success of commercial clubs such as Cream in Liverpool and Ministry of Sound in south London.

Both youth culture and popular music are central features of the culture industry which are shaped by an elite number of giant corporations which earn billions of dollars worldwide. Negus specifies that one recent form of globalization of youth and music is through the cultural marketing strategy of media synergy. He states synergy is about 'Diversifying into directly related technologies and areas of entertainment and using the opportunities that this provides for extending the exposure of specific pieces of music and artists' (1992: 5). On this basis synergy is able to maximize profit from interconnected areas of the leisure industry across different mediums. Here one global conglomerate, such as Time-Warner, owns the popular youth product as it develops through magazine, book, record, radio, television, video and movie. Western youth style is carried by visual representations of both popular music artists and their audiences. As youth culture becomes universally available it is promoted as a life style package to others, while its more conflictual 'local' edges are smoothed, creating what Featherstone (1995) sees as 'static fictions'. On this basis the youth culture is identified as an accessible life style which shows a taste preference, rather than a lived cultural existence which is shaped by an interaction of social structures.

Contemporary sociological theorists have defined this period as one of postmodernism, where culture plays a more significant role in shaping relations of consumption and production. According to postmodernist writers such as

Dick Hebdige (1988) and Angela McRobbie (1994) youth subculture is firmly located in marginality. This argument enables such theorists to explore the potential of the space i.e. marginality, as a location from which to critique dominant forms of power. Subculture is placed in the theoretical box of marginality for purposes of intellectual articulation, much in the same way that the concept of subculture was placed into the Marxist problematic of the base and superstructure by the creative analysis of the CCCS. For Stuart Hall (1988) the take-up of marginality-as-resistance under conditions of late capitalism results in potential incorporation. Marginality attracts attention due to its difference, but it then becomes a marketing strategy to feed competition and sell products. For Hall, a subcultural form that was perhaps unusual or challenging is reduced to a chic mask. This process was critically described in the lyrics by The Clash (1978) as 'turning rebellion into money', or as Adorno (1991) argues, the culture industry may be understood as responding to the desire for an individualized commodity.

We maintain that the generation of these commodities as cultural forms is derived from young voices which oppose centrality or experience centrality as oppressive. For Hall this results in problems of identity for different young people who have suddenly been recognized and given voice, because they may then lose their own sense of identity as aspects of their cultural habitus go global. Under postmodernist theory the power and meaning of youth culture is identified as deriving from its apparent marginality. The assertion is that such articulations from the margins consist of struggles for identity. Theoretically, young people are defined as possessing agency when they take part in a subculture which celebrates marginality. On this basis the subculture's 'Otherness' is the main ingredient for inversion, subversion and outrage. Hebdige remains silent on the material marginality of youth, while he romances cultural marginality through (post)structuralist theory by using the avant-garde literary expression of Jean Genet as a marker of resistance.

Initially it was the structuralist theory of youth culture developed by Hebdige (1979) which permitted youth culture to be subject to endless forms of different interpretations under semiotics. However, it was the postmodernist analysis which deconstructed youth culture from durable social structures such as class or gender through an assertion that such universal structures forced uniformity on individual expression. The marriage of structuralism and postmodernism as a form of analysis to explore youth culture places too much priority upon virtual rather than more material explanations.

Post-Fordist capitalist production recognizes the market potential of youth culture and its popular music as inherently potent in the sense of exerting power over youth and vulnerable in the sense of being exploitable. These features then become selling points drawing emotional responses. On this basis both the 'realities' and 'representations' of marginality become marketing opportunities for global capital. Capitalism exploits youth cultural marginality for its potential to sell the commodity, but there is no commitment to understanding the marginal status of young people in society. As Jameson (1991) notes, the culture industries are set for the pursuance of the next form of marginality to seize upon, while young people are left with the consequences of increased regulation and greater surveillance of their actions. Wallace and Kovacheva argue that the postmodernist approach 'Tends to ignore the real material inequalities between different groups of young people and their differential access to cultural consumption' (1996: 190). We maintain that for the subculture of origin, style is formed under relations of oppression where locale factors, including class, gender and ethnicity, give agency to young people in the production of a cultural identity.

For the young under late capitalism the contradiction of youth cultural consumerism rests between the pressure and pleasure to 'make changes' to their bodies and appearance. But this commercial edge is also where personal feelings become marketed as forms of commercialized cultural products. Here within popular youth culture individualistic consumerism meets an idealized life style which presents a striking contrast to the social reality of low income and poverty. On this basis exclusion from participation in the materialist world of youth cultural symbols leads to an implosion of dissatisfaction amongst young people. While it may not be fashionable to suggest that the state needs to take a more pro-active role it would seem that if the young are to progress into the adult world, without being damaged by the hegemonic experiences of youth culture, then tackling social marginalization through advancing forms of participative social, economic and cultural citizenship are essential. As mentioned earlier, one continuity between the previous Conservative hegemony and the new Labour government is that loosely connected forms of protest by young adults remain a powerful force. The involvement of young people with differing degrees of direct action from school pupils doing GCSE projects on the banning of live exports, College students supporting Greenpeace, to high profile young anti-road protesters, gives an appearance that the current notions of citizenship are too narrow and if the concept is to be of any value it has to embody cultural diversity.

Youth Marginalization, Resistant and Re-active Citizenship

The theorizing of 'youth citizenship' often fails to recognize the structural and institutional processes that marginalize large sections of the youth population which leads to a situation where they are reduced to 'passive' actors for theoretical manipulation. The effects of this are compounded by the increased marginalization of the young through the restriction and removal of rights, especially to paid work and the wage. This chapter asserts that youth culture in late modernity does have power and significance for the young. Not only is it important for their sense of autonomy and independence, but also as a site where identities are created. Within the debates surrounding young people's citizenship, this area of cultural activity is usually denied or ignored.

Returning to and exploring the notion of 'agency' and 'creativity', it is possible to suggest that the processes of marginality may have unforeseen consequences. Such processes may produce 'resistant' and 're-active' forms of cultural citizenship, which may have longer term consequences for young people. Re-active citizenship can be seen as a means where the state applies an objectifying and disabling gaze upon youth, thus making young people the object for competing discourses of transgression and 'normalization'. Here citizenship is forced on youth via notions of self 'adjustment' rather than through self-directed responsibility (France, 1998). Young people's re-active citizenship is negative, although this reaction is not in opposition to citizenship per se, but rather it contests the imposed ideology of cultural citizenship and thus is a logical response towards their marginalized economic and social position (France and Roche, 1998). Here, cultural citizenship under these circumstances is primarily about regulation and control of young people.

The postmodern preoccupation with consumption as a form of individual expression divorced from social and cultural factors which structure and restrict choice has resulted in a reductive analysis. During the Thatcher decade of the 1980s, market researchers such as Mintel (1988) asserted that young people held conservative attitudes and took part in a new conformism. It was stated that 'youth culture was dead' as a result of New Right economic policy which led to the social marginalization of young people (Frith, 1984). However, the 1980s ideal combination of youth and consumption fragmented under mass youth unemployment and the preceding youth riots: youth was not a model consumer but a social order problem. However, during the 1990s advertising and marketing began to exploit the apparent 'shocking' drug chic narratives and 'negative' images of youth marginality for an even harder mainstream commercial sell (Taylor, 2000).

Throughout the 1990s the youth labour market has been in decline and young people are being structurally directed into an intermediate status of student or trainee (Furlong and Cartmel, 1997). The status of citizenship is deferred for young people located within institutional settings. During the 1990s these educational institutions were the key site for critical socialization of children, teenagers and young adults into different values. Jones argues that 'Education and training policies are forcing working class families to behave in middle class ways: they assume that parents are willing and able to offer extended support to their children, and they assume that young people are willing and able to accept an extension of the period of childlike dependency' (1996: 5). In this context colleges and universities became the new spatial locations for the development of cultural citizenship related to youth culture and consumption (see Skelton and Valentine, 1998). At the same time the wholesale removal of young people from the labour market into differential levels of training and education corresponds to the growth of diversity within youth cultures, for example the dance scene. The impact of these social policies has been to establish a dual form of social marginalization and also to create youth cultural activities which enable participation and identity for young people.

One possible consequence of young working class people's experience of extended transitions is that it occurs within the context of an emancipatory ideology of education. It is here that increased access to values of middle class youth culture have infiltrated previous working class cultural forms. One contradictory outcome is that the further extension of education and training, even though it has resulted in young people experiencing increased economic dependency, has also created an opportunity for them to experiment with styles, sexualities and cultural identities. It is possible to suggest that one result of this extended transition for young people within an education setting has been the increased experimentation with recreational illicit drugs. The sites of university and college with their focus on intellectualism, radicalism and diversity are the home of the counter culture. For Whiteley counter culture is 'largely concerned with alternative modes of living which involved, to a greater extent, the use of drugs as a means of exploring the imagination and self-expression' (1992: 3). Through access to resources at subsidized rates within the college sector, education offered a space and context for young people to be culturally and symbolically active. In the 1990s a broad-based student culture was a meeting ground for the advertising worlds where the glamorization of drug related product identities encountered the recreational play of the newly disaffected youth under the 'long transition'.

The nature and understanding of illicit drugs within middle class youth culture contradicts that which is found within the state and media and primarily follows an intellectual rationale through an assertion of both identity and rights (Nelson, 1989). One problem for young people is that the apparent 'normalization' of drugs within youth culture may lead to further social exclusion and increase their marginality because of the nature of this transgression (Blackman, 1996; Parker et al., 1998). Here the diversity of young people's youth cultural activities allows experimentation for young people to both 'play with' and participate in alternative counter cultures in opposition to the dominant culture, including ecstasy-rave culture, Critical Mass bicycle protest and anti-road protest groups. This generates diverse forms of youth cultural protest which in turn assert demands for cultural citizenship. Here it is possible to identify a logic to young people's transgression, or as Best argues, the contradictory nature of popular cultural products and ideals is that 'they can be the site of both hegemonic and counter-hegemonic ideological productions depending on the context of their reception or production' (1997: 19). Thus we argue that young people's public presence offers real and symbolic challenge but these contestations will in turn be reversed by adults with power, and turned back on young people to deny their cultural and social voices.

Under labour market restructuring, and the lack of a legitimate opportunity structure, some young people have adapted the free market ideology to create their own economic rewards which can be defined as a culture of enterprise but operating outside the law. A number of studies of young people who have limited opportunities in the legitimate labour market have documented their involvement in the informal economy, to gain an income sufficient to allow them participation in a youth culture (Blackman, 1997; Craine, 1997). On this basis a key feature of young people's social marginalization is their lack of a material base which would allow activity in the 'public face' presentation of a youth culture. Inability to use a disposable income restricts the expression of youth cultural identities. This form of cultural exclusion amongst peers may lead some young people into circumstances of risk behaviour and criminality, leading to the ultimate exclusion of penal confinement. In this sense, Roman theoretically argues that 'youth is constituted not only as metaphorical spectacle but also as an economic liability' (1996: 16).

In both examples of illicit drugs and alternative careers, youth marginality creates opportunities and spaces where the young use culture as a means of constructing 'resistant' and 're-active' identities. For young people, youth culture may be one means of expression to challenge notions of imposed citizenship. Because of the removal of legitimate opportunity structures young people use illegitimate means to create identities and forms of anti-materialist cultural citizenship which are 're-active' (McKay, 1998). Not only has this led to increased exclusion from school and possible incarceration, but also the state has indicated that it intends to increase implicit controls on the young and put in force more regulations on their freedoms.

Note

We would like to thank the editor for his support and direction. We would also like to thank Debbie Cox and Jan France for their critical comments.

References

Abrams, M. (1959) *The Teenage Consumer*, 5, July, London Press Exchange Papers.

Abu-Lughod, L. (1989) 'Bedouins, Cassettes and the Technologies of Public Culture', *Middle East Report*, July-August: 7–11/47.

Adorno, T.W. (1991) *The Culture Industry*. London: Routledge.

Amit-Talai, V. and Wulff, H. (eds) (1995) *Youth Cultures: a Cross-Cultural Perspective*. London: Routledge.

Baudrillard, J. (1985) 'The Ecstasy of Communication', in H. Foster (ed.), *Postmodern Culture*. London: Pluto Press, pp. 120–148.

Benjamin, W. (1970) *Illuminations*. London: Jonathan Cape.

Best, B. (1997) 'Over-the-Counter-Culture: Retheorising Resistance in Popular Culture', in S. Redhead (ed.), *The Club Culture Reader*. Oxford: Blackwell, pp. 18–35.

Blackman, S.J. (1995) *Youth: Positions and Oppositions – Style, Sexuality and Schooling*. Aldershot: Avebury Press.

Blackman, S.J. (1996) 'Has Drug Culture Become an Inevitable Part of Youth Culture? A Critical Assessment of Drug Education', *Educational Review*, 48 (2): 131–142.

Blackman, S.J. (1997) '"Destructing a Giro": a Critical and Ethnographic Study of the Youth "underclass"', in R. MacDonald (ed.), *Youth, the Underclass and Social Exclusion*. London: Routledge, pp. 113–129.

Blackman, S.J. (1998) ' "Disposable Generation?" An Ethnographic Study of Youth Homelessness in Kent', *Youth and Policy*, 59: 38–56.

Brown, S. (1995) 'Crime and Safety in whose "Community"?', *Youth and Policy*, 48: 27–48.

Clarke, J., Hall, S., Jefferson, T. and Roberts, B. (1975) 'Subcultures, Cultures and Class: a Theoretical Overview', in S. Hall and T. Jefferson (eds), *Resistance Through Rituals*, Working Papers in Cultural Studies, 7/8, University of Birmingham, Centre for Contemporary Cultural Studies, pp. 9–74.

Clash, The (1978) (White Man) In Hammersmith Palais. London: CBS Records.

Cohen, A. (1955) *Delinquent Boys – the Subculture of the Gang*. London: Collier-Macmillan.

Cohen, P. (1972) 'Subcultural Conflict and Working Class Community', in Working Papers in Cultural Studies, CCCS, University of Birmingham, Spring: 5–51.

Cohen, P. (1997) *Rethinking the Youth Question*. London: Macmillan.

Cohen, S. (1972/1980) *Moral Panics and Folk Devils*. Oxford: Martin Robertson.

Coles, B. (1995) *Youth and Social Policy*. London: UCL Press.

Collin, M. with Godfrey, J. (1997) *Altered States: the Story of Ecstasy Culture and Acid House*. London: Serpent's Tail.

Connor, S. (1989) *Postmodernist Culture*. Oxford: Blackwell.

Craine, S. (1997) 'The Black Magic Roundabout: Cyclical Transitions, Social Exclusion and Alternative Careers', in R. MacDonald (ed.), *Youth, the Underclass and Social Exclusion*. London: Routledge, pp. 130–152.

Department of Employment and Education (1998) *The New Deal Pathfinders*. Report to Education and Employment Committee, House of Commons.

Evans, K. (1995) 'Competence and Citizenship: Towards a Complementary Model for Times of Critical Social Change', *British Journal of Education and Work*, 8 (2): 14–27.

Featherstone, M. (1995) *Undoing Culture: Globalization, Postmodernism and Identity*. London: Sage.

France, A. (1996) 'Youth and Citizenship in the 1990s', *Youth and Policy*, 53: 28–43.

France, A. (1998) ' "Why should we care?" Young People, Citizenship and Questions of Social Responsibility', *Journal of Youth Studies*, 1 (1): 97–111.

France, A. and Roche, M. (1998) 'Regenerating Exclusion: Citizenship, Youth and Urban Mega Projects', in M. Roche (ed.), *Sport, Leisure and Citizenship*. Basingstoke: Falmer, pp. 139–166.

Frith, S. (1984) *The Sociology of Youth*. Ormskirk, Lancashire: Causeway Books.

Furlong, A. and Cartmel, F. (1997) *Young People and Social Change*. Buckingham: Open University Press.

Gilbert, E. (1957) *Advertising and Marketing to Young People*. New York: Printers' Ink Books.

Gilroy, P. (1987) *There Ain't No Black in the Union Jack*. London: Hutchinson.

Giroux, H.A. (1992) *Border Crossings*. London: Routledge.

Goodwin, A. (1993) *Dancing in the Distraction Factory: Music Television and Popular Culture*. Minnesota: University of Minnesota Press.

Griffin, C. (1993) *Representations of Youth*. Cambridge: Polity.

Hall, S. (1988) 'Interview with Stuart Hall', *Block*, 14, pp. 11–15.

Hall, S. and Jefferson, T. (eds) (1975) *Resistance Through Rituals*. London: Hutchinson.

Harris, D. (1992) *From Class Struggle to the Politics of Pleasure*. London: Routledge.

Hebdige, D. (1979) *Subculture: the Meaning of Style*. London: Methuen.

Hebdige, D. (1988) *Hiding in the Light*. London: Routledge.

Holland, R. (1995) 'Friday Night, Saturday Night: Youth Cultural Identification in the Post-industrial City', Department of Social Policy, Working Paper No. 2, University of Newcastle.

Hoogvelt, A. and France, A. (1998) 'Results of New Deal Clients Study', Report to Community Task Team, University of Sheffield.

Jameson, F. (1991) *Postmodernism, or the Cultural Logic of Late Capitalism*. London: Verso.

Jones, G. (1996) 'Deferred Citizenship: a Coherent Policy of Exclusion?', Occasional Paper, No. 3, National Youth Agency.

Jones, G. and Wallace, C. (1992) *Youth, Family and Citizenship*. Buckingham: Open University Press.

Levitas, R. (1996) 'The Concept of Social Exclusion and the New Durkheimian Hegemony', *Critical Social Policy*, 46 (16): 5–20.

Lovatt, A. and Purkis, J. (1996) 'Shouting in the Street: Popular Culture, Values and the New Ethnography', in J. O'Connor and D. Wynne (eds), *From the Margins to the Centre: Cultural Production and Consumption in the Post-industrial City*. Aldershot: Arena, pp. 249–274.

MacDonald, R. (1994) 'Review of Redhead, S. (ed.) *Rave Off: Politics and Deviance in Contemporary Youth Culture*', in *Youth and Policy*, 43: 100–101.

McKay, G. (1996) *Senseless Acts of Beauty: Cultures of Resistance since the Sixties*. London: Verso.

McKay, G. (ed.) (1998) *DIY Culture: Party and Protest in Nineties Britain*. London: Verso.

McRobbie, A. (1994) *Postmodernism and Popular Culture*. London: Routledge.

Marcus, G. (1986) 'Contemporary Problems of Ethnography in the Modern World System', in J. Clifford and G. Marcus (eds), *Writing Cultures: the Poetics and Politics of Ethnography*, Berkeley: University of California Press, pp. 165–193.

Marshall, T.H. (1950) *Citizenship and Social Class*. Cambridge: Cambridge University Press.

Miles, S. (1995) 'Towards an Understanding of the Relationship Between Youth Identities and Consumer Culture', *Youth and Policy*, 51: 35–45.

Mintel, (1988) *Youth Lifestyles*. London: KAE House.

Mitchell, T. (1996) *Popular Music and Local Identity*. London: Leicester University Press.

Muggleton, D. (1997) 'The Post-subculturalists', in S. Redhead (ed.), *The Club Culture Reader*. Oxford: Blackwell, pp. 185–203.

Negus, K. (1992) *Producing Pop: Culture and Conflict in the Popular Music Industry*. London: Edward Arnold.

Nelson, E. (1989) *The British Counter-Culture, 1966–1973*. London: Macmillan.

Parker, H., Measham, F. and Aldridge, J. (1998) *Illegal Leisure: the Normalization of Adolescent Recreational Drug Use*. London: Routledge.

Parsons, T. (1942) 'Age and Sex in the Social Structure of the United States', *American Sociological Review* (7): 604–616.

Polhemus, T. (1994) *Streetstyle*. London: Thames and Hudson.

Redhead, S. (1990) *The End of the Century Party: Youth and Pop Towards 2000*. Manchester: University of Manchester Press.

Redhead, S. (ed.) (1993) *Rave Off: Politics and Deviance in Contemporary Youth Culture*. Aldershot: Avebury Press.

Redhead, S. (ed.) (1997) *The Club Culture Reader*. Oxford: Blackwell.

Rees, H. (1986) *14: 24 British Youth Culture*. London: Boilerhouse.

Reynolds, S. (1998) *Energy Flash: a Journey Through Rave Music and Dance Culture*. London: Picador.

Rietveld, H. (1998) 'Repetitive Beats: Free Parties and the Politics of Contemporary Dance Culture in Britain', in G. McKay (ed.), *DIY Culture: Party and Protest in Nineties Britain*. London: Verso, pp. 243–267.

Roche, M. (1992) *Rethinking Citizenship*. Cambridge: Cambridge University Press.

Roman, L. (1996) 'Spectacle in the Dark: Youth as Transgression, Display and Repression', *Educational Theory*, 46 (1): 1–22.

Skelton, T. and Valentine, G. (eds) (1998) *Cool Places: Geographies of Youth Cultures*. London: Routledge.

Taylor, D. (1989) 'Citizenship and Social Power', *Critical Social Policy*, 20, Autumn: 19–31.

Taylor, D. (2000) 'The Word on the Street: Advertising, Youth Culture and Legitimate Speech in Drug Education', *Journal of Youth Studies* (forthcoming).

Thompson, E.P. (1963) *The Making of the English Working Class*. London: Penguin.

Thompson, E.P. (1991) *Customs in Common*. London: Penguin.

Thornton, S. (1995) *Club Culture: Music, Media and Subcultural Capital*. Cambridge: Polity.

Turner, B. (1994) 'Postmodern Culture/Modern Citizens', in B.V. Steenbergen (ed.), *The Condition of Citizenship*. London: Sage, pp. 153–168.

Turok, I. and Webster, D. (1998) 'The New Deal: Jeopardised by the Geography of Unemployment', *Local Economy*, Feb. 1998: 309–327.

Wallace, C. and Kovacheva, S. (1996) 'Youth Cultures and Consumption in Eastern and Western Europe', *Youth and Society*, 28 (2): 189–214.

Whiteley, S. (1992) *The Space Between the Notes*. London: Routledge.

Willis, P. (1972) 'Pop Music and Youth Groups', unpublished PhD thesis, Centre for Contemporary Cultural Studies, University of Birmingham.

Willis, P. (1977) *Learning to Labour*. Farnborough: Gower.

Willis, P. (1978) *Profane Culture*. London: Routledge.

Willis, P. (1990) *Common Culture*. Milton Keynes: Open University Press.

Wyn, J. and White, R. (1997) *Rethinking Youth*. London: Sage.

13

RACE, MULTI-CULTURALISM AND DIFFERENCE

John Solomos

In contemporary discourse ideas about race, racism and ethnicity have become the subject of intense debate and controversy. It seems that almost everybody is talking about the role of racial and ethnic categorization in the construction of social and political identities. Yet it is paradoxically the case that there is still confusion about what it is that we mean by the use of concepts such as *race* and *racism*, as evidenced by the range of terminological debates that have tended to dominate much discussion in recent years (Goldberg, 1993; Miles, 1993; Solomos and Back, 1996). It is perhaps partly the result of this focus on terminology that much of the academic debate in this field has remained somewhat abstract and unsatisfactory.

I must make clear straight away that I shall not spend much time debating whether or not there are races, whether or not it represents a scientific error to actually use the term race. This is not because I take notions such as race as given or unproblematic. I, along with the vast majority of researchers in this field, do not regard race as a scientific category. Efforts to divide human beings into groups on the basis of alleged genetic or phenotypical differences have proved to be spurious and misleading, and in some cases politically disastrous (Kohn, 1995). Rather it is by now widely accepted that it is best to see race as a means of representing difference such that contingent attributes, such as skin colour, are transformed into essential bases for identities. But this is not to deny that race remains, at the level of everyday experience and social representation, a potent political and social category around which individuals and groups organize their identity and construct a politics. As such, race is socially constructed; and blackness and whiteness are not categories of essence but defined by historical and political struggles over their meaning.

In my recent research on race and political identities in Birmingham I have attempted to illustrate this point by showing how race and ethnicity are essentially political resources, that can be used by both dominant and subordinate groups for the purposes of legitimizing and furthering their own social identities and interests (Solomos and Back, 1995). Indeed a key theme running throughout the analysis of race and changing political cultures is that it is precisely through contestation and struggle that identities based on race and ethnicity gain meaning as both political and social categories. In this sense racialized identities are not simply imposed, since they are also often the outcome of resistance and political struggle in which racialized groups play a key and active role. For this reason it is more accurate to speak of a racialized group rather than a racial group since race is a product of racism and not vice versa.

If race and ethnicity are about the representation of difference, it is also necessary to be aware of the complex ways in which they are structured by relations of power. Sites of difference are also sites of power, a power too whereby the dominated comes to see and experience themselves as 'Other'. Dominant representations of difference may function to exclude and exploit, and to justify unequal access and involvement in specific institutions. Every regime of representation is a regime of power formed, as Foucault reminds us, by the fateful couplet, power/knowledge (Foucault, 1980; Stoler, 1995). Those in positions of power in a society can validate and impose their own definitions of normality, and define boundaries for the purpose of excluding, enclosing or exploiting others. These definitions carry with them particular notions of value and entitlement, and so defend privilege either directly or through the operation of codes, norms and rules that may appeal to universalism, but which actually represent the social interests of dominant groups.

From a historical perspective it is clear that part of the power of racism lies in the way in which racist ideologies operate by constructing impassable symbolic boundaries between racially constituted, or racialized, categories. A recurrent theme in racist discourses is the attempt to fix and naturalize the difference between belongingness and otherness. A principal means of accomplishing this is to perceive the self as carried in the genes rather than transmitted via culture, as distilled through what appears to us as most 'natural' and immediate: the body. Corporeal properties, and most fetishistically, skin colour, thus come to furnish an 'epidermal schema' not only for anchoring difference but for distinguishing the pure from the impure, the included from the excluded. To the extent that the body comes to signify difference so too does it become a site and target for strategies of normalization and discipline, a site for an obsessive imperative that aims to expunge any kind of syncretism which questions the authenticity of the 'truth propositions' about these em-bodied polar identities of 'black' and 'white'. We see this in the constant preoccupation in racist discourses with questions of 'racial purity' and the dangers of hybridity and miscegenation. The concern with policing racial boundaries and ensuring that 'purity' is maintained can and indeed has taken many forms. In the United States and in South Africa, albeit in very different forms, there were attempts to control and regulate miscegenation through legislation and state intervention. During the Nazi period in Germany the attempt to construct racial purity took the form of systematic genocide aimed at Jews and other groups and programmes of euthanasia aimed at 'undesirable' elements in German society.

The point I am trying to make through these examples is that race and ethnicity are not 'natural' categories, even though both concepts are often represented as if they were (Appiah, 1989; Mosse, 1985; Wolf, 1994). Their boundaries are not fixed, nor is their membership uncontested. Racial and ethnic groups, like nations, are imagined communities. They are ideological entities, made and changed in struggle. They are discursive formations, signalling a language through which differences are accorded social significance, may be named and explained. But what is of importance for us, as social researchers studying race and ethnicity, is that such ideas also carry with them material consequences for those who are included within, or excluded from, them.

Recent developments in Western and Eastern European societies are a case in point. The rise of extreme right wing and neo-fascist movements and parties has resulted in the development of new forms of racist politics and in the articulation of popular racism and violence against migrant communities. At the same time we have seen a noticeable rise in anti-Semitism in both Western and Eastern Europe, evident in both physical and symbolic threats to Jewish communities. In this environment it is perhaps not surprising that questions about immigration and race have assumed a new importance, both politically and socially, helping to construct an environment in which the future of both settled migrant communities and new groups of migrants and refugees is very much at the heart of public debate (Habermas, 1994; Miles, 1994; Wrench and Solomos, 1993).

Developments such as these show why it is impossible in the present political and social environment to ignore the impact of race and ethnicity on the social and political institutions of most advanced industrial societies. Whereas until the 1980s it was still relatively common to treat questions about racism, ethnicity and nationalism as relatively marginal to the agenda of both social scientists and policy makers it is perhaps no exaggeration to say that in many ways these issues have moved right to the core of public debate. Indeed, what has become evident in recent years is how almost every aspect of contemporary social and political relations is deeply inflected with a racial or ethnic dimension. In this context as we enter the twenty-first century it is vital that we develop a grounded and historically based view of the role that racialized social relations play in contemporary societies and are likely to play in the future.

This is partly because the terms of both official and popular discourses about race and racism are in a constant state of flux. The recent changes we have seen in European societies are perhaps the most clear example of this volatility, represented both by the development of new racist political movements and by intense official debate about what kinds of policies should be pursued to deal with such issues as immigration and the political and social rights of migrants (Ford, 1992; Wrench and Solomos, 1993). But it is also the case that similar transformations are evident in other parts of the globe. Castles and Miller's (1993) account of the changing politics of migration in various parts of the world illustrates the complex variety of factors that have helped to construct political understandings of the position of migrant communities in quite disparate geographical and social contexts. Numerous other accounts have shown how ideas about 'race', 'nation' and 'ethnicity' are constantly changing as a result of both governmental regulation and popular mobilization.

There is by now a wealth of historical research that shows that the social and political impact of ideas about race needs to be seen in the context of the experience of modernity and postmodernity which has shaped our societies over the past two centuries (Habermas, 1987, 1994). But if modern racism has its foundations in the period since the late eighteenth century there is little doubt that it has had a major impact on the course of historical development during the twentieth century and seems destined to continue to do so. It seems clear as we enter the twenty-first century that racist ideas and movements are continuing to have an impact on a range of contemporary societies in a variety of ways (Winant, 1994). What is more we have seen in recent years the growth and genocidal impact of new forms of racial and ethnically based ideologies in many parts of the globe, including most notably in the 1990s in both West and East Europe and parts of Africa. It is almost impossible to read a newspaper or watch television news coverage without seeing the contemporary expressions of racist ideas and practices, whether in terms of the rise of neo-fascist movements in some societies or the implementation of policies of genocide and what is euphemistically called 'ethnic cleansing'.

Such trends need to be situated within the changing socio-economic environment of contemporary societies. It is also important to situate them within processes of cultural and social change. By this we mean that it is of some importance not to lose sight of the complex social, political and cultural determinants that shape contemporary racist discourses and movements and other forms of racialized discourse and mobilization. Indeed what is clear from recent accounts of the growth of new forms of cultural racism is that within the language of contemporary racist movements there is both a certain flexibility about what is meant by race as well as an attempt to reconstitute themselves as movements whose concern is with defending their 'nation' rather than attacking others as such. It is perhaps not surprising in this context that within the contemporary languages of race one finds a combination of arguments in favour of cultural difference along with negative images of the 'Other' as a threat and as representing an 'impure' culture (Enzensberger, 1994; Gilman, 1985; Mosse, 1985).

It is also quite evident in the present environment that subordinate groups may use difference to stress their own separateness, and to authorize their own representations. They may seek to legitimize their definitions of cultural differences, including those against others from within their own collectivity. They may 'seize the category', claim it for their own and invert it, attaching positive value where before it was negative. This at times can lead, as we shall see later, to a strange convergence in the language of the racist right and of the black or ethnic nationalists, as both infuse categories such as race or ethnicity with essentialist, and supposedly naturally inherited, characteristics.

Race, Politics and Identity

The arguments presented above are held together by a notion that I have already hinted at, namely that race and ethnicity are intrinsically political resources, used by both dominant and subordinate groups for the purposes of legitimizing and furthering their own social identities and social interests. In this contest, nothing – not boundaries, or criteria for allocating or withholding membership, or the consequences that flow from membership – is unchanging. And it is perhaps because race and ethnicity are intrinsically forms of collective social identity that the subject of identity has been at the heart of both historical and contemporary discussions about these issues. The question of identity is certainly the one that everyone wants to talk, debate and write about at the present time. As a keyword in contemporary politics it has taken on so many different connotations that sometimes it is obvious that people are not even talking about the same thing. Nevertheless, it is quite evident that contemporary studies of race and ethnicity are concerned centrally with the ways in which constructions of identity have an impact on the social and political role of minorities.

The preoccupation with identity can, at one level, be taken as an outcome of concerns about where racialized minorities in societies such as our own actually belong. At a basic level after all identity is about belonging, about what we have in common with some people and what differentiates us from others. Identity gives one a sense of personal location, and provides a stable core of one's individuality; but it is also about one's social relationships, one's complex involvement with others, and in the modern world these have become even more complex and confusing. Each of us lives with a variety of potentially contradictory identities, which battle within us for allegiance: as men or women, black or white, straight or gay, able-bodied or disabled. The list is potentially infinite, and so therefore are our possible belongings. Which of them we focus on, bring to the fore, identify with, depends on a host of factors. At the centre, however, are the values we share or wish to share with others.

In exploring questions around the changing dynamics of identity we therefore need to ask: Who is constructing the categories and defining the boundaries? Who is resisting these constructions and definitions? What are the consequences being written into or out of particular categories? What happens when subordinate groups seek to mobilize along boundaries drawn for the purposes of domination? What happens to individuals whose multiple identities may be fragmented and segmented by category politics?

One of the problems with much of the contemporary discussion of 'identity politics' is that the dilemmas and questions outlined above are not adequately addressed. This is largely because much discussion is underpinned by the presumption that one's identity necessarily defines one's politics and that there can be no politics until the subject has excavated or laid claim to his/her identity. Inherent in such positions is the failure to understand the way in which identity grows out of and is transformed by action and struggle. This is one of the dangers as I see it of the preoccupation of exactly who is covered by the category 'black' in contemporary British society. The usage of the notion of black to cover a variety of diverse communities has been rejected by some scholars in favour of other categories such as Asian, Muslim or African Caribbean. Yet others have sought to argue for a notion of 'black' grounded in 'racial' particularity. But the danger of these approaches is that one is presented with no more than a strategy of simple inversion wherein the old bad black essentialist subject is replaced by a new good black essentialist subject whose identity necessarily guarantees a correct politics.

Part of the dilemma we have to face is that collective identities are not things we are born with, but are formed and transformed within and in relation to representation. That is, we only know what it is to be English or German because of the way Englishness and Germanness have come to be represented, as a set of meanings within a national culture. It follows that a nation is not only a political entity but something that produces meanings – a system of cultural representation. People are not only legal citizens of a nation; they participate in the idea of the nation as represented in national culture. A nation is a symbolic community and it is this that accounts for its power to generate a sense of identity and allegiance.

National cultures then are composed not only of cultural institutions, but of symbols and representations. A national culture is a discourse – a way of constructing meanings which influences and organizes both our actions and our conceptions of our selves. National cultures construct identities by producing meanings about 'the nation' with which we can identify; these are contained in the stories which are told about it, memories which connect its present with its past, and images which are constructed of it. As Benedict Anderson has argued, national identity is an 'imagined community', and differences between nations lie in the different ways in which they are imagined (Anderson, 1991).

But how is the modern nation imagined? What representational strategies are deployed to construct our common-sense views of national belonging or identity? What are the representations of, say, 'England', which shape the identifications and define the identities of 'English people'? These are by no means easy questions to answer, and there is a clear need for more detailed historical and contemporary research about how national identities are constructed and reconstructed through time and space. Recent studies by historians such as Linda Colley have highlighted above all the ways in which many of our own taken-for-granted images of 'British' identity are the product of processes centred around a struggle to forge cultural, religious, class and other boundaries in the period since the eighteenth century (Colley, 1992).

More importantly, perhaps, what such research has shown is that the formation of collective identities is based on selective processes of memory and remembering, so that a given group recognizes itself through its recollection of a common past. From this perspective national identity is a specific form of identity based on collective memories about 'the nation' and its origins and history. But it is also clear that the defence of a given 'national identity' inherently involves images of 'other nations', and it is for this reason that debates about cultural differences easily slip into the most hackneyed nationalism, or even racism, and the nationalist affirmation of the superiority of one group over another.

Take, for example, the notion of 'national tradition' and the ways in which it shapes many contemporary debates about education, religion and related issues. Part of the power of nationalist rhetoric is to be found in the construction of naturalized images of 'national culture', 'tradition' and related notions. Whatever the power of these images, however, it is clear that tradition is not a matter of a fixed and given set of beliefs or practices that are handed down or accepted passively. Rather, as Patrick Wright and others have argued, tradition is very much a matter of present day politics and the way in which powerful institutions function to select particular values from the past and to mobilize them in contemporary practices (Dodd, 1995; Wright, 1985). Through such mechanisms of cultural reproduction, a particular version of the collective memory and thus a particular sense of national and cultural identity, is produced.

A key process in play in contemporary British cultural life is one in which a romantically sanitized version of the English/British past is being busily re-created: a quite reactionary vision of pastoral England/Albion. Raphael Samuel describes this as the creation of a 'born-again cultural nationalism', which operates across a number of fields (Samuel, 1988). Thus we see the boom in the conservation and heritage movement; the re-evaluation of English landscape painting; educational reforms aimed at returning to 'traditional standards' in English and History as core components of the curriculum. The 'England' being reconstructed in being around a tradition that is unproblematically white, a tradition which tends towards a morbid celebration of England and Englishness from which blacks and other minorities are systematically excluded.

In other words the making of identities is an active process that involves inclusion and exclusion. There is no identity that is without the dialogic relationship to the Other. To be 'us', we need those who are 'not-us'. The imaginary process of creating traditions and of activating collective memories extends through time.

One of the issues that we have become increasingly aware of in recent years is that the history of identity politics is not one that has moved unproblematically from resistance to a broader politics of democratic struggle. While the growth of identity politics has been seen by some as challenging cultural homogeneity and providing spaces for marginal groups to assert the legacy and importance of their respective voices and experiences, it has often failed to move beyond a notion of difference structured in polarizing binarisms and an uncritical appeal to a discourse of authenticity. Identity politics may have allowed many formerly silenced and displaced groups to emerge from the margins and to reassert and reclaim suppressed identities and experiences. In doing so, however, they have often substituted one master narrative for another, invoking a politics of separatism, and suppressed differences within their own 'liberatory' narratives (Bhatt, 1994; Giroux, 1993).

Stuart Hall's critique of black essentialism highlights some of the inherent limits of 'identity politics'. Hall argues that essentialist forms of political and cultural discourse naturalize and dehistoricize difference, and therefore mistake what is historical and cultural for what is natural, biological and genetic. The moment, he argues, we tear the signifier 'black' from its historical, cultural and political embedding and lodge it in a biologically constituted racial category, we valorize, by inversion, the very ground of the racism we are trying to deconstruct. We fix the signifier outside history, outside of change, outside of political intervention. This is exemplified by the tendency to see the term 'black' as sufficient in itself to guarantee the progressive character of the politics articulated under that banner, when it is evident that we need to analyse precisely the content of these political strategies and how they construct specific 'racial' meanings through politics (Hall, 1991; see also Fuss, 1989).

We have, Hall argues, arrived at an encounter, the 'end of innocence', or the end of the innocent notion of the essential black subject. What is at issue here is the recognition of the extraordinary diversity of subject positions, social experiences, and cultural identities which compose the category black, that is, the recognition that is essentially a politically and culturally constructed category, which cannot be grounded in a set of fixed trans-cultural or transcendental racial categories and which therefore has no guarantees (Hall, 1990). What this brings into play is the recognition of the immense diversity and differentiation of the historical and cultural experiences of minority communities in societies such as our own. This inevitably entails a weakening or fading of the notion that race or some composite notion of race around the term black will either guarantee the effectivity of any cultural practice or determine in any final sense its aesthetic value.

It is interesting to note in this regard that new right political discourses have also become increasingly preoccupied with defending the importance of ever more fixed notions of culture and nation. They have sought to reconstruct primordial notions of ethnic exclusivity that celebrate national identity and patriotism in the face of criticism from multi-culturalists and anti-racists. Central to such discourses is the attempt to fuse culture within a tidy formation that equates nation, citizenship and patriotism with a racially exclusive notion of difference. It is also crucial to recognize that the new right, just as much as ethnic nationalists, have given enormous prominence to waging a cultural struggle over the control and use of the popular media and other spheres of representation in order to articulate contemporary racial meanings and identities in new ways, to link race with more comprehensive political and cultural agendas, and to interpret social structural phenomena (such as inequality or social policy) with regard to 'race' (Smith, 1994). It has to be said that for the new right the appeal is by and large no longer to racial supremacy but to cultural uniformity parading under the politics of nationalism and patriotism. The emphasis is on heritage, the valorization of an elitist view of self and social development, the view of civilization as synonymous with selected aspects of Western tradition. In this sense, difference in the language of the new right is removed from the language of biologism and firmly established as a cultural construct, but only to be reworked within a language that naturalizes race and nation as essentialized categories.

Citizenship, Multi-culturalism and Anti-racism

At the heart of contemporary discourses about identity there lie questions about what it means to 'belong' or to be excluded from particular collectivities. It is to this issue that I want to move onto now, particularly as regards the question of 'citizenship rights' in societies that are becoming increasingly multi-cultural. Within both popular and academic discourse there is growing evidence of concern about how questions of citizenship need to be reconceptualized in the context of multi-cultural societies. Indeed in contemporary European societies this can be seen as in some sense the main question which governments of various kinds are trying to come to terms with. Some important elements of this debate are the issue of the political rights of minorities, including the issue of representation in both local and national politics, and the position of minority religious and cultural rights in societies which are becoming more diverse. Underlying all of these concerns is the much more thorny issue of what, if anything, can be done to protect the rights of minorities and develop extensive notions of citizenship and democracy that include those minorities that are excluded on racial and ethnic criteria.

There are clearly quite divergent perspectives in the present political environment about how best to deal with all of these concerns. There is, for example, a wealth of discussion about what kinds of measures are necessary to tackle the inequalities and exclusions that confront minority groups. At the same time there is clear evidence that existing initiatives are severely limited in their impact. A number of commentators have pointed to the limitations of legislation and public policy interventions in bringing about a major improvement in the socio-political position of minorities.

This raises a number of questions. First, what kinds of policies could tackle discrimination and inequality more effectively? Secondly, what links could be made between policies on immigration and policies on social and economic issues? What kind of positive social policy agenda can be developed to deal with the position of both established communities and new migrants in the twenty-first century? All of these questions are at the heart of contemporary debates and have given rise to quite divergent policy prescriptions. It is quite clear that in the present political environment it is unlikely that any sort of agreement about how to develop new policy regimes in this field will be easy to achieve. On the contrary, it seems likely that this will remain an area full of controversy and conflict for some time to come.

But it is also the case that some key issues are coming to the fore in public debate. A case in point is the whole question of citizenship in relation to race and ethnicity. Policy debates in Britain, unlike other European societies, have often not looked seriously at the issue of political and citizenship rights of migrants and their descendants. This is partly because it is widely assumed that such issues are not as relevant in this country. But it also clear that ethnic minorities in Britain and elsewhere are questioning whether they are fully included in and represented through political institutions. It is not surprising, therefore, that an important concern in recent years has been with the issue of citizenship and the rights of minorities in British society. This is partly because there is a growing awareness of the gap between formal citizenship and the de facto restriction of the economic and social rights of minorities as a result of discrimination, economic restructuring and the decline of the welfare state.

The relationship between identity, difference and culture needs to be located within a broader reconceptualization of substantive democracy that can include a place for the 'rights of minorities'. The value of such a politics is that it makes the complicated issue of difference fundamental to addressing the discourse of substantive citizenship; moreover, it favours looking at the conflict over relations of power, identity and culture as central to a broader struggle to advance the critical imperatives of a democratic society. Primary to such a struggle is rethinking and rewriting difference in relation to wider questions of membership, community and social responsibility.

In essence we need to get away from the idea that solidarity can only be forged when we all think alike. Solidarity begins when people have the confidence to disagree over issues because they 'care' about constructing a common ground.

Solidarity is not impermeably solid but depends to a certain degree on antago-nism and uncertainty. If a radical democracy is to function and provide a point of articulation between and across difference, then, a key question must be posed: What kind of society do we want? We need to retain some kind of moral, ethical and political ground – albeit a provisional one – from which to negotiate among multiple interests. Without a shared vision of democratic community, argues Peter McLaren (1993) we risk endorsing struggles in which the politics of differ-ence collapse into new forms of separatism. We have to be mindful that in trying to avoid the Scylla of the 'tyranny of the whole' that we do not meet up with the Charybdis of the 'dictatorship of the fragment'.

The controversies about the Rushdie Affair, the rights of religious minorities and a number of other similar issues across Europe have highlighted the increased prominence of these issues in current political debates. The growing public interest about the role of fundamentalism among sections of the Muslim com-munities in various countries has given a new life to debates about the issue of cultural differences and processes of integration (Asad, 1990, 1993). By high-lighting some of the most obvious limitations of multi-culturalism and anti-racism in shaping policy change in this field such controversies have done much to bring about a more critical debate about the role and impact of policies which are premised on notions such as multi-culturalism. But they have also highlighted the ever changing terms of political and policy agendas about these issues and the fact that there is little agreement about what kinds of strategies for change should be pursued.

The full impact of current debates on the future of immigration is not as yet clear, but it seems likely that they will have an influence on how such issues as multi-culturalism and anti-racism are seen in the future. In the context of national debates about the position of ethnic minority communities the impact is already evident. In Britain, for example, there are already signs that the Rushdie affair has given a new impetus to debates about issues such as immigration, integration and public order. The hostile media coverage of the events surrounding the political mobilizations around the Rushdie affair also served to reinforce the view that minorities who do not share the dominant political values of British society pose a threat to social stability and cohesion. Some commentators have argued that as a result of the Rushdie affair more attention needs to be given to the divergent political paths seemingly adopted by sections of the African-Caribbean and Asian communities. Whatever the merit of such arguments it is clear that in the current environment one cannot develop any analysis of contemporary racial and ethnic relations without accounting for differentiation within both majority and minority communities.

The Politics of Difference and Belonging

Finally, I want to take up a question that is at the heart of the issues I have been talking about in this chapter, namely the question of whether it is possible to create a kind of society that can acknowledge difference, and not simply diversity. In other words whether there is a capacity to use difference as a resource rather than fear it as a threat. Recent trends in Britain seem to indicate that a mythic longing for cultural homogenization is alive, not just among nationalists and racists who are celebrating Great Britain, but among the minority communities and anti-racists as well.

The preoccupation in much of the recent literature in this field with issues of identity and the assertion of the relevance and importance of understanding the role of new ethnicities has not resolved the fundamental question of how to balance the quest for ever more specific identities with the need to allow for broader and less fixed cultural identities. Indeed, if anything, this quest for a politics of identity has helped to highlight one of the key dilemmas of liberal political thought (Moon, 1993; Squires, 1993). Amy Gutmann captures this contradiction well when she argues:

> One reasonable reaction to questions about how to recognize the distinct cultural identities of members of a pluralistic society is that the very aim of representing or respecting differences in public institutions is misguided. An important strand in contemporary liberalism lends support to this reaction. It suggests that our lack of identification with institutions that serve public purposes, the impersonality of public institutions, is the price that citizens should be willing to pay for treating us all as equals, regardless of our particular ethnic, religious, racial or sexual identities. (Gutmann, 1992: 4)

Yet what is quite clear is that the quest for ever more specific as opposed to universal identities is becoming more pronounced in the present political environment. The search for national, ethnic and racial has become a pronounced, if not dominant, feature of political debate within both majority and minority communities in the 'postmodern' societies of the twenty-first century.

One of the dilemmas we face in the present environment is that there is a clear possibility that new patterns of segregation could establish themselves and limit everyday interaction between racially defined groups. Hazel Carby, writing of the situation in the United States, argues that many suburban middle class white Americans are effectively cut off from contact with inner city blacks. She contrasts this with the explosion in the number of books published by black women and men which provide narratives of black lives, and which are often read by these same middle class whites. She makes the poignant point that:

> For white suburbia, as well as for white middle-class students in universities, these texts are becoming a way of gaining knowledge of the 'other', a knowledge that appears to satisfy and replace the desire to challenge existing frameworks of segregation. Have we, as a society, successfully eliminated the need for achieving integration through political agitation for civil rights and opted instead for knowing each other through cultural texts? (Carby, 1992: 198)

The growing evidence of a 'crisis of race' and of racialized class inequalities in the United States is a poignant reminder that the Civil Rights Movement and other movements since then have had at best a partial impact on established patterns of racial inequality and have not stopped the development of new patterns of exclusion and segregation.

The arguments developed by Carby and others have to be situated carefully in the rather specific context of the racial politics that have shaped American society in the post Civil Rights Movement era. But it is also clear that there is evidence that within contemporary European societies there is the danger of institutional-izing new forms of exclusion as a result of increased racial violence and racist mobilizations by the extreme right. It is no surprise in the present environment of fear, violence and physical attacks on foreigners that commentators such as Hans Magnus Enzensberger warns of the danger of violence and 'civil war' becoming an endemic feature of many cities in contemporary Europe unless the conditions which produce racism and xenophobic nationalism are fully understood (Enzensberger, 1994). Yet others warn of the dangers faced by liberal democra-cies in the context of the growth of 'corporate national populism' and 'post-modern racism' (Zizek, 1993: 224–226; see also Zizek, 1989).

Pronouncements such as these are of course intentionally melodramatic and they are meant to be both a warning as well as a description of the present situa-tion. But given our recent experiences in quite diverse local and national political environments who would argue with any real faith that we can ignore them? Can we be sure that the resurgence of racist nationalism does not pose a very real dan-ger for the possibility of civilized co-existence between groups defined as belong-ing to different racial, ethnic and national identities?

One of the great ironies of the present situation is that trans-national economic, social and political relations have helped to create a multiplicity of migrant net-works and communities that transcend received national boundaries. Categories such as migrants and refugees are no longer an adequate way to describe the realities of movement and settlement in many parts of the globe (Huyssen, 1995). In many ways the idea of diaspora as an unending sojourn across different lands better captures the reality of trans-national networks and communities than the language of immigration and assimilation. Multiple, circular and return migrations, rather than a single great journey from one sedentary space to another, have helped to transform trans-national spaces.

This links up with a question which I have been asking myself a lot these days, namely: What degree of cultural relativism is compatible with democratic princi-ples and the maintenance of a democratic state? In the present environment this is by no means an easy question to answer. But answer it we must if we are to avoid some of the divisive and destructive aspects of the move towards 'identity poli-tics'. One obvious trend is to conflate culture and ethnicity, and this tends to privi-lege a form of categorizing that emphasizes ethnic constructs at the expense of other cultural practices, for example, those that generate the embodiment of gender and class relations. This is evident in most discussions of multi-culturalism and cultural diversity. This conflation gives rise to unitary categories such as 'black culture' or 'Asian culture' used without further analysis, despite obvious complexities of regional, class, gender, or historical, and social differences within such categories. Even more serious is the tendency to conflate human values such as liberty, freedom, justice, democracy with particular ethnic communities and to identify them and celebrate them as the qualities of particular national or ethnic groups. It is precisely questions such as these that we should be exploring both in terms of research and in terms of the curriculum that we teach.

References

Anderson, B. (1991) *Imagined Communities: Reflections on the Origin and Spread of Nationalism* (Revised edn). London: Verso.

Appiah, K.A. (1989) 'The Conservation of "Race"', *Black American Literature Forum*, 23 (1): 37–60.

Asad, T. (1990) 'Ethnography, Literature, and Politics: Some Readings and Uses of Salman Rushdie's *The Satanic Verses*', *Cultural Anthropology*, 5 (3): 239–269.

Asad, T. (1993) *Genealogies of Religion: Discipline and Reasons of Power in Christianity and Islam*. Baltimore: Johns Hopkins University Press.

Bhatt, C. (1994) 'Race, Ethnicity and Religion: Agency, Translocality and New Political Movements', unpublished PhD Thesis, Birkbeck College, University of London.

Carby, H. (1992) 'The Multicultural Wars', in G. Dent (ed.), *Black Popular Culture*. Seattle: Bay Press.

Castles, S. and Miller, M.J. (1993) *The Age of Migration*. London: Macmillan.

Colley, L. (1992) *Britons: Forging the Nation 1707–1837*. New Haven: Yale University Press.

Dodd, P. (1995) *The Battle Over Britain*. London: Demos.

Enzensberger, H.M. (1994) *Civil War*. London: Granta Books.

Ford, G. (1992) *Fascist Europe: The Rise of Racism and Xenophobia*. London: Pluto Press.

Foucault, M. (1980) *Power/Knowledge: Selected Interviews and Other Writings 1972–1977* (ed. Colin Gordon). London: Harvester Wheatsheaf.

Fuss, D. (1989) *Essentially Speaking: Feminism, Nature & Difference*. New York: Routledge.

Gilman, S.L. (1985) *Difference and Pathology: Stereotypes of Sexuality, Race and Madness*. Ithaca: Cornell University Press.

Giroux, H. (1993) 'Living Dangerously. Identity Politics and the New Cultural Racism: Towards a Critical Pedagogy of Representation', *Cultural Studies*, 7 (1): 1–27.

Goldberg, D.T. (1993) *Racist Culture*. Oxford: Blackwell.

Gutmann, A. (1992) 'Introduction', in C. Taylor et al., *Multiculturalism and 'The Politics of Recognition'*. Princeton: Princeton University Press.

Habermas, J. (1987) *The Philosophical Discourse of Modernity*. Cambridge: Polity Press.

Habermas, J. (1994) *The Past as Future*. Cambridge: Polity Press.

Hall, S. (1990) 'Cultural Identity and Diaspora', in J. Rutherford (ed.), *Identity: Culture, Community, Difference*. London: Lawrence and Wishart.

Hall, S. (1991) 'Old and New Identities, Old and New Ethnicities', in A.D. King (ed.), *Culture, Globalisation and the World System*. London: Macmillan.

Huyssen, A. (1995) *Twilight Memories: Marking Time in a Culture of Amnesia*. New York: Routledge.

Kohn, M. (1995) *The Race Gallery: The Return of Racial Science*. London: Jonathan Cape.

McLaren, P. (1993) 'Multi-culturalism and the Postmodern Critique: towards a Pedagogy of Resistance and Transformation', *Cultural Studies*, 7 (1): 118–146.

Miles, R. (1993) *Racism After 'Race Relations'*. London: Routledge.

Miles, R. (1994) 'A Rise of Racism in Contemporary Europe?: Some Sceptical Reflections on its Nature and Extent', *New Community*, 20 (4): 547–562.

Moon, J.D. (1993) *Constructing Community: Moral Pluralism and Tragic Conflicts*. Princeton: Princeton University Press.

Mosse, G. (1985) *Toward the Final Solution: A History of European Racism*. Madison: University of Wisconsin Press.

Samuel, R. (1988) 'Little England Today', *New Statesman and Society*, 21 Oct.

Smith, A.M. (1994) *New Right Discourse on Race and Sexuality: Britain, 1968–1990*. Cambridge: Cambridge University Press.

Solomos, J. and Back, L. (1995) *Race, Politics and Social Change*. London: Routledge.

Solomos, J. and Back, L. (1996) *Racism and Society*. Basingstoke: Macmillan.

Squires, J. (ed.) (1993) *Principled Positions: Postmodernism and the Rediscovery of Value*. London: Lawrence and Wishart.

Stoler, A.L. (1995) *Race and the Education of Desire: Foucault's History of Sexuality and the Colonial Order of Things*. Durham: Duke University Press.

Winant, H. (1994) *Racial Conditions: Politics, Theory, Comparisons.* Minneapolis: University of Minnesota Press.

Wolf, E.R. (1994) 'Perilous Ideas: Race, Culture, People', *Current Anthropology,* 35 (1): 1–12.

Wrench, J. and Solomos, J. (eds) (1993) *Racism and Migration in Western Europe.* Oxford: Berg.

Wright, P. (1985) *On Living in an Old Country: The National Past in Contemporary Britain.* London: Verso.

Zizek, S. (1989) *The Sublime Object of Ideology.* London: Verso.

Zizek, S. (1993) *Tarrying With the Negative: Kant, Hegel, and the Critique of Ideology.* Durham: Duke University Press.

INDEX

Compiled by Jackie McDermott